Rationalist Pragmatism

Philosophy of Language: Connections and Perspectives

Series Editors: Margaret Cameron, Lenny Clapp, and Robert Stainton

Philosophy of Language: Connections and Perspectives comprises monographs and edited collections that explore connections between the philosophy of language and other academic disciplines, or that approach the core topics of philosophy of language in the Anglo-American analytic tradition from alternative perspectives. The philosophy of language, particularly as practiced in the Anglo-American tradition of analytic philosophy, has established itself as a thriving academic discipline. Because of the centrality of language to the human experience, there are myriad connections between the core topics addressed by philosophers of language and other academic disciplines. The number of researchers who are exploring these connections is growing, but there has not been a corresponding increase in the venues for publication of this research. The central purpose and motivation for this series is to address this shortcoming.

Titles in the Series

Rationalist Pragmatism

A Framework for Moral Objectivism

Mitchell Silver

LEXINGTON BOOKS
Lanham • Boulder • New York • London

Published by Lexington Books
An imprint of The Rowman & Littlefield Publishing Group, Inc.
4501 Forbes Boulevard, Suite 200, Lanham, Maryland 20706
www.rowman.com

6 Tinworth Street, London SE11 5AL, United Kingdom

British Library Cataloguing in Publication Information Available

Library of Congress Cataloging-in-Publication Data Is Available

ISBN 978-1-7936-0539-9 (cloth)
ISBN 978-1-7936-0541-2 (pbk)
ISBN 978-1-7936-0540-5 (electronic)

To
Joel M. and Joel G.
for nigh half a century of dialectic marbled with ironic laughter.

Contents

Preface   ix

Introduction: Ideal and Nonideal Moral Theory   xv

1   The Quest for Justification   1

2   Objectivity and Truth   19

3   Others   49

4   Meaning, Morality, and Social Agreement   59

5   Morality's Motivational Powers   95

6   No Double Standards   115

7   Our Morality   135

8   Political Implications   149

Appendix: On Weighing Goals   167

Works Cited   183

Index   191

About the Author   201

Preface

I start with the urge to preach, to say what is right and what is wrong. The impulse is less didactic than self-justificatory. I want to think of myself as good. For me, this desire shares psychological and philosophical space with the desire to think of myself as rational. Goodness and rationality, although hardly the whole of my character ideal, comprise its central and essential substance, and so I seek *reasons* for commitment to my idea of goodness, in the hope that the idea will endorse the *goodness* of Reason, thereby laying a virtuous circle as the foundation of my ideals.

This book of self-justification aspires to make clear the compatibility of my character ideals by demonstrating that a good person can be a rational person. Indeed, its loftiest ambitions aim higher; I want to show that a rational person must be a good one. However, this view has long, and recently with renewed vigor, been challenged. Some challengers say Reason is as comfortable with amorality as it is with morality. Others go further, denying that morality can have any place in a fully rational outlook. In what follows I want to take on these challenges. I want to preach goodness using Reason as scripture so that I may be justified in my eyes.

The self-justificatory impulse of this book, if its argument has merit, can only be satisfied by an objectivist morality. Justification, responsibility, mutually recognizing selves, truth, and rationality are the central concepts that enable self-justification by enabling standards for judging conduct that we correctly apply to all selves—an objective morality. Objective morality makes self-justification possible. Whether my argument for objective morality is motivated by a noble or neurotic desire for self-justification is an issue beyond the manifest topic of the book. But readers can infer what they will.

Some things are right and some things are wrong. In this book, I will mostly be concerned with how that is possible. Only if it is possible that some things are right and some are wrong can we sensibly attempt to sort out which is which. The sorting of right from wrong is named "normative ethics," and inquiry into the nature of normative ethics is termed "meta-ethics." The division is not quite that neat, for a metaethics always has normative implications. A significant motive for writing this book is my belief that faulty metaethics may empower defective normative ethics. I will defend four major claims in what follows: (1) We recognize the truth of a set of beliefs by its utility. (2) The recognition of truth is fundamentally social. (3) Moral beliefs are potentially true. (4) The best articulation of the most general moral truth is "Actions should be judged by a single set of standards."[1]

The first claim is in the pragmatist tradition, and while pragmatism has seen a resurgence of interest and advocacy among professional philosophers, it remains a minority view. Common understanding distinguishes even more sharply between what we should accept as true and what is useful to believe.

The second claim has been maintained and variously developed by philosophers and social theorists for over two centuries. While particular arguments in support of the irreducible social nature of knowledge remain controversial, as do their implications, the irreducibility itself is widely accepted.

Academics label belief in unqualified right and wrong, my third major thesis, "moral objectivism," and in one version or another it represent the majority view of professional philosophers.[2] So too in common understanding; although when pressed to do moral theory many might give lip service to a nonobjectivist position, most people, most of the time, act and speak as though some acts really are wrong, some really right.[3] I am with the majority of both philosophers and others in holding that there are true and false moral judgments, but believe the only credible philosophical framework for moral objectivism includes a pragmatic conception of justification. The position I develop I call "Rationalist Pragmatism," and I hope to justify the name in due course.[4]

Lastly, while there are many different formulations of a moral "golden rule," from *the* Golden Rule, through Hutcheson's "Greatest Good for Greatest Number," to Kant's "act only in accord with universalizable law,"[5] I will argue that the principle of "No Double Standards" best comports with the metaethical structure that houses moral truth.

The skeleton of that structure is briefly described: morality is rationality between persons; rationality is the effective pursuit of goals guided by justified beliefs; beliefs are justified when they are known, beliefs can only be known if they are objective, and objectivity is achieved when all persons' goals are taken equally seriously. The attempt to flesh out this skeleton is made in chapters 1 through 5. The subsequent chapters explore the moral implications of this theoretical framework.

I remain ambivalent about the ordering of the chapters. I've a taste for wanting to do first things first, and am inclined to think of definitions, presuppositions, and their immediate implications as first things. Hence metaethics before ethics. "As a philosopher, true to form, I begin a discussion of content by looking at form."[6] However, those with limited patience for the abstractions of metaethics may choose to start with the normative discussions of chapters 6–8, and, should they find the moral principles delineated there appealing, might find themselves more inclined to examine the supporting metaethics of the first five chapters.

At the end of his preface to the first volume of *The Origins of Political Order* Francis Fukuyama defends his engagement as a nonspecialist with areas of specialist inquiry in which he, unfamiliar with the primary sources, is inexpert and therefore vulnerable to error.[7] Fukuyama, however, thinks the value of synoptic and comparative history is worth the potential loss of precision and nuance. The present book is premised on an analogous judgment regarding philosophy. I can hardly claim deep knowledge of the specialist philosophical literature in epistemology, logic, philosophy of language, action, or even some niches of ethical theory—all areas I nonetheless touch upon because they are relevant to this book's ambition. Prudence might recommend scaling the ambition back rather than plunging into waters whose shoals and tides I have not mastered. Yet philosophy, perhaps more than any other intellectual endeavor, calls for such recklessness. No region of philosophical inquiry is self-contained. It is not merely that different philosophical specialties rub up against each other at the boundaries, but rather that core questions in every area involve taking, often unacknowledged, positions in other areas. What makes this especially troublesome is that those unacknowledged positions are usually highly contested. A biologist can make her case on the role of a particular gene secure in the knowledge that all of her intended audience accepts that natural selection can create adaptations, but no theoretician of beauty can safely assume her readers come with a common view of truth and goodness. Hence, philosophy stands in particular need of both attempts to tie things together and efforts by its practitioners to lay out their metaphysical and epistemological cards, even if the game is putatively restricted to moral theory. This I try to do, knowing that treating of a large topic and laying out those cards has me playing in fields whose recesses I haven't thoroughly explored. I write in the hope that the intricacies of specialist arguments and distinctions that I am ignorant of, or positions I take with a minimal defense, although surely making the project needful of some elaborations and modifications, will not prove fatal to it.

A further justification for risking naïve mistakes by attempting breadth has to do with the mission of philosophy. There is a special imperative in philosophy to seek broad understanding, which, after all, is philosophy's central aspiration.[8] Uncontextualized philosophical findings are worse than useless; they are pure scholasticism. While it is not every philosopher's job (at least not all the time) to fit their inquiries into a larger context, setting the highly detailed, exquisitely narrow, professional philosophical investigations into larger contexts is the only way to realize their value—the only way to explain why minutely focused philosophical work matters.

Finally, presenting a broad view is worth doing in a small book that has a chance of being read by those who, although interested in the subject and willing to endure the abstraction, density, and obsessive analyses of serious philosophy, are unwilling to devote months to the massive tome which would be required to dot every specialist i and cross every technical t implicit in a large thesis (not that complete thoroughness could ever actually be achieved). This small book that stakes out many philosophical positions in service of a large thesis is the result of these considerations.

A philosophical view of some complexity is most perspicuously presented in provisional pieces that are revised in the course of assembly. Objections will occur to even the most sympathetic reader as the unrefined cogs and springs of the view make their first few appearances. Serious objections for some readers will doubtlessly survive full assembly, but I hope that as the ideas are developed, polished, and integrated, many naturally arising objections will be addressed. In the end you may have sufficient reason to reject my view, but I plead for some patience before you reach that judgment.

After an introductory *apologia* for my method, I will begin my sermon proper with the subject of the hoped for justification, the self. I write in the firm conviction, as fundamental as any I have, that there are *other* selves, and in the somewhat less firm, but still strong, conviction, that many of those other selves share my interest in self-justification. Morality, like sanity, begins in the rejection of solipsism. Moral philosophy begins in the belief that some of those other selves want, as I do, to do the "right" thing, if there is such a thing.

Belief that there are other selves that share an interest in self-justification is more than an initial assumption; it is, in Kantian terms, a transcendental condition of the entire endeavor. The justification of myself to myself must travel through others, for the justification is not a Popeye-an "I am what I am"; rather it is the Spike Lee-an "I do *the* right things," and, to be real, this rightness requires others. More of this to come, but the upshot is a quest for "moral objectivism," a morality that is the same for me and you, all of you.

I do not doubt that a careful reader, and certainly one with specialist knowledge, will have little difficulty finding mistakes. But the book would be considerably more error prone had it not been for helpful friends and colleagues. *Rationalist Pragmatism* was largely written during the tenures of Mickaella Perina and Christopher Zurn as Chairs of the University of Massachusetts/

Boston Philosophy Department, and they did their utmost to make it a place conducive to philosophical reflection. Nelson Lande's persistent urgings stimulated much of the department's philosophical life from which I benefited. Many members of the department attended lunch talks where early versions of chapter 2, sections 5 and 6 were discussed. Those meetings generated a number of useful suggestions, as did a presentation of chapter 2, section 3 to a group of UMB philosophy alumnae. Steven Levine and Jeremy Wanderer were generous with their knowledge and time when I needed guidance on an issue in pragmatism or semantics. I am grateful to all my UMB colleagues and students for their contribution to this work.

Joel Greifinger read an early partial draft, and his always sharp observations were of general help, but most particularly his comments caused me to engage more seriously with Habermas, and to realize I needed to explain how my idealized epistemology would function in nonideal contexts (chapter 4, section 7). Hadass Silver also read an early draft and persuaded me that the issue of measuring the value of competing goals required the substantial treatment it now gets in the appendix. Hadass' reading of a later draft led to useful changes regarding the ordering of topics. Arthur Goldhammer offered a cryptic but encouraging remark that helped push me to complete the project.

For their patient support throughout the editorial process, from *Lexington Books*, I wish to thank Jana Hodges-Kluck, Trevor Crowell, Sydney Wedbush, Syed Zakaullah, Arun Rajakumar, Len Clapp, and especially Rob Stainton. Two anonymous readers for *Lexington Books* made suggestions that improved the book. I am grateful to them all.

Of course, none of the people mentioned above bear any responsibility for the resulting book.

Joel Marks, however, does. After decades of debating the relative merits of Kantianism and Utilitarianism with me, Joel dramatically and suddenly rejected all moral beliefs as false and pernicious. This "anti-epiphany," as he called it, he partly attributed to my critique of modern liberal theism,[9] and he challenged me to explain why that critique did not apply, *mutatis mutandis*, to morality. It was this spur which first moved me to think through the philosophical grounds for my belief that some actions are right and some are wrong.

However, although Joel Marks bears responsibility for its existence, he bears no blame for the book's contents. His meticulous reading and generous, extensive commentary on a late draft was a heroic effort to save me from what he saw as blunders of logic, fact, or style. I have no doubt that the many recommendations of his I accepted made this a better book, but there were also many I rejected, so Joel is guiltless of all remaining infelicities. His interest in the project sustained it through a long gestation, and I am deeply appreciative of that, even if he thinks the baby ugly.

It surely is not always easy living with someone who spends much time staring into space thinking about truth and goodness when he might otherwise be doing truly good things, but Ora Gladstone tolerates it, and even helped proofread the index. I am grateful for her forbearance. Isaac and Hadass make the objectivity of moral goodness psychologically impossible for me to disbelieve.

NOTES

1. In each assertion, by "truth," or "true" I mean what some feel the need to call "objective truth" or "objectively true." In general, I feel no such need, and think the modifier redundant. Nonetheless, it is sometime convenient to refer to a belief as "subjectively true," and so in certain contexts clarity requires using the expression "objectively true."

2. Like many philosophical labels "moral objectivism" has been slapped on a host of differing doctrines. What I mean by it must await developing its elements, but for now I'll simply say it asserts that there are true principles of action.

3. I recognize that some recent work in experimental philosophy (e.g., Pölzler 2018) casts some doubt on this claim, but hardly enough to shake me from this conviction. See chapter 5, section 4.

4. Cf. Misak (2000). Although not *directly* influenced by Misak's work, this book explores many similar themes and arrives at many of the same positions she anticipated. For a comparison of her views and my Rationalist Pragmatism see chapter 4, section 10. Brandom (2011) who has also used the term "Rationalist Pragmatism," to describe his views, is in some ways closer, in other ways less close, to the form of Rationalist Pragmatism I espouse than is Misak. See chapter 4, section 9 for a more extensive discussion of Brandom's rationalist pragmatism.

5. See Kant (1785), Hutcheson (1723). Also Bentham (1789) and Mill's (1861a) versions of the principle of utility.

6. Nozick (1993, 140).

7. Fukuyama (2011, xiv).

8. "Philosophy is the discipline that surveys all things that we think are true and tries to figure out how they can be true together." Antony (2016).

9. Silver (2006).

Introduction

Ideal and Nonideal Moral Theory

This book is an exercise in "ideal moral theory" insofar as it tries to lay out the fundamental structure of morality. Ideal theory, conceived of as describing a perfectly just polity or a complete set of fundamental moral principles, recently has been unfavorably contrasted with "nonideal" theory, which it is claimed, unlike ideal theory, attends to particular injustices and moral wrongs. The contrast and criticism are not new. Marx's critique of "utopian" socialism and orthodox pragmatists' reluctance to define "the good," are motivated by many of the same concerns that inform contemporary arguments against ideal theory.[1]

There are three basic complaints about ideal theory. The first is that the proposed ideals are useless because they are impossible for us. They are castles in the air, populated with fully reasonable beings, which we are not, shaped by uncorrupted institutions, which we don't have, and immaculately conceived outside of history, which nothing is. In a word, the ideal is unreal, and only the realistic is valuable.

The second complaint is that imagining the ideal makes one blind to actual injustices, or at least unresponsive to them. So, for example, because racism would not be part of any proposed ideal world, the construction of an ideal gives no guidance for a just response to racism. The ideal theorist, it is claimed, doesn't begin with our experience of actual injustices, and therefore will tend to finish without addressing our strongly felt moral intuitions.

The third criticism leveled at ideal theorizing is that ideal theory envisions a perfected condition (that is what makes a theory ideal), but our norms are and ought to be conceived as evolving, constantly subject to reformation due to new experience and new knowledge. The good is never achieved, and it is a mistake to even imagine it achieved. Nonideal theorists, especially from the pragmatic tradition, argue that the fixity of the ideal in ideal theory misconstrues the source of value.

These criticisms are not without merit when directed against certain ideal theories, or when directed against certain misapplications of any ideal theory, but they fail as a general indictment of imaging and defending ideal moral institutions and practices.

To begin with, in an important sense, all normative theory "idealizes," whether "ideal" or not. Unless the theory is of the "whatever is is right" variety, it moves beyond reality. Theories which merely describe the actual and explain how it came to be and operate are not normative theories. The normative evaluates the actual and compares it to some possibility, or compares some possibilities to each other. What is not the case, at least not yet the case, is always part of the normative theory mix. So the mere unreality of the ideals of ideal theories is no fault insofar as they are normative theories. Attempting to conceive of the best is simply the most extreme form of normative thought. Complaints that ideal theory departs from reality are complaints against doing any kind of normative theory.

If the charge is that the ideal trucks in impossibilities, then that is a different matter. Ideal theory should recommend the best possible world, but no better. Perfection in normative theory should be conceived of as good as it can get, not as as good as we might want. "Impossible!" is a grave accusation, and if warranted, a fatal offense. However, the charge of impossibility can only be sustained against a particular ideal theory combined with a theory of the possible. Possibility is always relative to a set of constraints delineating the possible. The logically possible may be physically impossible, the physically possible, biologically impossible. When a theorist claims some ideal normative construct is impossible, we need to ask which constraints she takes to be fixed. Just which unchangeable laws condemn Thomas More's *Utopia* to remain nowhere? Since all normative theory strays from the actual, the realists must state the boundaries they set for wandering. Ideal theory usually is explicit in the constraints it accepts.[2] Such methodological honesty sets a good example for nonideal theory's less totalizing normative endeavors.

Constraints that critics are entitled to take as fixed in their critique of ideal theories are where we have been and where we are now. A possible good, which we cannot get to given our past journey and current location, might as well be nowhere. Without knowing how a condition might be achieved by us, its description and justification might be of aesthetic value, but is of no practical value. The sensible heart of the criticism of ideal normative theories is that they lack transition programs, and without a detailed itinerary, we cannot have any confidence that their destination is a possibility for us. There may be no way to get there from here.

This criticism points out ideal theory's *incompleteness* as a blueprint for reaching the good, but it does not establish ideal theory's *irrelevance*, let alone its baneful effects. And while ideal theories typically offer no complete transition program, nothing about them dismisses this work. Doing ideal theory does not imply that we can ignore formulating educational programs and political strategies rooted in our best social theories and most informed historical understanding. Idealizing may be only one of the theoretical tasks contributing to moral and social betterment, but it is a useful one. Like the more specialized or narrowly focused theoretical work, ideal theory can help us understand how to achieve a more perfect world. Ideal theory's vision sets a direction for the next concrete step. There can be no transition program without knowing what we are transitioning to.[3] That ideal theory provides no detailed instructions for the journey only shows that it is not the only theoretical work needed for moral progress. But who said it was?

As to the claim that ideal theorizing is insensitive to our moral intuitions and pressing moral concerns, I'd claim that rather than blind us to actual injustice, ideal theory illuminates them. We judge an ideal theory by how well felt injustices are explained and unfelt ones revealed. If the felt injustices aren't accounted for it is a deficiency of the ideal theory under consideration, not of ideal theorizing as such. If we are not sensitized to previously unfelt wrongs, the theory is of little help in making moral progress, but other ideal theories might helpfully uncover many and deep real injustices unnoted by contemporary moral consciousness.

Does ideal theorizing commit us to a stultifying vision? I do not dispute that our conception of the good changes, but ideal theory need not deny this. Justifying an ideal does not disallow future justifications of modifications of that ideal. An ideal theory need not claim its ideals are the last word in ideals, and it can even incorporate openness to new values and norms into its idealization. Ideal theory gives direction to our first steps. It strategically informs what is to be done now. But setting a direction does not lay rail tracks onto an unbending utopia parkway.

Related, but subtler criticisms of ideal theories are provided by Elizabeth Anderson. She argues, although she doesn't put it quite this way, that idealizing leads to inadequate or positively harmful transition programs, or rather, that thinking of moral progress as implementing a transition program is misconceived. She claims that even tentatively held ideas of "the best," are unnecessary and may misdirect us away from what is actually better; knowledge of the "best" is not needed for knowledge of the better, and what's worse, may prevent improvement.[4]

It is quite true that we need not know what is best to know what is better, but we must know what is good to know what is better, and trying to understand what is best is a way of getting clear on what is good. Nothing is justifiably believed better than anything else without a conception(s) of the good and reasons to think that the "better" condition has more of the good(s) than the "not as good." However tentatively held, an idea of goodness is required to believe things could be better. But how, asks the critic, does inquiry into what is best clarify what is good? Might it not instead defame or obscure the goods that are at hand, and ignore or acquit present evils?

Granted, idealizing can, as Anderson fears, distort evaluation and moral judgment; it can be dismissive of perspectives that would not ideally exist (e.g., the perspectives of members of an unjustly despised group),[5] but do exist and need to be heeded. It can ignore a good that is only good in the nonideal context (affirmative action?), or endorse one that is only good in the ideal context (open borders?). But nothing essential to ideal theory entails such mistakes. Ever conscious of the context of constraints it works within, well done idealizing will be highly alert to the morally relevant changes wrought by further constraints. In a world without homophobia, perhaps it is just to refuse on a whim to sell a couple a wedding cake. It might be useful to know that given the delight humans take in indulging their whims, an ideal society would allow the whimsical refusal to sell wedding cakes. However, knowing that does not prevent us from knowing justice must weigh different considerations in a world burdened by homophobia. The idealizing might even highlight the injustice of refusing to sell same sex couples wedding cakes by making explicit the conditions that justly permit giving wide latitude for whimsical desires and how the absence of those conditions forbid whimsical discrimination.

Ideal theory's relation to nonideal theories is similar to nonideal theories' relation to reality, and serves a similar function—it describes what is better.[6] Insofar as any distinction can be made between nonideal and ideal theorizing, the latter simply takes on only the constraints the theorist believes will always be inescapable for rational beings, or slightly less idealized, human beings, while the former takes on constraints the theorist believes early twenty-first century humans are stuck with for the time being.

The utility of doing ideal theory is made more perspicuous if we conceive of it not as attempt at constructing the "best"—that of which there can be no better—but instead as an of unending striving to imagine the "still better." The transitive nature of "the better" relationship enables ideal theory to shed light on the comparative worth of more immediate options. So, for example, if two reforms promise equal, but different advances to a more just society, but only one of them offers a feature, which although of no value now, would be a virtue in an ideal society, that gives us some reason to pursue the reform that includes the potentially virtuous feature. Suppose we could increase satisfying, productive employment through investment in dedicated vocational programs or in vocational tracks embedded in liberal arts schools, and had little evidence that one would be more effective than the other. If a liberally educated general population is part of our ideal, then we have a reason to prefer integrating vocational training into a liberal educational context.

To be sure, we must be alert to a virtue in ideal conditions being a vice in our actual conditions, or allowing a large virtue in an imagined future prevent the pursuit a slighter but more immediately available good. Perhaps in current conditions mixing a liberal and vocational education would engender student resentment and thwart the training effort, or would diminish its results; the speculative good of a liberal education to the individual or society would seldom justify forgoing an immediately and more certain beneficial policy. Ideals can mislead. But the misuse of idealizing hardly demonstrates its uselessness, and the dangers its abuse poses don't erase the benefits its circumspect engagement promises.

Finally, Anderson argues that ideal theory cannot learn from experience because it is not judged by experience. Ideal theory, she claims, sets the standards by which experience is evaluated, so our judgments of experience are forced to adjust to our theory rather than our theory adjusting to judgments formed by experience.

I believe this picture misrepresents ideal theory, depicting philosophical method as dogmatic theology. Ideal theory does not, at least not typically, present its findings as revealed truth, or matters of faith, irrefutable by logical or empirical evidence. Ideal theory demands no commitment to evaluate experience on the theory's terms regardless of the intuitive appeal or consequences of those evaluations. Our moral intuitions are formed by personal, social, and cultural experiences of every type, and those same historically formed moral intuitions have the most prominent jury seats when pronouncing on the plausibility of an ideal theory. To speak of the norms provided by ideal theory as standards external to experience is to describe the formal role they have been nominated for, not the reasons for their election. And even once elected, the norms of ideal theory are liable to impeachment if experience demonstrates they perform poorly in office.

Idealizing, like nonideal theorizing, creates a normative structure and pronounces it good. But unlike God's pronouncement at the end of each creative day, the ideal theorist declaration of goodness comes with reasons. Our intuitions and ongoing experience not only continually assess those reasons, they assess the practices those reasons have realized.[7]

NOTES

1. For a sampling of contemporary critiques of ideal theory see Anderson (2010) and Mills (2005). While related, criticisms of ideal theory should not be confused with criticism of the role of theory in morality. There are those who believe all

theorizing about morality useless or unhelpful, whether ideal or nonideal. See Fotion (2014).

2. Cf. Rousseau's (1762) taking men as they are and laws as that might be, Rawls (1971) making men self-interested but envy free.

3. Later I deal with the objection that we don't need to know the ultimate destination to know where we should go next. The point here is only that we need at least a proximate destination to move at all.

4. Anderson (2010, 3).

5. Anderson (2010, 5).

6. This is more specific than Parfit's (2011, 95) defense of idealization as revealing of information.

7. In *As if: Idealizations and Ideals* (2017), Kwame Anthony Appiah offers a similar justification of theoretical idealizations. However, there are three ways in which Appiah's defense of idealizing differs from mine that are worth noting. Firstly, following Hans Vaihinger, Appiah describes idealizing as treating falsehoods as true. I think that is a misleading and unnecessary characterization. Instead, I think of idealizing, especially in moral and political theory, as treating possibilities as actual. This may seem to amount to the same thing because it is false that the possible is actual. But insofar as moral and political idealization is a species of practical reasoning, that is, figuring out what is to be done, it is future oriented. From our epistemic standpoint, no future event is in fact actual; *all* events are only possibilities. The decision to treat some current actualities as enduring and others as changeable is not a matter of recognizing some truths and ignoring others. Rather it is a matter of accepting (resigning yourself to?) the inevitable realization of some possibilities (treating them as if they will become actual) and then exploring which other possibilities are compatible with the inevitable ones. Ideal moral and political theory takes the possibilities whose realization appear dependent on voluntary, contingent human action, evaluates them, and commends, *ceteris paribus*, the best contingent possibilities' realization. This way of describing idealization removes the connotation that idealizing is irrational because it traffics in falsehoods.

Second, Appiah's embrace of pragmatism is more hesitant than mine, leaving the justification of idealizing more lightly anchored than it need be. Appiah emphasizes, quite rightly in my view, that idealizing's justification requires that it be useful (2017, 156). But he offers no general account of utility, relying mostly on a gut pluralism (2017, 111) that claims we know utilities when we see (or imagine) them only in specified circumstances. This approach disallows more comprehensive idealizations because we cannot say what *they* are good for.

This second difference leads to a third: Appiah is reluctant to say what is good, and as I argue above, however tentative and undogmatic such account is, it is needed to provide an account of the better. While the best may be an enemy of the better, neither is recognizable without goodness. The robust epistemological pragmatism that this book adopts gives a general answer to the question what idealizations are good for—discovering ethical truth—and thereby secures them a central role in normative theory. Ethical truth itself, like all truth, receives its justification pragmatically. What a pragmatic justification of truth amounts to is discussed in chapters 3, 4, and the appendix.

Chapter 1

The Quest for Justification

1. THE SELF

Much of traditional Western religious thought contends that selves are simple unified soul substances. The Cartesian mind is a philosophical variant of this tradition. Separable from its body, or any particular perception, thought, or emotion, the self is the thing that senses, thinks, feels, and has a body. Traditional Eastern thought often holds that there are no selves. Here selves are either mythical beings with no reality at all, or illusory beings, all appearance, shimmering inconsequentially on the surface of reality.[1] It is not my purpose to argue against either of these traditional ideas of the self, rather I acknowledge these views, and dismiss them. Instead of rebutting opposing views of the self, I will simply roughly describe the conception of the self I accept.

The self is a complex, ever-changing entity, extended in time, which performs a set of functions we label "mental." Prominent among these mental functions, using crude, broad, but familiar categories, we find believing, perceiving, and acting. The intimate and unique causal relations these functions have with each other, especially relations of memory, and the ongoing awareness of these relations, constitutes a particular self. As best we can tell, such relational complexes are most fully realized in human brain tissue. You, and I, do not *have* logical, emotional, moral, and aesthetic capacities, we do not *have* beliefs, feelings, dispositions, perceptions, aches, pains, loves, hates, memories, principles, fears, motives, and thousands of other mental properties—we *are* networked clusters of those capacities and properties. Although some of those features play more enduring, central, and influential roles in the grouping, no small subset of properties is definitive of the group. Empirically, your brain may be essential, but conceptually no one aspect is necessary or

1

sufficient to you being you. But want of a strict definition does not make you a mythical creature or an illusion. It makes you vague. We all have loose boundaries. Our beginnings, ends and synchronous catalog of constituents all elude precision. But if the real were restricted to the precise, and responsible philosophical talk restricted to the real, at best we might be able to speak of subatomic particles, and that would make for a dull sermon. So there *you* are. More or less.[2]

Selves, and the goodness and rationality, of which they are capable, develop from humans' peculiar social nature. Moreover, they can only be manifested in society. Society is the stone out of which selves are carved and only in relation to other selves can selves maintain their form. The autonomy of the self, the self-sovereignty which is the fulfillment and measure of the self's reason and goodness, rather than being independent from others, is achieved and exercised with and through others. Later, I will say more about the social production and sustenance of the self.

2. OUR FREEDOM

This conception of the self is the setting of a coherent notion of "free will." Indeed, to a large extent, selves are conceived and formed to explain freedom. The potpourri of variously related elements that cause human actions are theoretically welded into an entity of which we can predicate character, responsibility, and agency. Selves are the things that are free.[3]

The ancient debate on free will has concerned itself with the question of whether the will can be free in a determined world, that is, a world whose entire condition, down to the last detail, is a function of its fully specified condition in the previous instant. In the history of a determined world, each and every event ensues from the constellation of earlier ones. Given the initial constellation, the events of this world admit of no alternatives.

My acts are of this world, and if they are determined by the state of the world from the first syllable of recorded time, or first fluctuation of unrecorded first being, well before I am at all, then surely *I* have not determined my acts. And if I do not determine my acts, I am unfree. Or so say the free will deniers.

I take no position on metaphysical determinism, and think it irrelevant to an adequate conception of free will, which needs only that there be *sufficient* determinism, that is, that we live in a world where we can truly say that some things are caused, among them our acts. A free act of will is simply an act that is caused by certain processes of the self. "Free" is the name we give acts with a favored pedigree. Although no act has untainted ancestry, and there is no perfect freedom, to the *extent* that an act is the result of careful deliberation, considered values, enduring and cherished desires, clear logic, true beliefs, realistic hopes, reasonable fears, and a recursive reflective awareness of these processes, all of which are possible *constituents* of a self, the self has acted freely. It matters not a whit how the self came to include these elements. An uncreated God-like self that had these elements eternally and necessarily, and because of them chooses to sacrifice his only begotten son so that others may live, acts no more freely than a man who has acquired them from contingently fluttering butterfly wings last week, and because of them chooses to perform a painful act of loving altruism. Who you are is conceptually independent of how you became who are,[4] and what you did is even further removed from how you came to be the sort of being that does that sort of thing. Even if you were the creation of an intelligence that crafted you to inevitably perform specific acts, still, should the proximate causes of those acts be your thoughts, values, principles, and uncurtailed reflective deliberations, your acts would be free. You would not be your creator's puppet merely acting out her will, rather you would be her like-minded collaborator, the immediate instrument of your fully aligned *mutual wills*. First, causes are not the only causes, and rarely the most salient. For my purposes, the most salient causes are reasons, for my object is to show how they can cause goodness.

There is much more that needs to be said to counter those who believe a fully determined world leaves no room for a meaningful human freedom. I believe it has been said by others.[5] My goal here is simply to state the notion of freedom that is operative in what follows.

3. THE ADVERSARIES

Goodness, at least the moral goodness discovered by sound moral judgments, has its skeptics. I spoke earlier of a renewal of ancient challenges to the possibility of objective moral justification. The details of the challenges will emerge as we develop a response to them. However, a preliminary distinction between types of moral doubters will be useful.

First, we have the deniers of the possibility of moral justification, those for whom "doubt" puts things rather mildly. These deniers—we may call them "amoralists"—find the world empty of anything truly meriting the term "morality."[6] There is doctrinal variety among the amoralists, but they hold in common the view that moral justification requires something that either could not exist, or simply does not exist. Amoralists believe moral justification needs some supernatural, transcendent moral standard, which some amoralists hold incoherent, others hold coherent but fantastical, and all hold nonexistent. If Santa does not exist there can be no gifts from Santa, and similarly amoralists believe if transcendental moral standards don't exist, there can be no moral justifications. According to amoralists my quest for self-justification is as deluded as a child's wish to get a gift from Santa, for the standards needed for moral justification are as unreal as Santa.

Other opponents of morality do not deny its reality; instead, they lower its status, limit its domain, and shrink its authority. Call these opponents "relativists."[7] With the amoralists, the relativists disbelieve in any supernatural, transcendent moral standards, but unlike the amoralists, such disbelief is prelude to demotion of moral justification, not denial of its existence. Relativists, in contrast to amoralists, hold that moral justification needs no transcendent standards, but the absence of such standards in the relativists' eyes results in considerably more tepid justifications than is commonly sought by the seekers of moral goodness, myself included.

I share with the amoralists and relativists disbelief in supernatural, transcendent, moral standards, but I think we are in no need of such—indeed, they would be of no help in achieving, robust, objective, moral justification. All we need is Reason—natural, this-worldly, historically evolved, Reason.

4. REASON

Like a pious polemic that would prove the divine provenance of a holy book by citing its opening verse—"This is the word of God"—any reasons given for the value of Reason, any justification of justificatory practice, only convinces the faithful. Justification is the provision of good reasons, and there are no good reasons without it. I am not trying to justify Reason, a point I'll make repeatedly, because, I would not be accused of the presumption. Reason cannot be its own character witness. Nor can anything else *justify* Reason. The temptation to seek other Gods to testify to one's own monotheism is idolatry masking as piety. The will to justify that which justifies, is incoherent (my faith's term for sinful), and the truly rational must rest content *within* their rational faith.

I set the bar low for membership in the church of Reason. I count among the faithful everyone to whom I have ever professed anything in the expectation that I would be understood, and anyone who has made a profession to me with the same expectation. This "professional" relationship is transitive, and forms a fellowship that includes all who have offered or will offer into our common reservoir of beliefs their beliefs, and understand it as a truth offering. Regardless of the degrees of separation, stretching across space and time, if there is a chain linking communicants, I view them as belonging to the same community of devotees of truth. I term this community "the social system," and it embraces every person you or I have ever known of or will ever know of, as well as every embraced person's embraced persons. The nature of the embrace is simple: to say or write "this is so." The social system consists of those who have opinions about what's true and what's not, and whose opinion may come our way. When I say "us," that is whom I speak of. The social system is the set of connected makers of claims. Active church members offer justifications for their claims, but even reticent worshippers of truth take their beliefs to be justifiable. It is what one needs to be, and perhaps all one needs to be, a self.

Rationality (Reason's less reified name) is the capacity to be sensitive to reasons.[8] If a reason can serve as a cause of one's belief, then one is capable of rational belief. If a reason can serve as a cause of one's action, then one is capable of rational action. Philosophers have called the first theoretical reason, the second practical reason. Neither theoretical nor practical reason is a widespread capability. Like most capabilities, it comes in degrees, but full-blown cases seem to be limited to humanity. Admittedly, there are aspects of Reason in the capabilities of computers and nonhuman creatures, and there is room for debate regarding the rationality of smart phones and simians, of Watson and Washoe.[9] However, no ape or algorithm at present gives us grounds for believing that it approaches the rational capabilities of humans, even if the most rational of humans, let alone a typical one, is only partly characterized by rationality. As far as we can tell, only humans routinely cross the rational threshold, even if they spend a good deal of time on the nonrational side of the boundary.

Although reasons are its elemental elicitors, rationality is manifested by one's relationship to structured constellations of reasons called "justifications." Indeed, a statement or a belief only becomes a reason as part of a justification. I use the term "justification," unless otherwise indicated, only to refer to sound justifications. That issue will be discussed later.

Rather than thinking of rationality as sensitivity to individual reasons, we ought to think of it as sensitivity to justifications. Reasons are the pixels for our rational sense, but justifications are its images. When we are rational, we are responding to a justification as a whole—to the justification's constituent reasons in relationship to each other—rather than to the individual reasons. When it is raining, we have reason to wear boots, but only because we wish to have dry feet, the boots are waterproof, we will be leaving the house, and so forth. By itself, the fact that it is raining justifies nothing, and it would not be rational to always put on boots whenever it is raining, even though rain is a reason to wear boots.

What sort of things are reasons, the building blocks of justifications, the sensitivity to which makes for rationality? Strictly speaking reasons are propositions, expressed as sentences or beliefs. Less formally, reasons are what the sentences or beliefs are about, and as such, reasons come in many ontological types.[10] They may be external astronomical facts or internal biological ones. A full moon can be a reason for a hayride, high cholesterol a reason for a statin. They may be social institutions, or rules, or principles. A wedding may be a reason to buy a gift, a third strike to call a batter out, and a solemn oath to remain loyal. Reasons may even be beliefs and sentences, for beliefs can be about beliefs, sentences about sentences. The umpire's belief that a shoulder high pitch is a strike is a reason for the batter to swing at it, the beauty of a sentence a reason to memorize it. Indeed, no ontological type could be ruled out as a potential reason, for anything can be the subject of a proposition, including other propositions.

Not all propositions are reasons. What makes a proposition a reason is that it has a role in a justification of a belief or of an action. The proposition "it is raining," becomes a reason when it is employed to justify my belief that I ought to wear boots or justify my actual donning of the boots. A proposition playing a role in a justification of a belief or an action need not be a proposition which does any work to create the belief or action it justifies. The rain may justify my wearing boots, even if their chic styling is the sole cause I wear them. All of our beliefs and actions are caused, and some are caused by propositions, but only some of those propositional causes, and those only some of the time, will also find a place in a justification of the belief or action. At those times, when a cause of a belief or action could also be a proposition doing justificatory work, it will have taken on an added designation: it will be a reason, and we will be acting *from* reason when reasons are both causes of our action and their causal efficacy is attributable to the role that they play in the justification of that same action. We act from reason when the proposition "it is raining" is part of a sound justification for wearing boots *and* the justification caused us to put them on.

A reason need not cause anything, and beliefs and actions need not be caused by reasons constituting a justification. But when beliefs or actions are so caused, we are in the domain of the rational. The more extended examples in the following sections should further clarify when beliefs and actions are rationally caused and when not.

5. JUSTIFICATIONS

The reasons forming a justification relate to each other as premises and conclusions, for a justification is an argument. But unlike some other arguments, a justification solicits a commitment to a belief or an action. In theoretical reasoning, a justification seeks belief, in practical reasoning, action.[11] A justification implicitly claims to be decisive, or, at least, worthy of commitment all things considered. It suggests that after subarguments have been summed and counterarguments weighed, its deliverances ought to be accepted. Only an argument which is understood as soliciting belief or action in accordance with its conclusion is a justification.[12]

Like any argument, and on the same basis as any argument, a purported justification can be sound or unsound. Its premises may or may not be true, and, if true, they may or may not entail or provide strong support for its conclusion. Therefore, we must further refine the notion of rationality; rationality is a sensitivity to *sound* justifications.[13] It is an inclination to believe the conclusion of a sound theoretical justification or to act in accordance with the conclusion of a sound practical justification.

This conceptualization is an idealization. It describes Reason when it is successfully being itself. But, what passes for Reason, is often not the thing itself. We colloquially refer to failed attempts at reasoning as a kind of rationality. We feel rational when we are sincerely trying to be rational, that is, whenever we are moved by an (usually implicit) argument. Alas, sensitivity to unsound purported justifications is common among the creatures we call rational—and indeed, this quasi-rationality may be as close as we usually get to true rationality. I think we are frequently moved by justifications, but because rationality is sensitivity to *sound* justification, our actions are rarely fully rational. Vague, if not outright false premises, often undermine full rationality, and even when all the premises are precise and accurate, the arguments that motivate us are usually too complex to be supposed free of faulty inferences. Even with the best epistemic will in the world, we will more often than not act with less than full justification. Quasi-rationality is the rational faculty gone astray, but this is not necessarily the faculty's fault. We often lack the resources to discover the flaw in a purported justification. "Quasi" in quasi-rationality simply means a mistake is being made, and mistakes lurk in all unsound justifications, or they would not be unsound. However, mistakes are often guiltless and unavoidable. Our inability to be perfectly rational no more makes us irrational than our (related) inability to be perfectly good makes us evil. Still, in the complete absence of a capacity to respond, on occasion, differentially to sound and unsound justifications, or at least to understand the distinction, we would not even have this quasi-rationality. An aspiration to rationality is an essential ingredient of rationality.

At least as common as quasi-rationality, but more distantly related, is pseudo-rationality. We often construct justifications, whether sound or unsound, to decorate our beliefs or actions, although these proffered justifications play absolutely no role in generating the belief or action. We call this "rationalizing," pretending rationality, rather than being rational. To adapt an epigram, rationalizations are the compliments that prejudice, habit, feeling, and instinct pay to Reason. Our approval and pride in rationality is demonstrated by how often we assign our beliefs and actions rational parentage, regardless of the true circumstances of their birth. Sometimes pseudo-rationality is meant to fool others. More often, we are after self-delusion. Frequently, both self and other are the target dupes. A politician may use bad arguments to persuade voters to elect him, but these arguments are probably most effective at persuading the politician that he ought to be elected. It is pleasant for him to think that Reason caused him to seek office, regardless of the true cause. This is pseudo- rather than quasi-rationality, because the politician is not running as a result of mistaking an unsound argument for sound. Rather the argument played no role at all in his seeking office. Whether sound or unsound, the argument, causally speaking, was pure window dressing.

Surely many of our beliefs and actions are not caused by justifications, let alone sound justifications, and so our rationality is very partial. We can act and believe without reason, for no reason at all, even against reason, and we often do. We can act and believe in accord with reason, although we might not be acting *from* reason when we do so. That too is surely common. Still, if with sufficient frequency, we believe or act because of Reason, or perhaps more importantly, if at any given time we are liable to be moved by reasons, we are capable of Reason. Capabilities need not be exercised to exist, but it is consoling to note, that our rational capabilities, however underutilized, are not left completely idle. Justifications, including some which may be sound, do cause us to believe things and do things—at least once in a while.

An illustration may be helpful: it is raining and I put on my boots. The rain, in company with a number of other elements, is a reason for me to put on my boots, because there is at least one justification for my wearing boots that includes the rain.[14] But that justification which includes the rain may have nothing to do with how I dress. It may happen that I put on my boots as a fashion statement in complete ignorance of the rain. In that case, the rain would still be a reason for me to wear boots; however, I would not have acted from that reason. Indeed, the rain may not be a *reason* causing me to put on the boots *even if* it causally contributed to my wearing the boots and *is* a reason for me to put on the boots. Maybe the rain sounded like hoof-beats on my roof, which caused me to dream of cowboys, which caused me to wear my boots. So the rain, while being a reason for me to wear boots, and a cause of my wearing boots, in this instance would not have been, *in its role as a reason*, a cause of my wearing boots. I was not acting rationally when I put on the boots (although, because the rain did justify boot-wearing, I was acting in accord with reason). A reason is a constituent of a justification, and rationality is the capacity to believe or act because of a justification. The *justification* for my putting on boots that included rain was not why I wore boots.

This description of believing or acting out of reason does not require con-sciousness of the role that reason may be playing. A justification, in whole or in part, might be causally effective without one's being conscious of it. Indeed, we philosophy teachers are often engaged in excavating and bringing *to* consciousness justifications which have shaped our students' beliefs and actions. This is not to deny that we probably spend considerably more time constructing justifications for beliefs and actions whose causes are quite other than that those dialectically constructed justifications. But these rationalizing processes should not to be sneered at. Building a sound justification is a first step in being moved by it.

Benjamin Franklin quipped that the advantage of being a rational animal is that you can rationalize anything.[15] It was not meant as a compliment, and the cynical construction of insincerely offered rationales are indeed a vice. But our rational aspirations, the capacity and penchant to construct and be moved by justifications and to judge ourselves by standards of rationality, are unavoidably accompanied by their natural, although perverted, cousins— sophistical rationalizations. Pseudo-rationality honors the real thing even as it betrays it.

The inclination to believe the conclusion of a sound theoretical justification or to act in accordance with the conclusion of a sound practical justification, attests to a desire for consistency, the soul of rationality.[16] Practice, has a higher threshold of rationality than does theory, because there are more way to act inconsistently than there are to believe inconsistently. The possibility of truth is sufficient to confer theoretical rationality. Beliefs' rationalities are only challenged by other beliefs, for even evidence doesn't contest theory until it inhabits belief. Rain is not inconsistent with my belief it is not raining, but a belief that it is raining is. Rational belief need only get along with other beliefs. But rational action must be compatible with a more diverse ontological array: an action can conflict with a belief or an action. There is inconsistency in believing that you ought to, all things considered, never torture cats, while knowingly torturing a cat, for the action is inconsistent with a judgment of the action—a belief. An action can also fail to be consistent with another action. It is irrational to torture a cat right now, while also attempting to prevent that cat from being tortured right now, regardless of any relevant judgments. When the right hand does not know what the left hand is doing, they may have incompatible goals, in which case the hands' owner stands guilty of irrationality. All of the goals of an agent's actions must be realizable in the same possible world if the actions are to qualify as rational. And so practical is more complex than theoretical reason.[17] The beliefs constituting a practical *justification* must meet all of the requirements of theoretical rationality, and then some: first, the rationality of a practical *justification* requires the theoretical rationality we term "soundness." Next, the rationality of *acting from* sincerely held judgments, which we call "character," or "will power," is needed, as is the rationality of practice itself, which, when it avoids subtle inconsistencies, we may term "strategic coherence," avoiding blatant inconsistencies we call "sanity." Finally, it is the burden of this book to persuade you that there is an additional criterion of practical rationality, morality, consistency in the treatment of self and others.[18]

6. JUSTIFICATION AND EXPLANATION

When we say "let me explain myself," we usually mean "let me justify myself." In "explaining ourselves," seldom do we say *how* we came to do a questioned deed; mostly, we want to "explain" that its doing was blameless. This is justifying, not explaining, but the confusion is understandable, for while explanation and justification are distinct, they are entangled and are often playing a game of one-upmanship.

There are formal and informal explanations. The informal explanations of daily life aim either to provide enough information to enable the adequate performance of a relevant task, or to satisfy the curiosity of a relevant inquirer. To be a truly good informal explanation, besides succeeding at the provision of sufficient information or the satisfaction of curiosity, the explanation must consist solely of true statements. If you ask why I bought a bed from Ikea, and I explain that my old bed broke, and I've been satisfied with other Ikea products, the explanation counts as good if you have no lingering questions about what drove me to the purchase. If I ask you how to assemble it, your explanation is good if it provided me all the information needed to complete the task.

The orthodox view of formal, that is scientific, explanation, goes by the daunting moniker "the deductive-nomological" model of explanation.[19] In the deductive-nomological model, that which is to be explained is explained when it is shown to be a deductive consequence of statements that include at least one law. The boiling of a particular liquid is explained by noting that (1) the liquid is water; (2) the liquid's temperature has been raised to 100 degree centigrade, and (3) (here comes the law) all water boils at 100 degree. Given statements 1, 2, and 3, it deductively follows that the liquid boil, and so its boiling is explained. It is well explained if 1, 2, and 3 are true.

The notoriously murky idea of causation, which was cavalierly invoked in the discussion of Reason above, lurks about both the informal and formal conceptions of explanation. The statements in the deductive-nomological model can be viewed as citing the causal factors for the boiling (the heat and the kind of thing being heated) and the claim that they are indeed causal factors in such situations (the "law" that water boils at 100 degree centigrade). Regarding the less formal "explanations," it seems that curiosity is normally satisfied when we believe we have seen the causes of the curious phenomenon (we believe an old broken bed and good experience with the Ikea brand would cause buying a new Ikea bed), and to know what causes an achievement is to have all the information (albeit perhaps not all the skill or resources) to achieve it. Hence, we can speak generally of "explanations," whether everyday informal ones or formal scientific ones, as causal accounts (although I will leave "causal account" philosophically undefined and rely on unanalyzed intuition of the notion) of the things explained.

Whether we possess them or not, there are causal accounts of all that we do, and the true causal accounts doubtless would cite all manner of facts and "laws." Not only do different sorts of acts likely have different sorts of causes, but highly similar acts may have very dissimilar causes. One man reddens because he is allergic to peanut butter, another because he is embarrassed that he ate too much peanut butter. The resulting complexions may be identical, not the causes. One woman kills her pained, dying husband because of a merciful, loving heart, another the quicker to get her hands on the dying man's fortune, a third because she is hallucinating and imagines herself to be playing Othello and her dying husband to be performing Desdemona. The act of smothering may have been the same in all three instances, the causes of each act quite different.

In principle, everything is liable to being explained, for presumably a causal account, however difficult to find, is there to be found. The existence of everything, the occurrence of every event, the sequence in every process, the performance of every act—in principle there is some story that uncovers the causes, and thereby the thing, event, process or act is explained.

Justification has no necessary connection with causation. Sometimes justifications cause things or invoke causal claims, sometimes they don't. Our interest in justifying may ultimately be that we wish to cause an action or belief, but justifications need make no causal claims. Justifications make claims of adequacy—claims that a belief or act meet a relevant standard or belong to a relevant category. A belief or act's adequacy may well be affected by its causes, but it is determined by some criterion of adequacy—whether a benchmark of correctness, a standard of rightness, or a principle of goodness, truth or beauty. The existence of those justifying criteria may or may not have played a role in the causal story that created the item of interest. A yardstick may have been used to create a football field of regulation length, or merely invoked to demonstrate that it is of regulation length. It can build the field or prove its adequacy, or both. This possibility has confused many and led them to deny that there is anything more one can do beyond explanation, or to assert that to explain all is to justify all. But to only explain, regardless of how thorough and accurate the explanation, is to justify nothing. An explanation need never invoke any standard of adequacy or include a judgment as to whether the facts meet the standard. An explanation tells us how something came to be, a justification tells us how to categorize it.

However, these distinct processes of explanation and justification can engulf one another. Like all things, justifications can be explained, and like all things that are subject to judgments of adequacy, explanations are liable to justification. To further complicate things, explanations can be explained and justifications justified. Finally, whenever we are sincerely attempting rationality (acting *from* Reason, not merely in accord with Reason), the explanation and justification of our belief or action overlap. The rain both justifies and causes me to wear boots when I act from Reason. I am sometimes kind *because* I accept a principle endorsing kindness, and that same principle may justify my kindness. A true explanation of how something came to be often does most of the work required to categorize it correctly.

But justifications and explanations do not always coincide. Commonly, justificatory principles play no causal role: I may be kind (or cruel) because of unreflective sentiment. Sometimes a justificatory principle causes but fails to justify an act: I am kind to my plants *because* I believe nothing should suffer, but if plants are incapable of suffering, my kindness principle does not justify my behavior. (This is not to deny that my kindness to plants may be justifiable on other grounds, grounds which are not playing a causal role in this particular case. Perhaps kindness to plants sharpens gardening skills). Whenever justifications and explanations do coincide, the relevant beliefs are playing a dual role. We may have one set of beliefs in play, but distinct functions are present when that set serves to explain and justify.

The possible divergence of justification and causation enables a further source of confusion: the failure to distinguish between justifying an act and justifying its particular motivation. A kind act may be justified, even when motivated by greed, an unjustified motive. No true principle may support the general cultivation of greed, nor even its occasional empowerment, and yet greed may cause a fully justifiable act (surely many a justifiable gift-giving has occurred because of some greedy hope for reciprocity or vainglory: behold the names on hospital wings and contemplate the cause of their funding. Yet the gift was justifiable).

The dance of explaining justifications, justifying explanations, explaining explanations, justifying justifications, has no end of steps and moves. After a few basic turns, most people are made dizzy by the dance, that goes on (to their mind) ad nauseam. Philosophers are obsessive choreographers of the explanation/justification tango and are exhilarated at a dance that makes others wish to throw-up.[20]

7. THE SOUNDNESS OF PRACTICAL JUSTIFICATIONS

When applied to action, the phrase "sound justifications" rings hollow in the ears of the denigrators of morality. If this skepticism regarding the justification of action is correct, then there is no such thing as practical reason, for justification is the heart of practical reason, as it is of theoretical reason. But the skepticism is unwarranted; justifications of practice operate as sure-footedly in their own domain as justifications of belief do in theirs. True, the domains are at a remove, but there are no grounds for judging practical reason the lesser realm. Each domain is a human capability composed of similar types, functioning in similar ways; it is apt that they share the name of Reason. But some central inhabitants of each domain belong to different species, neither of which can *directly* produce the offspring of the other. Nonetheless, the kinship relationships within each species are the same, and they live a common life, the life of Reason, in constant intercourse and mutual support. Although they do not breed the other type, their union is not barren. Their progeny is the rational made real. Sound justifications, theoretical and practical, causally empowered, combine to create a more rational world.

Being a sound justification in either domain is a matter of logic and truth. If the premises of the justificatory argument are true, and by the rules of standard logic they entail or make probable the conclusion, the justification is sound. This is the conventional account of soundness: true premises and good logic. The use of logic in practical reason is standard and involves nothing contentious. It *follows* from the principle that one ought not cause avoidable suffering, and the fact that eating animals causes avoidable suffering, that one ought not to eat animals. The logic of practical reason is no more at issue than the logic of theoretical reason.

The possibility of sound practical reason is questioned not on its logic, but on the grounds of its premises' truth, with the skeptics arguing against the very possibility that all of the premises needed for a justification of a practice can be true. The moral skeptic denies that a principle of action can be (objectively) true, and no justification of an action can be sound without including a *true* principle of action. This radical claim should not be confused with the commonplace observation that moral disagreement is found at every level of moral discourse. We often dispute the truth of particular premises of the prudential and moral arguments of daily life and politics, and also when we contest the normative theories that posit adjudicating principles. The moral skeptic's point, however, is a metaethical one: *no* principle of action can be true, and so no practical justification can be sound. The "ought" statement, the "imperative" claim, the principle of action which is a necessary premise in any justification of practice is simply, according to the moral skeptic, not a candidate for truth. Some skeptics say this is so because the principle "says" nothing, others because what it says is metaphysically false.[21] So, beyond the question of whether it is true that one ought not to cause any avoidable suffering, is the question of whether any proposition expressing a principle of action can be true. If it cannot, then there are no practical justifications with *all* true premises, and therefore no sound ones. And that would mean that in the realm of action there can be no rationality, for if there are no sound justifications of practice, there can be no sensitivity to sound justifications of practice. That would be a lethal result for my project of rooting goodness in Reason. Fortunately, practical principles can be true, but unfortunately defending that claim requires an excursion into the theory of truth.

NOTES

1. A vast oversimplification of a diverse philosophical/religious intellectual realm that contains a large range of subtle views on selfhood. See Garfield (2015) for an excellent, concise account of this range. Still, I think it fair, if somewhat broad-brush, to characterize the core of the Eastern philosophical view of the self as I do, even if some streams in that tradition come close to the view of the self I will presume.

2. Cf. Parfit (1984).

3. See Silver (2002).

4. When I say "Who you are is conceptually independent of how you became who are" and "It matters not a whit how the self came to include the elements constituting self-hood," I am not denying its necessarily social origins and nature, I am only asserting that given the reality of those properties which constitute selfhood, a reality which perhaps could have only emerged from a certain history, the powers of the properties are immanent in the present.

5. In contemporary philosophical taxonomy, the position I take on free will is "comptibilist," or "soft-determinist." Hume (1748) is the classical source for this position. I think Dennett (1984, 2003) provides its most subtle and thorough justifications.

6. For example, Marks (2013), Garner (1994). Marks and Garner don't deny there is widespread, and consequential *belief* in morality, but they hold that belief to be false, and think it better if morally inflected terminology disappeared. Others find some positive uses for moral terms, but in my view still qualify as amoralists, for example, Mackie (1977), and Joyce (2001).

7. Relativists, an older and more common breed than amoralists, come in even more varieties than do amoralists, and some varieties I consider relativists might bristle at the "relativist" label.

8. That we have this capacity is nicely asserted by Robert Nozick: "We are creatures who are amenable to being inducted into a world of norms." Nozick (1993, 27). I'll use the term "rationality," to refer to the capacity to engage in Reason, the semantic process that renders truth. I'll use the upper case "R," to distinguish Reason from a

reason which is an element in a bit of reasoning. Partfit (2011, 111) call's rationality "responsibility to reasons" rather than my "sensitivity" to reasons.

9. An IBM computer that plays Jeopardy well and a chimpanzee that spoke ASL poorly.

10. As the reader who continues for a while will see, I take talk of beliefs and sentences being "about things" and "propositions" as a convenient shorthand. See chapter 4 for the sense in which beliefs and sentences are, and are not, "about things," and for further details regarding meaning.

11. Although we might treat any argument for a belief or action as a prima facie "justification," it is best to reserve the term for those overall arguments making a claim for truth or rightness.

12. We can think of "argument" as labeling the locutionary content and "justification" as the illocutionary, or perhaps the implicature of beliefs were those beliefs to be manifested as speech. See Austin (1962) and Grice (1961).

13. If it is unsound then, strictly speaking, it is only a purported justification. I am using "sound" as synonymous with "good" when modifying arguments. Valid deductive arguments with all true premises, are sound, as are (in my usage) inductive arguments with all true premises that are logically stronger than any arguments to contradictory conclusions. Although most logicians reserve the term "sound" only for good deductive arguments, here I follow Paul Herrick (1994) in applying it to inductive arguments with true premises and sufficient logical strength.

14. For example, I do not like wet feet, I ought to avoid what I do not like, if it is raining then the best way to avoid wet feet is to wear boots, it is raining, therefore I ought to wear boots.

15. Franklin (1787, 18).

16. The nature of consistency is discussed in chapter 3, section 2, chapter 4, section six, and especially chapter 5, section 2.

17. Although actions can be inconsistent with each other, ultimately, this reflects an inconsistency at a theoretical level or between at least one of the inconsistent actions and a belief. See chapter 5, section 2, especially note 19 of that chapter.

18. I am not claiming that "reality" is overall less constraining of rational "factual" beliefs than it is of rational practical principles. Insofar as factual beliefs must be most responsive to a narrower range of reality than principled belief, factual beliefs have it easy. But that range tends to be far less fluid than the realities practical principles are most sensitive to, so the candidates for rational factual belief are more fixed than those for rational belief of practical principles. In the sections on pragmatic justification and objectivity, I discuss the sense in which all rational belief must be sensitive to all of reality. In chapter 2, section 6, and chapter 4, sections 4–7, I argue that nonetheless some aspects of reality will be more influential in determining various domains of belief.

19. Hempel (1962).

20. For those with a stomach for more details and examples: I voted for Barack Obama in 2008. An Initial Justification (IJ) of my act may go as follows:

> IJ a. It is right to vote for the candidate most likely to respect human rights and bring peace and prosperity to the nation by constitutional means.

IJ b. Barack Obama was the candidate most likely to respect human rights and bring peace and prosperity to the nation by constitutional means.

IJ c. Therefore, it was right to vote for Barack Obama.

But perhaps we are less interested in a justification of my vote than we are in an explanation of it. Here is an Initial Explanation, the one I like to think is true:

IE a. I accept the principle that it is right to vote for the candidate most likely to respect human rights and bring peace and prosperity to the nation by constitutional means.

IE b. I believed that Barack Obama was the candidate most likely to respect human rights and bring peace and prosperity to the nation by constitutional means.

IE c. As a result I voted for Barack Obama.

Although similar, and easily conflated, the IE and the IJ are quite different. The latter makes no reference to the acceptance of any principles, only to a principle itself, nor does the IJ refer to belief in any facts, only to the facts themselves. And unlike the IE, the IJ suggests no causal relationships. While my acceptance of certain principles and my belief in certain facts may have caused me to vote as I did, the principle and the fact adduced in the IJ do not *cause* the rightness of my vote, they *imply* it.

Now it is true that the D-N model of scientific explanation also has the "explaining statements" serve as premises that imply the statement explained (the "explanandum"). So isn't this explanation the same inferential form I am claiming for justification? Yes, but it has a different deep inferential structure because it is trying to get at causation. In an explanation, we are not trying to prove the explanandum true. We assume it is true, and claim to show how it, in fact, came to be true. A good formal explanation doesn't simply involve true premises that imply the explanandum. The explanation also asserts (in that "as a result") that if the premise with the law were not true, the explanandum wouldn't be either. If IEa were false, we are meant to infer that I would not have voted for Obama, for it claims to be part of the explanation of my voting for Obama, not just evidence that I did. But if IJa were false, my voting for Obama might still have been justified on other grounds.

There are other possible justifications and explanations, besides IE and IJ of my vote. An alternative explanation (AE) might go as follows:

AE a. I am a baby boomer, New Left veteran, humanities Ph.D., Newton Massachusetts' resident, and secular Jew, with a microscopic Wall Street portfolio.

AE b. All such baby boomer, New Left veteran, humanities Ph.D., Newton Massachusetts residents, secular Jews, with a microscopic Wall Street portfolios vote for the liberal candidate.

AE c. Obama was the liberal candidate

AE d. So I voted for Obama.

Whether AE or IE is the correct or a better explanation of my vote is immaterial to the justification offered as IJ. The justification of the act stands apart from any explanation of it. Perhaps political scientists and sociologists would be inclined to think that the AE is the better explanation of my vote. We may ask them to explain why I offered the IE as to account for my vote. In other words, how would they explain my explanation. Perhaps they would offer us a the following "social science" explanation, SSE, of IE:

SSE a. All people want to believe that their acts are motivated by principles and a correct understanding of the facts.

SSE b. Silver is a person.

SSE c. IE claims that Silver's vote was motivated by principles and a correct understanding of the facts.

SSE d. So Silver believes that IE explains his 2008 Obama vote.

I am partial to a different explanation of IE. My "personal explanation" of IE is

PE a. People offer explanations they believe to be true.

PE b. I believe that my acceptance of the principle that it is right to vote for the candidate most likely to respect human rights and bring peace and prosperity to the nation by constitutional means along with my belief that Barack Obama was the candidate most likely to respect human rights and bring peace and prosperity to the nation by constitutional means led me to explain my voting for Obama by referring to that acceptance and belief.

PE c. As a result, I explained my vote for Barack Obama with IE.

We now have two competing explanations (SSE and PE) of my initial explanation (IE) of why I voted for Barack Obama in 2008. We can go on to attempt to explain SSE or PE, or shift modes and try to justify one of them, that is, try to show that its premises, for example, SSEa, SSEb, SSEc, are true, and that its conclusion, SSEd, follows from the premises. The justification would be subject to explanation or justification. And so it goes.

21. I am using "skeptic" to mean a denier of objective morality rather than just one who is doubtful about it. The primary school of skeptics in the morality "says nothing" category are emotivists/expressivists, for example, Stevenson (1944), and Ayer (1936), who hold that moral statements make no claims, but rather give voice to attitudes or feelings—a sort of "Boo" or "Hooray." Expressivists do not neatly fit into my division of moral skeptics into relativists and amoralists. Like amoralists, they maintain that there are no, indeed cannot be, true moral claims. Like relativists they believe that morality actually exists as a variety of effects of various groups or individuals. The "metaphysically false" view of moral principles is held by amoralists.

Chapter 2

Objectivity and Truth

1. CATEGORIZING THEORIES OF TRUTH

Philosophers might do well to follow Jesus' example and remain silent when asked "What is truth?" Truth resists a fully satisfying analysis, and the most plausible efforts have an air of circularity that reinforces belief in the concept's unanalyzable, primitive centrality. But silence is a poor strategy for a defender of morality if it leaves in place a misleading notion of truth that casts doubt on the possibility of rational action and just conduct.

Insofar as my project requires a theory of truth, it is mostly a partial theory, a theory of how truth can be recognized—a theory of justification. All theories of justification are implicitly question begging;[1] at best we can say that a theory of justification is justified by its own lights. However, if the justificatory circle is consistent, big enough to encompass a range of phenomena, organizes a cluster of ideas into a stable structure, and makes the familiar uses of our words and attitudes more understandable, even an ungrounded circle can clear and prepare ground on which to build. Although the core of the concept of truth cannot be disassembled into more basic components, truth's role in our thought can better be understood by illuminating its proper setting. As important as making a place for morality, a correct theory of justification can dislodge philosophically common, but confounding and false concepts of truth used to undermine morality. While I will not endorse or describe a full theory of truth, I will argue against some types of truth theories, and I will build my case for an objective morality on a particular theory of justification.

Richard Kirkham has persuasively argued that theories of truth vary in their purposes.[2] Some theories aim to tell us what the word "truth" means. Other theories of truth aim at discovering a class that is extensionally equivalent to the class of all true things, that is, a group whose members are defined by properties that do not speak of truth, but yet contain only and all true things. Finally, there are theories of truth that tell us not what "truth," means, nor the necessary and sufficient conditions for being true, but how to recognize truth.

We need not long linger over theories of truth's meaning, or what philosophers call truth's "intension." Determining what a word means is largely a task for lexicographers. I am doubtful that philosophy makes much progress by learning that the truth is "what the case is," or "how things are," or "the accurate account of reality." Such phrases may help teach English, but they don't provide philosophical insight. The search for synonyms of "truth", the Meaning Theories of Truth, makes minimal demands on metaethics, and believers in morality easily meet those demands.[3] Defenders of morality have no cause to dispute "truth's" dictionary definition. It is *true* that one ought not to torture cats because it *is the case* that one ought not to torture cats. Later, when we get to the theory of meaning I employ to support moral objectivism, that theory (inferentialism) will be seen to apply as readily to propositions containing "is true" as it does to any other proposition.

Extensional theories of truth are of two types: those which tell us that two groups simply do have the same members (contingent extensional equivalence), and those which claim they *must* have the same members (necessary extensional equivalence).[4] Theories of contingent extensional equivalence tell us something about truth, and theories of necessary extensional equivalence (henceforth, following Kirkham, "essentialist" theories) tell us more. But by themselves, both sorts of theories may leave us no closer to the truth about truth, for we may have no means of identifying either of the equivalent classes. Maybe all ghosts are dead people and all dead people are ghosts (note: "dead person" doesn't mean "ghost"), but their equivalence does not necessarily tell you how to positively identify a ghost or a dead person. That job requires theories of ghosts or dead people that offer criteria for identifying them. And while it *may* be useful to know that equilateral triangles and equiangular triangles will always, everywhere, be one and the same, unless we are also able to measure or at least approximate length or angles, we remain in geometrical ignorance of particular triangles. Theories of truth which only tell us what truth *is* may not tell us how to recognize it.[5] We want a theory of truth which tells us when it is reasonable to believe we are in its presence—a theory of justification.

Theories of justification instruct us how to recognize the truth and distinguish it from impostors. It is a theory of justification, if anything, which will explain how principles of action can be justifiable, and, ultimately whether ours are actually justified. And while a theory of justification cannot dispense with the idea of truth, for to justify a belief is to justify it *as true*,[6] a theory of justification need no more "analyze" truth than a theory of vital signs needs to analyze life. A nurse can reasonably conclude that someone is alive without defining "life," and anyone can reasonably conclude that a proposition is true without defining "truth."

Before adopting a theory of justification—a theory of how to recognize truth—it is useful to discuss where to look for it. To what kinds of things might we attribute truth? Although little that immediately concerns us hangs on it, we can proceed with fewer distractions if we settle on the *bearer of truth*: truth is, in the first instance, a predicate of beliefs.[7] Reality is whatever it is—with some properties and without others. But, without believers, reality would contain no truth.

2. CORRESPONDENCE: A MISLEADING FAMILY OF THEORIES

"Truth" is the term for beliefs that have a certain relationship to reality. An essentialist theory of truth's main burden is to describe that relationship.[8] Although no essentialist theory of truth is needed for a theory of justification, some essentialist theories disqualify certain kinds of beliefs as potentially justifiable.[9] One major branch of morality's degraders infers from its essentialist analysis too many, including—potentially incompatible, true moralities—these are the moral relativists. Another branch, from the same essentialist analysis, infers that there is no morality at all—the amoralists. Both branches presume a common conception of truth: the correspondence theories of truth.

There are many correspondence theories of truth. What they share is the claim that the bearer of truth, when it is actually bearing truth, in some sense stands for an element of reality. The language to define this "standing for," and the manner it is achieved distinguish correspondence views from each other. The elements of reality stood for may be called "objects," "events," "facts," "referents" or "state of affairs"; the things doing the standing may be "beliefs," "propositions," "words," "signifiers," and "sentences"; and the standing relationship might be a picturing, mirroring, conventional associating, representing, or describing. These listings are hardly exhaustive of the ideas or terminology of correspondence theories. For a correspondence theory, the thing that is true must in some way be similar or conventionally tied to that bit of reality that is under consideration, or referred to, or in mind. This "correspondence" relationship is what makes the potential bearer of truth true.

Suppose, as I have, that beliefs are the primary bearers of truth. A correspondence theory would then tell us that a belief is true if it corresponds to a feature of reality. Those who deny morality altogether argue that "in reality" there are no moral principles, so belief in any moral principle must be false, for it follows from their theory of truth, that if there is no *thing* that is a moral principle, no belief in a moral principle can be true.[10]

These deniers of morality are in thrall to an implausible theory of truth that requires entities to account for every aspect of truth. They take this ontological view of truth for realism, believing all real phenomena are things. It is an understandable mistake, for it is easy to slip from a genuine requirement of realism, namely that something about reality contributes to making beliefs true, to the distinct claim that true beliefs must correspond to some *thing* in reality. But the latter is an extravagant and unwarranted position. Is there a thing, or fact, that corresponds to 7+5=12? What "thing" makes it true, if it is true, that the birth of Galileo was a necessary antecedent of the scientific revolution? Is there an ontological correspondent to the truth that it is difficult to get clear on metaethics? A correspondence theory of truth, which needs a thing for every truth to correspond to, must either subscribe to a crowded Platonic heaven, where every general truth has a thing or collection of things making it true, all existing in an atemporal eternal realm, or restrict truth to concrete statements about elementary particles and their current positions.[11]

It is not the metaphysical extravagance suggested by correspondence theories alone that makes them problematic; they also provide no convincing account of the nature of the correspondence. Ever since people have reflected on the matter, it has been obvious that descriptions of ordinary experience are inadequate to describe the world more closely inspected or carefully considered. Philosophers from at least since Plato and the Vedantists have taught that there is a chasm between appearance and reality. Modern science has empirically confirmed the philosophical suspicion: things are not what they seem.[12] Surfaces appearing smooth to eye and hand are roughly textured when more minutely examined. Regions perceived as lifeless prove teeming with microorganisms. Solid objects are mostly empty space, and empty space is abuzz with activity. The advance of science can be told as a retreat from the understanding and vocabulary of ordinary experience, culminating in Relativity Theory and most especially in Quantum Mechanics, where the very forms and structures of human experience give way to mathematical models, models which some scientists refuse to even think of as "descriptions" of reality, but rather as tools for making exquisitely precise predictions. If reality makes our quotidian beliefs true it is not by being *similar* to the experiences which give rise to those beliefs. Even the reality inferred from our experiences isn't similar to them.

Correspondence between beliefs and their typical causes is both a more plausible explanation of what makes beliefs true, and closer to what I take to be the best account of how we *recognize* the truth. However, a causal correspondence theory remains unconvincing. In a causal correspondence theory reality is supposed to cause experiences which in turn cause belief, and beliefs are true if they are induced by experiences that were caused by the typical causes of just those experiences. A true belief then is one caused by the circumstances which usually lead to that belief.[13]

This story leaves us unable to have *common* false beliefs. The flat earth belief becomes true, as do all beliefs that arise naturally from experience, for surely there is something about reality which causes those common beliefs to become common. But systematic error is not transmuted into truth by virtue of being systematic. Causal connections between belief and reality are indeed involved in justifying our beliefs, but not because there is a uniquely correct correspondence between particular causes and particular beliefs. Causes are the most promising prospect for any correspondence account, but neither typical causes, nor isomorphism, stipulated connection, nor historical association confers truth on belief by transforming belief into a stand-in for an aspect of reality.[14]

Rejecting this implausible view of truth does not yet qualify moral principles as candidates for truth, it merely prevents summary disqualification. But we need not provide an alternative theory of truth, if by that we mean some definition or analysis of truth's necessary and sufficient conditions, in order to defend the possible truth of moral principles. Rather, we require a theory of justification, a theory of what counts toward holding a belief true. And this can be done without specifying what truth is. One need not be able to define love in order to justify the claim that Robert Browning loved Elizabeth Barrett. Indeed, a theory of justification presumes an understanding of truth's meaning. The meaning of "truth," however, does not require knowing its necessary and sufficient conditions. I make no commitment to a particular analysis of truth by claiming I know what "truth" means. Nor does a theory of justification—a theory of when we can be confident a belief is true—require we possess an analysis of truth.

Before offering a conception of justification that can render the moral truth we seek, we will note the many strengths of moral relativism, the ancient adversary that the champions of undiminished moral truth must confront.

3. MORAL RELATIVISM

A thoroughgoing general relativism would hold that there is no truth except in relation to a particular believer or group of believers, a view that I will later endorse in a modified version. But *moral* relativism usually makes a more specific claim: moral truth is relativistic even if general relativism is false.

A number of related but distinct doctrines get called moral relativism. One is a doctrine rooted in linguistic theory. It is the claim that the truth of any moral statement depends on who is making it; moral language must be evaluated in light of who is speaking. The view has an initial plausibility because linguistic relativism is clearly true of some statement types: I truly assert "*I* was born October 4, 1950," and you, with equal truth (at least for most readers) say "*I* was *not* born on October 4, 1950."

Is something like this going on in *all* moral statements? "Yes" argues the moral relativist: my claim "torture is wrong" and your claim "torture is *not* wrong," may both be true in spite of the apparent contradiction. The "I" in each of the birthday sentences is readily understood as speaking of different people. The relativist sees a far more subtle equivocation in the "wrong" attributed and denied in the two torture sentences, but no less equivocal for being obscured. What counts as "wrong" depends on an implicit standard, and the relativist argues that underlying our torture claims are different standards leading to our divergent evaluations of torture. This does not mean we are adducing different evidence on which to base our statements, but rather that our statements are about different things. The statements may broadly both be about torture, but they are specifically about different aspects of torture. My claim that torture is wrong may be about whether it causes pain; yours may be about whether it effectively elicits information. Were this equivocation made manifest the appearance of contradiction disappears. Just as our birthday sentences may both be true because it is logically possible for me to have been born October 4, 1950, and for you not to have been, our torture sentences may both be true because it is logically possible for torture to cause pain *and* to elicit information. I am not you, and causing pain is not eliciting information.[15]

What is usually meant by "moral relativism," begins as a corollary of the above linguistic claim: if moral statements are implicitly (and unconsciously) referring to different moral principles, and thereby make different statements, then a set of moral statements may all be true in spite of their apparently conflicting surface grammar. My "torture is wrong" really asserts "by my standards torture is wrong," and your "torture is not wrong" should be interpreted as "by your standards torture is not wrong." Here we find no disagreement, only a use of different principles.

The next step to moral relativism declares each standard as "good," or "correct," or "true," as any other moral standard. Because the relativist assumes the correspondence theory of truth, and finds no transcendent moral standard with which to evaluate our historically formed principles, the principles are alethic as well as ontological equals. No moral principle is more correct or more justified than any other moral principle. One morality is just as good as another. So concludes the relativist.

The most persuasive framing of this line of relativist thought speaks of perspectives. Moral judgments, like all judgments, are formed in and emerge from a perspective. To re-purpose an image of Thomas Nagel's[16]—there is no judgment from nowhere. Nor is there evaluation from nowhere. Whether a moral judgment is true depends on the principles of the judger, which are constituents of her perspective. Again, moral claims are true (or false) only when judged from a particular perspective. Different perspectives will result in different, potentially conflicting, truth evaluations, and no supreme perspective serves as the final court of appeals.

That there are a variety of moral principles the moral relativist thinks an established fact. While I have some sympathy with the anti-relativist claim that this appearance is a result of diverse empirical and metaphysical beliefs rather than evidence of *fundamental moral* disagreement, I'm willing to concede that there may indeed be different basic moral principles employed by different agents, and it is beyond question that on important moral issues there is disagreement, whatever the grounds of that disagreement may be.

The tendency of moral disagreement to resist resolution even upon extensive inquiry needs explanation.[17] The relativist's explanation is that there are many true principles, and each principle decides the issue a different way. Perhaps the resort to different standards is not the only possible explanation of moral disagreement, but it is an explanation.

Not only does the relativist have a ready account of moral disagreement, she is certainly correct that whatever moral standards human beings have, be it one or many, that standard is a result of our biology and history. Our moral beliefs are a contingent matter. Even if it is the case that there is a single human moral standard, it might have been a different one had we been wired differently or had our cultural evolution taken a different path. If many moral standards don't exist, they might have. Whether a moral standard is one shared by all humans, or one being used and defended by a particular human, the fact that it could have been other than it is shakes confidence in its truth: "there but for fortune I might have been a rule-utilitarian." The relativist's confidence that she has *the* correct answer isn't merely shaken; she thinks their contingency robs all moral principles of the possibility of being justified. Therefore, all of them must be *arbitrary*.

Here, I believe, the moral relativist fails to distinguish contingency from arbitrariness. Contingency is a causal concept; if, given causal laws and circumstances, multiple effects are possible, then what actually happens is contingent, that is, its occurrence is random or depends on further, unspecified facts.[18] Contingency is simply the notion that things could have been otherwise. My nose (for all *anyone* knows) might have resembled my father's rather than my mother's; that it resembles Mom's is a contingent fact. Perhaps omniscience would reveal that everything (or nothing) is actually contingent. Perhaps God knows there was no chance I could have had Dad's nose; but given our lesser knowledge, some things appear to be contingent and some don't. We know enough to know that any offspring of my parents would necessarily be human. No contingency there.

Among the things that could have been otherwise are our moral principles. Humans may never have evolved, and so had no principles, or the cultures and history that produced contemporary moral principles may have been different. Perhaps any *agents* that exist would necessarily have practical principles, and perhaps agents of certain kinds necessarily have principles of certain forms, but as the relativist notes, diversity of moral principles seems to demonstrate the contingency of any particular standard.

Arbitrariness, however, is a justificatory notion, and speaks of the presence or absence of a *specific type* of cause: a belief or an action uncaused by a reason is arbitrary. I am indifferent to whether I write in blue or black ink. I reach for the blue ink pen rather than the black ink pen. But I neither have, nor even believe I have, a *reason* for using *blue* ink. My use of it is arbitrary. A man asks his son rather than his daughter if the child is interested in learning how to fix the flat tire. He thinks he has a reason, so his choice of child to teach does not appear arbitrary to him, or indeed to all those who share his beliefs about innate gender interests and abilities. But for those of us who believe those beliefs are false, he has a motive but he has no reason (although we grant he thinks he has a reason), and, in our judgment, his choice is arbitrary at best.[19]

There surely are causes for our arbitrariness, but the causes, even if known, do not make belief or action less arbitrary so long as those causes are not reasons. Should a future master neurologist scan our brains and find the configuration of gray matter in our skulls that causally accounts for all of our beliefs and actions that are unmotivated by reason, the beliefs and actions will be explained, but still arbitrary.[20] The arbitrary may not be contingent, for an event may be causally necessary without any of the causes being reasons,[21] and, more to the point, the contingent need not be arbitrary, for although an event is caused by reasons, given the laws of nature and given circumstances, other causes may have obtained. Reason may have prevented the United States and the Soviet Union from going to war at the time of the Cuban missile crisis, but nothing we know made that escape causally inevitable. Avoiding nuclear war in 1962 was not an arbitrary act, but it was a contingent event.

Contingency, therefore, is not relevant to the charge that all moral standards are arbitrary. Although moral standards may never have come into being, it yet may be the case that Reason brought some of them into being. However, if reasons played no role in causing a moral principle, the charge of arbitrariness would be warranted. So, are there reasons to hold moral principles?

There are no *moral* reasons for holding moral principles. As the generator of moral reasons, *fundamental* moral principles themselves are uncaused by *moral* reasoning.[22] Still, like a constitution which is immune to being judged constitutional or unconstitutional, and yet may be judged by other standards, we can evaluate how basic moral principles fare judged by a nonmoral standard, a standard which may generate nonmoral reasons to hold the moral principles.[23] The nonmoral standard that gives moral principle the possibility of escaping arbitrariness can be nothing but Reason itself. Morality is not arbitrary if it is a subset of Reason. Reason itself, although contingent, is neither arbitrary nor nonarbitrary—rather it is the arbiter of the arbitrary.

The standard that all forms of rational principles and procedures claim to meet, including moral ones, is the tendency to reveal truth. Deductive rules of inference promise to preserve truth flawlessly as beliefs combine and transform into other beliefs. Inductive principles promise insight into the probable truth regarding the unobserved based on the observed. There may be no noncircular way for them to justify their claim that they do serve truth, but deduction's and induction's roles in rationality presume there is a truth to be served.[24]

Moral principles too must offer a domain of truth they reveal, otherwise, they would be arbitrary, and there would be no reason to adopt one morality rather than another. If there were no moral truths, rationally speaking, any moral principle would be as useless as any other, for none could be a truth revealer if there were no moral truths to reveal. If "Thou shalt not steal" is no more true or false than "Never give a sucker an even break," then, if we take rationality to be about tracking the truth, neither principle could be rational, and adherence to either principle would be arbitrary.

Of course, if these were not fundamental moral principles, but rather derived from others, they might not appear arbitrary in in the absence of a realm of moral truth. Suppose one accepted "never give a sucker an even break," because, along with some beliefs about the best way to acquire wealth, it followed from "Do that which will ensure wealth," which itself followed from "Do that which your heart most desired." Does that not justify "never give a sucker an even break?" Does that not make it a reasoned choice of principles, a nonarbitrary choice? It would, but only if "Do that which your heart most desires," along with the other premises in the derivation of "never give a sucker an even break," were *true*. At the bottom, only the possibility of truth can save a belief (and therefore an action in accordance with a judgment) from arbitrariness, for reasons, the antithesis of the arbitrary, are by nature seekers of truth.

It must be granted that no *moral* argument can demonstrate that a particular fundamental moral principle reveals moral truth more reliably than an alternative fundamental moral principle, for that demonstration would employ a moral principle and thereby beg the question. However, the relativist is not disputing particular moral truths, but the idea that there are *objective* moral truths. To answer the relativist, we must show that it is possible for a morality to get at the moral truth better than an alternative, even if we cannot yet, and perhaps never will, definitively demonstrate that it has actually done so.[25] And to show that it is possible for a morality to get at the moral truth better than an alternative, there must be moral truth.

In sum, if morality exists at all, then relativism is surely correct that one or another particular moral perspective is inescapable, that moral standards are not external to human beings but are rather human creations which might have been other than they are, and that there is a strong appearance of a variety of deeply held yet incompatible moral principles. However, neither the perspectival specificity, nor the contingency, nor the multiplicity, nor the human genesis of moral standards self-evidently implies that they are all equally correct, equally true. Nonetheless, in light of the relativist insights, the anti-relativist is burdened with showing how a moral standard can be correct, leaving others incorrect. Although basic moral principles are not deficient because unjustifiable in moral terms, to respond to the relativist challenge they must be able to justify the truth of their implications. The problem is not that moral principles are morally unjustifiable, it is whether there is anything *they apply to* that is eligible for justification, that is, that might be true. Can moral judgments, any moral judgment, be true?

Before shouldering the anti-relativist burden of describing a nonrelativist moral truth, we should note the heavy load the relativist must carry, which makes being an authentic relativist a rarity. While this does not lighten the anti-relativist burden, feeling the weight of relativist baggage, may encourage taking on the nonrelativist responsibility to provide an account of moral truth.

If we ask the relativist to adjudicate between my condemnation and your tolerance of torture, she would say "you are both right according to the standards you each employ." We could readily agree, but that is not what we are asking; we want to know which of us she thinks has come to the right view on torture according to *her*, the relativist's, sincerely held moral standards. She can of course claim to have no moral standards (although that is not the typical relativist position—it is more the amoralist one) and so no view on the matter.[26] But a standard-less life is not an easy one, for without standards, there are no means of evaluating actions, and yet to live one must act. Indeed, a standard-less being would hardly qualify as an ongoing agent; she would enact an endless stream of rationally unconnected whims, as if she has no good, only impulses. Without standards, she acts not because she *judges* anything worthy of achievement, but only because she (with or without reflection) finds herself nonrationally driven toward some ends and not others. As a purely theoretical stance, the abjuring of any practical standards puts a relativist in the position of holding that her relativism has no moral implications whatsoever.

The relativist might object that her life isn't without standards, only without *moral* standards. But if her standards do not evaluate and recommend *action,* they are practically vacuous, and if they do, they are moral standards despite her demurral. However, even if one granted (which I do not) a conceptual distinction between morality and practical rationality,[27] any metaphysical grounds for rejecting moral standards would apply with equal force to any standards of practice. If there is nothing you ought to do, there is nothing you ought to do.

Alternatively the relativist might (indeed usually does) admit having *moral* standards, and perhaps say her standards take torture to be wrong, but her relativism requires her to acknowledge that your standards, which are tolerant of torture, are no less true than her own. This may not prevent her from being seriously committed to her standards and the wrongness of torture,[28] but it is then a commitment without any rational foundation, and her condemnation of torture reflects standards which she takes seriously but which she thinks *you* have no *reason* to take seriously. Although not as difficult as being without standards, having to act with utmost seriousness on standards you believe no more correct than those which support contrary actions also saps the will. But if the relativist does not really take her standards seriously, she doesn't really hold those standards. To truly hold moral standards as a relativist one has to experience one's judgments as both righteous and ultimately arbitrary. Not an easy psychological trick.

Still, in spite of the difficulty of living a relativist life, indeed even were it impossible to live as an ever-mindful relativist, we would have to acknowledge its (or amoralism's) truth if we could not provide a credible alternative account of how there can be moral principles revealing of moral truth.

4. A PRAGMATIC APPROACH TO RECOGNIZING THE TRUTH

A pragmatic theory of *recognizing* true beliefs—which is independent of a pragmatic theory of truth's meaning or essence—claims that truth is *known* by its fruit.[29] We recognize a belief as true because holding it is, all things considered, helpful to *achieving our goals.*[30] You are ultimately justified in believing that the cat is on the mat, not because you have certain visual evidence (it looks like the cat is on the mat), and testimony (your companion reports that the cat is on the mat), but because, when you believe the cat is on the mat, you successfully locate the cat. If in spite of appearances and all reports, upon wanting to pet the cat, you did better by going to the chair than to the mat, you would be more justified in believing that the cat was on the chair than on the mat. Many of one's firm beliefs discount certain experiences as illusory and certain testimony as mistaken. The most justified belief is the one that proves more serviceable than its competitors.[31]

This unrefined initial sketch of a pragmatic theory of justification is prey to obvious counterexamples. An old story about Jake, the winner of millions of dollars in the lottery, exemplifies the simplest. When asked how he came to play the winning number of 14300, Jake replied that he had dreamt of 120 diamonds dancing with 120 pearls. He multiplied the pearls and diamonds and chose to bet on the product—14300. When told he was in error, that $120 \times 120 = 14400$, not 14300, he replied, "So, you go be a mathematician!"

It would appear that Jake's belief that $120 \times 120 = 14300$ better helped him achieve his goal of wealth than the alternative belief that $120 \times 120 = 14400$. But it would be rash to conclude that a pragmatic theory of justification must thereby designate the first belief to be more justified than the second. Consider the larger story: Jake's belief, if consistent with his approach to arithmetic, would result in a steady stream of beliefs that ill served him. Others who had any quantitative dealing with him would think of him as an idiot. He would quickly be cheated out of his new wealth. His faulty tax returns could land him in jail. We could hardly expect him to be a successful investor. Every purchase he made would pose a danger. And if we try to imagine him an otherwise competent arithmetician, with this singular idiosyncratic belief, his prospects are no better. We make him into a man with no cognitive commitment to consistency, no belief in the basic principles of inference, no need to see how things fit together. It is difficult to think of him as successful in achieving his goals. Indeed, the belief that *we* take to be true is the one that would best serve him, namely that although $120 \times 120 = 14400$, he was fortunate to have had a different belief when choosing his lottery number, but that he could not expect to succeed in the future by maintaining the belief that $120 \times 120 = 14300$. If objectors reply that, nonetheless at the moment that Jake was choosing a lottery number, $120 \times 120 = 143000$ was the optimally successful belief, then again they are wrong. The most successful belief would have been "dreams do not foretell winning lottery numbers, $120 \times 120 = 14400$, and although I have no ground for choosing one 5 digit number over another, I expect 14300 to win and will act accordingly." Such a belief would best help Jake achieve his goals. It would certainly leave him with the same lottery winnings.

Jake's story points us toward the refinements that are part of an adequate pragmatic theory of recognizing truth. First, goal achievement isn't a one time, at one instant, matter.[32] More significantly, people have many goals and many beliefs, and therefore, although beliefs are the core carriers of truth, *they carry it as a collective.* Sets of beliefs are the things in which truth is fundamentally found or found wanting. More accurately, sets of beliefs are the things which are more or less justified, and a single belief's claim to truth derives from its contribution to the justifiability of the set of beliefs of which it is a member.[33] The set is defined as all of the beliefs currently attributable to a believer. The beliefs that the cat is on the mat and $120 \times 120 = 14400$ tend toward truth insofar as they increase the justifiability of the set to which they belong. A belief is justified because it makes the set of beliefs it is part of more justified. And it makes the set of beliefs more justified not merely because of its inherent properties, but rather because of its contribution to the set's effectiveness, which will depend, in the first instance (but not solely) on the other beliefs in the set. It might be useful to believe the cat is on the mat while believing the mat is in the bedroom, but less useful to believe the cat is on the mat while believing the mat is on a cloud.

Your belief set's usefulness also depends on factors external to the set, including other believers belief sets. The effectiveness of believing that you will meet Jake at 2 p.m. at the diner depends in large part on what Jake believes. Ultimately, the justifiability of a belief depends on all of reality, for a set of beliefs justifiability is determined by its effectiveness at achieving goals, and that effectiveness is affected by which goals are pursued and the context in which they are pursued. Considered in isolation, no belief is justified, because it has neither coworkers with which it might work well or poorly, nor a mission that defines the quality of its work. And workability, according to pragmatism, is the *measure* (which is different than the essence) of a belief's truth.

The denigrator of morality in the relativist mode might argue that this pragmatic theory of justification makes his case. Justification depends on effectiveness, and the measure of effectiveness is success at achieving given goals. Therefore, the measure of a belief's truth will vary with the goals of the believer. If sets of belief are justified not because they match reality, but because reality empowers those belief sets *relative* to a set of goals, then there is no single set of beliefs that are *absolutely* justified, no description of the world that is justifiable independently of any set of goals. This appears to be a rejection of the notion of objective justification, because goals always are *someone's*. Insofar as beliefs' justification depends on goals, they are only subjectively justifiable, justifiable relative to someone's goals. Here we seem to be stymied in our quest for justifications of action that are sound for any rational observer regardless of her personal set of goals.

Before attempting to overcome the apparent relativism of pragmatic justification, it should be noted that this sort of relativism does *not* claim that beliefs are justified because someone wants the beliefs to be true. The truth of a belief cannot be determined apart from the goals the belief might serve. In that sense beliefs are justified relative to goals. But their truth is quite independent of anyone's desire that they be true.[34] Beliefs are justified rather because they are needed as action guides in order to achieve goals. Suppose one wants to be creative; with the view on offer here, a justified belief would enable one to become creative. Perhaps, the belief that one must work hard to be creative is more effective at engendering creativity than any alternative belief. The belief that creativity requires hard work would then be justified, whether or not anyone wants to believe it. We might prefer to believe that hard work is not required to become creative, but our belief preferences do not justify our beliefs, our result preferences do. There is nothing of the "believing it makes it so" in this relativism, nor does it make mind-external reality irrelevant to justification. The effectiveness of a belief for a given end will be thoroughly dependent on the nature of reality. Reality marks our beliefs true because, given our goals, reality proves them good.

Nonetheless, however sensitive to reality this view of justification is, however demanding it is in evaluating beliefs, as it stands it still appears to make justification depend on features that *vary across individuals*. It looks as though your rationally held belief can be, at bottom, different from mine, your truth different from mine. It would appear that at best we might get a principal of action to provide "subjective truth," and subjective truth is insufficient for the kind of morality we are hoping to defend. For that we need unqualified truth, objective truth.

Pragmatic justification does not deny objectivity. Although we can only recognize truth because it achieves goals well, and all goals are subjective, we are nonetheless not stuck with subjective justifications as our only ones. That is because pervasive subjectivity does not crowd out objectivity. Only small-mindedness does. Before we can discover the nature of objective justification, we must grapple with the idea of objectivity.

5. OBJECTIVITY

Objectivity is what subjectivity is not. Subjectivity is the nature of things in their relation to a particular subject. Conceptually, objectivity is born of subjectivity, and the idea of subjectivity begins with the idea that there are other minds.[35] The minds are other because they differ in beliefs, perceptions, desires, powers, or judgments. When qualitative like-mindedness becomes qualitative identical-mindedness, otherness disappears. "Subjectivity" labels and explains other-mindedness. It is the notion that nature and history give each mind a different form and location, which together determine the particular matter and shape of its contents. Different minds, differently placed, have different "perspectives." If your thoughts are not my thoughts, it is because your perspective is not my perspective.

To say that a thought is subjective is to say that it is a result of that mind's, that *subject's*, perspective. But, taken literally, that is a trivial claim. How could any thought not be a function of the properties of the mind thinking it? The idea of subjectivity takes on some interest when it is used to explain *differences* by positing that different perspectives account for different thoughts, and it takes on more interest when the thought-differences it is explaining are not restricted to sensory perceptions, but expand to judgments of facts and values.

Subjectivity is inescapable. Thoughts are activities of the mind, and have no more being without thinkers than do dances without dancers.[36] And just as each dance must take on the features and location of the dancer, so must each thought of the thinker. But the ubiquity of subjectivity does not render objectivity illusory.

Objectivity is commonly, but incoherently, conceived of as thought scrubbed clean of the particularities of a particular thinker. Thomas Nagel, in the trope we alluded to before, has called this idea of objectivity "the view from nowhere." It is a mind without a perspective. Perhaps a solipsist can make sense of this idea, but you and I cannot. Views are always from somewhere. But, some views see more, because they include other views. These more encompassing views include what is seen in other perspectives, and often why those other perspectives fail to see things seen in the more capacious view. Objectivity, then, is not a transcendence of subjectivity; it is an expansion of subjectivity.[37]

Although often heuristically useful, it is a mistake to cast objectivity as the neutral, undistorted perspective arbitrating between partisan, blurry-eyed subjectivities.[38] "Undistorted" suggests observation uncontaminated by the observer. But the ideal of objectivity multiplies such "contaminations," not in the vain hope that they will cancel out each other and reveal the thing in itself, but rather in an endeavor to enrich our understanding of all the effects of reality that register in any observer. What appears in only a few, or even a single perspective, is not noise that objectivity tunes out, it is a note that objectivity strives to bring into harmony with all the other subjective strains. The conductor is as subjective as any other member of the orchestra, but she is working with more material.

Perspectives may be ranked along a subjective-objective spectrum by how well they incorporate and account for other perspectives. Were there to be a mind that saw what all other actual and possible minds saw (and felt, and thought), its perspective would still be subjective. God's-eye view is a particular eye view, even though it has achieved full objectivity, which is not the view from nowhere, but the view from everywhere.[39] More limited perspectives have lesser degrees of objectivity. Absent omniscience, there is no absolute objectivity, but still objectivity is a real property. People can be kind even though there is no perfectly kind person, and similarly objective even if there is no perfectly objective person.

Although every particular perspective is had by a particular subject, and so is necessarily subjective, it can move toward objectivity. The objective perspective is an ideal one, which reconciles all of the information contained in every possible subjective perspective. No subject of course has, or could have (disallowing mystical claims) this view from everywhere. But any subject can attempt to register information from other perspectives and thereby become more objective.

Objectivity, however, is not some sort of compromise between the judgments of various subjects. Nor is it a *negotiated* movement to consensus among actual subjects. Rather, it is the information in all perspectives that objectivity takes into account, and this accounting requires no agreement. Although subjective judgments are not to be ignored, for that there are such judgments is important information that a perfectly objective set of beliefs should understand, the objective beliefs do not have to concede correctness to any of these limited subjective judgments, at least not on any particular judgment.[40] Nor must objective practical judgments enjoin the actual pursuit of all goals. The view from everywhere is different from the collection of views from everywhere. It is the integration of the *content* of every perspective into a consistent, coherent perspective. It is the ideal perspective that every individual would achieve if she were perfectly objective. It is why, although consensus does not constitute truth, under conditions that permit the formation and expression of dissent, convergence of views is a sign of increased objectivity; we become objective by incorporating one another's experience. Having done so—having seen, heard, and felt what the other has seen, heard, and felt, we will increasingly conclude what she concludes.

An assertion of objectivity is commonly misinterpreted as dogmatic commitment, or pretention of infallibility. But beyond the obvious point that defending objectivity is not a defense of one's personal objectivity, the concept of objectivity is an, almost literally, open-minded ideal. It broadens the candidates for truth rather than dogmatically dismisses them, and, rightly conceived, unsettles certainty by enlarging the grounds for possible error. The ideal of absolute objectivity is not reached till all subjective judgments are considered and accounted for in a synoptic vision of reality. As long as there is a dissenter, or simply the possibility of a new, unaccounted for, subjectivity, confidence that one has attained objective truth must be restrained, and any belief, factual, moral, or aesthetic, must be held tentatively. Finally, although the believer in objectivity strives for an inclusive subjective perspective, she has no nonsubjective way of comparing the extent of the inclusivity of her perspective to that of others. The concept of objectivity entails the fallibility of your own perspective. Belief in objectivity is needed to keep you humble, especially about one's own objectivity.

Epistemically modest, the ideal of objectivity is metaphysically minimalist. It posits other minds with goals of their own, and the ontological bases of communication between the separate minds. In addition, the pragmatic context in which I place objectivity, posits a reality which has causal powers that render some sets of beliefs more effective than others. But nothing further is claimed about the nature of that reality in this conception of objectivity. Certainly, it does not imply there is some absolute description of reality, independent of its effects on subjects, which the objective perspective procures. There is nothing more in this objectivity than supposing a reality, which somehow shapes our subjective lives. All of them.

6. OBJECTIVELY TRUE PRINCIPLES

Effective goal achievement justifies belief, and the objectivity of the justification derives from the breadth of goals the effectiveness is measured against. Objectivity is effectiveness in light of goal inclusivity.[41] Just as information gleaned from every perspective makes description objective, the interests that emerge from every perspective makes action objective. A principle of action's objectivity grows with the membership of the set of goals used to test it. A perfectly justified principle of action, which a rational person will acknowledge objectively true, would be a member of that set of beliefs that would best realize all goals, without regard to the goal's origins.[42]

There may be different systems of belief that would be equally effective at achieving the most inclusive set of goals, so this conception of objectivity does not imply that there is a unique set of objectively justifiable beliefs.[43] But the possibility of multiple truths must be distinguished from the idea that nothing is true, or the idea that everything is true. Although not provably monogamous, pragmatically justified belief is far from promiscuous. There are an infinite number of sets of belief less efficacious than the most effective set(s) of beliefs, so there is no end of objectively *false* beliefs. Any principle of action not found in the best set of beliefs, is unjustifiable, and cannot contribute to a sound justification of action. Acting on such a principle is irrational. The theoretical pluralism of pragmatic justifications gives no scope for a robust relativism of the "all principles are true, no actions are wrong," variety.

Two additional considerations diminish the relativistic character of pragmatic justification. First, for neither individuals nor social groups are sets of goals static. Implicit in objectivity's universalistic ambition, is its temporal impartiality—objectivity is not measured by a temporal cross-section of goals. An objectively true belief retains its effectiveness as future, evolving, and unforeseen goals come into being. The unpredictability as well as diversity of goals stabilizes the objectivity of belief, or rather, one criterion of the objectivity of belief is its stability across temporal perspectives. The best all-purpose tools may be inferior to tools tailor-made for specific tasks, but they are less liable to obsolescence. Lasting, wide-ranging, and adaptable effectiveness is the mark of truth. As we learn in eighth grade science, the longer a belief is tested and the more various the circumstances in which it is tested, the better its confirmation. Beliefs that pass unanticipated tests earn special credibility. Principles of action, like other sorts of belief, are justified by their enduring efficacy. As the universe of goals expands, once serviceable principles prove parochial and lose claim to objectivity.

Principles of action are winnowed from objective ranks even more ruthlessly than other kinds of beliefs, for it is their manifest function to adjudicate between conflicting goals. The belief that the cat is on the mat does not directly tie its justifiability to any goal, however, much its justification rests on its relation to the totality of goals, the goals of all who have goals. It presents itself as indifferent to goals. Its acceptance as a fact, its justification, ultimately depends on its contribution to goal achievement, but no specific goal is alluded to or implied by the claim that "the cat is on the mat." However, the principle that implies one ought not to torture the cat, directly suggests that the acknowledged universe of goals is best served by belief in this principle. The callous child's amusement, the sadist's frustration, the cat-lovers anguish, and the cat's agonized suffering are immediately revealed as the arbiters of the principle's justifiability. The *exclusion* of any goal is simultaneously a step away from the principle's objectivity and a specification of its purpose. Principles of action wear their degree of objectivity on their sleeve because they so clearly point at the goals their invokers would use to justify their truth. With principles of action, goal achievement is the last and first evidence adduced in their defense, and the goals explicitly entered into evidence declare the principle's level of objectivity. Practical principles, which its denigrators view as morality's flimsy subjective foundations, are instead its most overtly objective concrete pillars.

Hallvard Lillehammer suggests three characteristics of the objective: liability to error, dependence on reality for correctness, and, under ideal conditions, the tendency of objective judgments to converge.[44] The "view from everywhere," notion of objectivity, even when applied to practical principles, features all three. Any given practical principle might not appear in any justified belief set, so it is liable to error. If the principle is justified, it is because it appears in a justified set of beliefs, known to be true because reality enables it to maximally satisfy the totality of goals; so the principle's justification depends on reality. Finally, under ideal conditions, wherein everyone recognized the maximal satisfaction of the same set of goals, namely the totality of goals, as the measure of justified principles, there is every reason to expect convergence of judgment. Groups that share goals tend to agree on principles of actions relative to those goals. Agreement on the ends will, along with instrumental experience, bring about agreement on the true means. If judgments converge more readily on factual beliefs than they do on beliefs of principle, it is attributable to the great overlap of *proximate* goals used to justify factual statements. The belief that the cat is on the mat serves the goal of locating the cat, a step on the way to feeding it, petting it, teasing it, admiring it, or protecting it. The enemies of cats and friends of cats alike share the goal of locating it. The same belief is useful to both, so both acknowledge its truth. All who share the goal of protecting cats will just as easily agree on the truth of the judgment that one ought not to torture cats as all who are interested in locating the cat will agree that it is on the mat.

Of course, a justification of the pragmatic approach to justifying principles of action as *objectively* true, cannot escape the ungroundedness that marks any ultimate *justification* of the truth of anything, when put under sufficient philosophical pressure. By what *justified standard* can one justify the pragmatic *standard of truth*? Any answer must beg the question.[45] Nonetheless, we have the same kind of reasons to believe "you ought not to torture the cat," is *objectively true,* if it is, as we have to believe "the cat is on the mat" is objectively true, if it is. Both will best serve the goals garnered from every perspective, even if their maximal satisfaction leaves some goals unachieved.

A pragmatic approach to justification is often taken as involving a "deflationary," concept of truth, a pale version of the original idea. This is false. Pragmatic justifications justify truths that are as stubborn and enduring as we can coherently wish. It does not claim that we are justified in believing whatever some individual, group of individuals, or even the totality of individuals *want* to believe, for what we want to believe may not serve us well. Nor does it claim that we are justified in believing whatever some individual or group of individuals in fact believe, for what we in fact believe may not serve us well. Finally, it does not claim that we are justified in believing the set of beliefs that would be most useful to an individual or any group of individuals that is a *proper subset* of all individuals, whether that subset is defined geographically, temporally, cognitively, or politically. What serves some well, may not, all persons considered, best serve the whole. What pragmatic justification *does* claim is that we are justified in believing only those beliefs that will be included in the set of beliefs which best serves all of us. What best serves all of us may not, probably will not, include beliefs which are most useful to only some of us.

The conception leaves justification the same for all. A justified belief doesn't change with circumstances. Although justification is relative to goals, the goals it is relative to are the totality of past, present, and future goals, and they fix what it is justified to believe as securely as any isomorphism or unvarying causal links to reality could. This conception of justification does not deny that there is a reality whose properties are independent of what we find useful to believe. But truth and objectivity are not properties of reality; they are properties of beliefs and expressions of beliefs. The correctness of those expressions or of those beliefs—linguistic entities and mental states that dispose us to respond in particular ways to reality's properties—can only be judged by the experiences engendered by the expressions and mental states. This is no more than a basic empiricist tenet: truth is recognized through experience. Reality makes what is true true, but truth is not a feature of non-human reality. Nor are expressions and beliefs justified by their being similar to reality, or re-presenting bits of it, or being typically caused by the same bits of it, or even by being caused by the original bits of reality that first gave the beliefs their usefulness.[46] Reality, *as a whole*, simply makes some *sets* of belief more useful than others. The most useful set is what we are justified in believing. What other justification could there possibly be?[47]

7. SOCIAL CONSENSUS AND OBJECTIVE JUSTIFICATION

Much philosophical angst and discussion in recent decades has been concerned with whether this sort of pragmatic view of justification and objectivity makes them *entirely* a matter of social agreement, free of any constraints imposed by nature. This has been the main content of the "deflationary" fear. I will discuss this question in more technical depth in chapter 4, but for now, answering in the manner of my former teacher Joel Kupperman, who was wont to value nuanced accuracy more than attention-grabbing dramatic pronouncements, yes and no.

The meaning of terms requires consensus, and, as only meaningful beliefs can be justifiable, there is a sense in which social agreement provides the grounds of justification. Reality has effects, it can even kill us. But that is not a judgment, not a claim, not a justification; an effect is meaningless, and so cannot be a true proposition, so is not a candidate for justifier or justified. Objectivity and justification are epistemological properties and cannot be predicated of mindless reality, nor can mindless reality make any assertions or denials. Reality can help or hurt us, but never agree with us or dispute with us. Meaning is essential to justification, and meaning is essentially social. That is one reason for the "yes"; social consensus is the ground of justification.

However, given a meaningful proposed standard, what actually satisfies it requires no social consensus. The justificatory evidence, according to the standard, are propositions regarding the *beliefs' effects* on goal achievement, and those effects are not exclusively generated by social agreement. Reality, including nontruth apt parts of it, determines what effects are caused by what beliefs. These beliefs' effects weigh heavily in justification, even if the effects *qua* effects play no role in the justification itself. Although not part of justifications (which are constituted solely by propositions whose meanings are a matter of social consensus) nature's effects are justifications' primary sculptors. Hence, the "no"; justification and objectivity do not float free of inputs from nature. We must agree on what the effects of our beliefs are, but our agreement does not cause the effects.

This realism gives nature substantial influence regarding which beliefs are justified. However, in addition to establishing propositional meaning, there is another consideration which makes social consensus loom large in this view of justification: if maximal goal achievement justifies, not only must we learn of all goals, we must inquire into their state of achievement. An agent is the best expert on what her goals are and their degree of achievement. An expert, of course, can be wrong, and even if right, is not an expert on all matters. An agent in general has no expertise on others' goals or their degree of satisfaction. That is why objectivity demands wide consultation. A stable, growing, social consensus constitutes strong, and in some cases the best evidence that a belief is justified. This does not mean that a belief held by a single believer, or indeed by no one, may not be justified. Any given social consensus is defeasible, and nature's effects can causally contribute to its rejection. But it does mean that a belief destined to forever have dissenters will forever remain doubtful. It may maximally achieve goals despite the dissent, but the dissent indicates that some goals are unachieved and raises the question whether the goal achievement attained really is maximal.

An analogy might prove helpful: A ball of twine covered in cowhide passing a man holding a stick near a piece of 1.5 square feet of house-shaped white wood or plastic lying on the ground is neither a strike nor a ball, for the social institution of baseball creates strikes and balls. Regardless of where the ball flew in relation to the "plate," without the institution of baseball there are no balls or strikes. Nor would stipulating a "strike zone," by itself create a baseball strike. Outside of the context of the game of baseball a ball thrown with a specific relation to a plate on the ground can be called whatever we wish, but to be a *baseball* strike it must have a host of implications, for example, three of them and a "batter" is "out." Social consensus, people cooperating in a mutually understood practice, creates baseball, which in turn allows thrown balls to be strikes.

Now although social consensus creates strikes, whether a pitched ball in a baseball game is a strike is not unaffected by the flight of the ball. A pitch in baseball becomes a strike or a ball when the umpire declares it so, but the spherical covered twine's trajectory (it is expected) influences the umpire's call.

Within the game of baseball does the umpire's call, regardless of its causes, fully determine whether a pitch is a strike? Officially, yes, but not really. Umpires, we all believe, can make the wrong call. After all, there is (a historically changing) written definition of the strike zone in the official rulebook (itself a consensus product), and we argue as if we too were umpires and say what call we would have made, influenced by the ball's trajectory and faithful to our strike-zone-consensus. Because baseball is a game that needs final decisions in finite time, we make one designated umpire's call the definitive determination of a particular pitch's status. But imagine if we were all deputized as umpires, and had unlimited time to make the call and that we were always liable to receive new evidence (new camera angles on new video replays), what then? After an eternity of contemplation of video replays was exhausted, any settled unanimous consensus among us (and *ex hypothesi* there would be no more of us nor more information relevant to the pitch) would be the strongest *possible* evidence for believing the pitch was a strike, and sufficient for considering it so. While we could understand the claim "still, perhaps it wasn't a strike," there would be *no reason* for any doubt that it was a strike. The belief it was a strike would be fully justified; an objective, completely rational belief. However, were there one adamant dissenter, she could be right, especially if she had better access to some relevant video tape, and that dissenter should give us pause.

In the practice of Reason, of determining truth, we are all umpires, and the effects of reality on our beliefs' serviceability are, like the flight of the ball, supposed to affect our call. And each of us has especially good, somewhat exclusive, access to relevant video tape (our personal goals and their state of achievement). Were the justifications of our beliefs indifferent to realities effects on us, it would be as if we created a game in which balls and strikes are determined by agreement among people not watching the game and totally unaffected by the route of the ball. Here social consensus, unconstrained by reality, would make the calls and get them right solely in virtue of the consensus. Balls and strikes would be stipulated by a consensus that was unshaped by and indifferent to reality. But that ain't baseball. And socially stipulated truth indifferent to reality ain't Reason.

The pragmatic standard of justification, optimal goal achievement, is, I suggest, Reason's *de facto* strike zone (there is no official agreed-upon rulebook—albeit not for want of philosophers' submissions). Ideal objective justification includes the perspective of all who have a perspective and are

participating in the "game" of Reason. All get to weigh in on whether everyone's goals have been maximally satisfied. As I will argue in the next chapter,
anyone judging truth by only their own goal satisfaction, or the goal satisfaction of a select group, is not using Reason's strike zone, and is not correctly
playing the game of Reason. No single person, or group of people, serves as
the umpire authorized to stipulate the call—the truth—of any belief. Reason's
"call" would only be certified when every perspective that was, is, or will be
is reconciled.[48] But such hypothetical reconciliation, although it would make
the belief fully justified (a strike beyond dispute in our analogy), would not
influence the belief's effects (the ball's flight route), which is determined
completely by natural causes. Nor would that hypothetical reconciliation be
uninfluenced by the effects of the belief, any more than an umpire's call is
uninfluenced by the actual trajectory of the ball. And although the umpire
and the totality of perspectives have the authority to certify strikes and truth
respectively, in both cases, there is a sense that they can blow the call.[49] Once
the strike zone is agreed upon a baseball has either passed through it or not;
once everyone's goals are made the measure of truth, a set of beliefs will
either maximally serve them or not.

  In this chapter, I have argued that objectivity is an ideal limit of intersubjectivity.[50] In the next chapter, I will argue that intersubjectivity is the basis
of selfhood, rationality, and morality.

NOTES

  1. See the case Alston (1993) makes for that proposition. Nozick (1993) argues
that a justification of instrumental rationality is subject to the same circularity. Later, I
will distinguish the question begging circularity inherent in any theory of justification
from a vacuous circularity that renders a theory useless.
  2. Kirkham (1992).
  3. In chapter 4, I sketch a general theory of meaning, but we can bypass a specific
assignment of meaning to "truth," except to note that any meaning of "truth," must be
compatible with the claim that "x is true" implies and is implied by "x." This I take
to be the key requirement of Tarski's semantic theory of truth (1933), and it presents
no problem for the possible truth of principles of action: "one ought not to cause
avoidable suffering is true" if and only if one ought not to cause avoidable suffering.
We need no reform of the common meaning of "truth," whatever that may be, to
make principles of action viable candidates for truth. When we proclaim a principle
of action is true, in our attribution of truth, we mean just what we mean when we say
of anything that it is true.
  4. "Games with bishops that move diagonally," does not mean "games with
rooks that move horizontally and vertically," although the two descriptions encompass the very same things. The different descriptions define extensionally equivalent

classes; they pick out the same things. Although two classes are in fact equivalent, they may not be necessarily equivalent. There might have been a game that had bishops without rooks, although there are none in our universe. A more prominent set of philosophical theories seeks classes whose equivalences are necessary. The class of triangles with equal sides, in any world, is the same as the class of triangles with equal angles. We can call these essentialist theories. Finding a class extensionally equivalent to the truth teaches us something about the truth—what things are true in our world. But an essentialist theory of truth tells us what things must be true in any world. It is the sort of truth about truth that is catnip for the philosophical imagination.

5. While it certainly helps to know what something must be when figuring out how to recognize it (knowing that a species with a kidney will be a species with lungs can help one recognize a species with lungs), and some essentialist theories may make any or some specific justificatory theory impossible (if ghosts are essentially *invisible* dead people, then seeing ghosts cannot possibly justify their existence, nor can failing to see them count as evidence against their existence), a justificatory theory need not be coupled with any essentialist theory. We can find the truth, and know that we have found it, without listing its essential properties (without knowing the essence of "being a dancer" we can be sure that anything that has performed a tango is a dancer). A justificatory theory need only identify sufficient conditions for knowledge, and therefore justificatory theories of truth do not entail equivalence theories.

Nor do equivalence theories of truth entail justificatory theories. While finding a class extensionally or essentially equivalent to truth *can* be part of a general justificatory theory, and an extensionally equivalent class may be *established* by a justificatory theory (if the only sure way to *know* that a team has won a baseball game was by seeing that it had scored the most runs, then we would have a justificatory theory that gave us the stipulated essential properties of a baseball winner), neither need be the case. All of Santa's helpers may be elves and all elves may help Santa, but that may not give us a clue for identifying either a helper or an elf, and although the only way to recognize an elf might be to establish that he/she rides on Santa's sleigh, because not all elves get to ride, sleigh ridership with Santa does not offer an equivalent class.

6. See Kirkham (1992, 51).

7. For the way in which statements, propositions, and sentences can be true see chapter 4 on meaning. In chapter 4, I will modify the claim that a belief can be the bearer of truth to indicate that, in my view, the more precise bearers of truth are collective systems of belief—sets of sets of belief—what I call a "social system of belief."

8. At least, that is the burden of a family of theories we may term "realist." Realist theories are often called "correspondence" theories, but I think it best to reserve that latter term for a subspecies of truth theories I discuss, and reject, in the text. The realist theory I advocate is not a member of this subspecies, but is of a kind typically called "pragmatic." Pragmatic theories are often considered nonrealist, but I think this is a mistake. The nonrealist theories of truth, "coherence theories," view the truth of a belief to be *solely* a function of its relations to other beliefs. A nonrealist theory still takes aspects of "reality" as determining truth, but only a very limited

domain of reality—mental and social reality. Pragmatic theories are thrown into the nonrealist camp because they too start and end in the mind and society. But they are realist because they take a route through nonmental reality in such a way that what nonmental reality is like helps make true things true. It just doesn't do it all by itself.

9. At least they do when combined with certain ontologies and analyses of moral terms.

10. Less severe demoters of morality (relativists) do find moral principles in reality. Lots of them. They are embedded in the hearts and minds of humankind. And a belief that corresponds to any of them is true. A true moral principle is simply a believed one. Principles believed are true because they correspond to themselves. We will discuss this relativism anon.

11. Lillehammer (2007, 76) points out that Putnam made similar claims: "one metaphysical reason that has led many philosophers to deny the objectivity of ethical judgment, namely, that it doesn't *fit the picture* of 'description of natural facts' . . . is no reason for classifying them as outside the range of notions of truth or falsity, good and bad argument . . . there can be 'objectivity without objects'" Putnam (2004, 77–78).

12. Bertrand Russell (1940) a staunch defender of truth as correspondence concedes that point.

13. A Millikanian (1990) view of representation, although similar to this kind of causal account of truth, I believe is more akin to the pragmatic/causal account of justification I endorse and will soon put to work. More on Millikan in chapter 4, note 10.

14. Beliefs however, are justified (as I will soon argue in the text) because they typically cause a useful *response* under standard circumstances. But that is not corresponding to the circumstances.

15. The above discussion simplifies and conflates a variety of linguistic relativisms. Some relativists allow that the propositions do not *refer* to different standards, but nonetheless different standards are employed in determining their truth. Many would argue that the word "wrong" is being used univocally, that is, has the same "meaning" in each torture sentence, but has different truth conditions in each use (and argue that a term's meaning is not constituted by its truth conditions). Questions regarding vagueness, context, comparatives, and indexicals are all relevant here, and give rise to technical distinctions that are important for the philosophy of language. But for our purposes, what is significant is the relativists' claim that different moral standards allow what appear to be syntactical contradictions to be simultaneously true. See Richard (2008).

16. Nagel (1986).

17. See Wong (1984).

18. This is a conception of *causal* contingency. Logical contingency is what is possible unconstrained by particular circumstances of any kind. Causal contingency is about possibility under specified conditions.

19. I say "at best," because in addition to being without a justification—that is, arbitrary, an act can be positively unjustified, that is, the negation of a justified act. Treating boys and girls as equals if justified makes the man's act both arbitrary and pernicious.

20. Granted, it feels unidiomatic to label a fully explained event "arbitrary," but this is due to the confusion between explanation and justification (see chapter 1, section 6), along with the fact that justifications and explanations often coincide and, when they don't, psychological explanations frequently attribute an unacknowledged quasi-justification as the cause of beliefs and actions. So, while knowledge of nonrational causes often appears to dilute arbitrariness, a word is wanted for beliefs and actions, presumably caused, but uncaused by anything resembling a reason. "Arbitrary" satisfies the need to name beliefs and action untethered to reason. Of course, if God created all causes for good reasons, then nothing is arbitrary *sub specie aeternitatis.*

21. Mortality may be a case in point. I know I must die, but I am unsure there is a good reason for my death.

22. A number of caveats are in order: first, what is fundamental among moral principles is vague, dynamic, and changeable, so the once unjustifiable justifier of today can be justified tomorrow by a newly adopted basic principle. Second, the foundationalist picture can be misleading. Moral principles, even if stably ranked and not reordered by new principles, reinforce, reflect and cohere with each other. However, in any such system, some elements will play a more central, system-defining role, and these will be its basic moral principles that are *morally* neither justified nor known to be unjustified.

23. This, if successful, would not by itself be a derivation of "ought" from "is," except insofar as "one ought to *believe* x" is derivable from "x is true." There may be reasons to believe a basic moral principle, but whether those reasons constitute reasons to act is a further question. The most significant "is/ought" divide is less between description and all prescription, than between prescription of belief and prescription of action. For more on "is/ought" derivation, see chapter 4, section 6.

24. Hume (1739) famously revealed that there is no noncircular justification of induction, causing great philosophical consternation. However, there is no noncircular justification of deduction either. Reason does not justify our deductive inferences, rather Reason itself is partially defined by acceptance of those inferences. Nelson Goodman (1955) has argued that the response to Hume's (old) problem of induction would be to acknowledge that Reason is also defined by accepting inductive (probabilistic) inferences. In both cases, we call the acceptance of the inferences "reasonable" because we believe, *although we cannot noncircularly demonstrate*, that they always (in the case of deduction), or usually (induction), yield truth, and therefore are objectively correct. A deductive rule of inference that sometimes did not preserve truth, or an inductive rule of inference that too often failed to preserve truth, would be objectively incorrect. I am arguing that, moral principles can similarly, be correct or incorrect. But there must be moral truth for that to be the case.

25. The situation is the same with nonmoral, or what we may term "factual" truth. Any demonstration of fact will be premised on other facts. While we can argue over which facts are most likely true, the argument presumes the possibility of a true factual proposition.

26. Having no standards does not necessarily make her a moral denier, that is, an amoralist who claims there is no such thing as morality. She could believe that there

is morality because others have standards. One can be personally amoral without denying that others can be moral, albeit each after his or her own fashion.

27. Of course there can be a sort of theoretical rationality regarding means and ends—what causes what—which does not involve moral reasoning, but nor is it practical reasoning; it does not conclude that anything *ought to be done*. It remains theoretical even in the guise of "If you want X, you should do Y" because it doesn't conclude you should do Y (or anything for that matter). It can seem like practical reasoning given a suppressed premise, "you should do what you want," but that is clearly a moral principle. So-called "instrumental reasoning" is either merely theoretical because it advocates no action, or embodies a moral principle (at a minimum, action X is permissible) because it does advocate action.

28. See Wong (1984, 106).

29. See Pierce (1877).

30. I use the term "goals," because I think it has fewer misleading connotations for my purposes than do some plausible alternatives. Our "interests," or even more so, our "good," suggest states of affairs that might be independent of anything we ever approve of or sanction. Moreover, however well they suit us, our goods and interests may not originate with us, but rather may be externally given to us. "Desires" although originating with us, is still independent of our will; one desires many things one has neither intention of pursuing, nor even desires to pursue. In addition, the object of a desire may be immediately obtainable and not involve a longer-term project connoted by "goal." "Values" is too abstract. One achieves states of affairs one values, or acts in accordance with certain values, but goals become concrete in a way that values resist. I believe we can best make sense of these other terms by using "goal" as the central notion in understanding beliefs' proper function.

31. Later, I will modify this claim to make the belief's justification its inclusion in a wider set whose justification is its (the wider set's) serviceability. But for now, we can speak of the serviceability of the individual belief.

32. James (1905, 108) points out that belief is not a momentary mode of consciousness. See also Pierce (1878, 97).

33. More accurately still, sets of individual belief sets are the bearers of truth. See chapter 4, section 4.

34. Cf. Pierce (1878, 97–98).

35. I start with this formulation, but later we will see that it is readily reversed. A sense of self, and hence the experience of being a subject, requires a recognition of other minds. Although these minds are understood as loci of subjectivity (they are, after all, minds) their otherness makes them external to, that is, objects for, the self. And so subjectivity can be said to be born of objectivity. Conjunctive twins really.

36. None of which is to deny the possibility that a thinker may be a constellation of thoughts in particular relations. But that doesn't obviate the fact that for there to be thought we must ascribe a thinker.

37. Cf. Nietzsche (1887, 119): "Henceforth, my dear philosophers, let us be on guard against the dangerous old conceptual fiction that posited a 'pure, will-less, painless, timeless knowing subject'; let us guard against the sneers of such contradictory

concepts as 'pure reason,' 'absolute spirituality,' 'knowledge in itself': these always demand that we should think of an eye that is completely unthinkable, an eye turned in no particular direction, in which the active and interpreting forces, through which alone seeing becomes seeing *something*, are supposed to be lacking; these always demand of the eye an absurdity and a nonsense. There is *only* a perspective seeing, *only* a perspective 'knowing'; and the more affects we allow to speak about one thing, *the more eyes, different eyes, we can use to observe one thing, the more complete will our 'concept' of this thing, our 'objectivity' be.*" [Emphasis added].

38. Richard Rorty (1979) contends that the "epistemological project" is an attempt to describe the undistorted perspective that reveals objective truth; Rorty argues that this attempt, which characterizes much of Western Philosophy, is deeply misguided. See note 49 of this chapter. I am sympathetic to Rorty's claim that striving for a pure, "undistorted" perspective is misguided, but disagree that that renders any epistemological project impossible. To deploy some Rortarian terminology, I will claim that objectivity is a kind of solidarity.

39. My student, Daniel Norman, pointed out to me that similar notions appear in some works of science fiction.

40. Later, I discuss and endorse the Davidsonian (1967) point that part of recognizing a subjectivity as such involves recognizing that it has a belief system that is substantially true.

41. This is hardly to say that full objectivity will reconcile all goals. Maximal goal achievement will still likely leave many goals unrealized, just not unrecognized. See more on this in the appendix.

42. Of course, the objective truth of a principle must also be judged by how well it weighs goals, not merely how many goals it gives any weight. But, although an epistemological problem with some special challenges for the would-be objective agent, this is not a conceptual issue specific to the justification of objective principles of action. A principle that was measured only against the goals of the believer-agent would still be confronted with the task of weighing those goals in order to judge which of competing principles was most subjectively justified. In neither the purely subjective case, nor the more objective cases, is justification simply a matter of counting the number of goals achieved. Goals have weight, and appropriate weighing techniques are required for any rational actor, whether or not they strive for objective rationality. For a discussion of weighing goals and related issues see the appendix.

43. That is, there might be conflicting true principles of action, principles which belong to belief sets that do equally well at realizing the totality of goals. It nonetheless seems unlikely: the best possible realization of the totality of goals is a vast, intricate and precise state of affairs, sets of beliefs are tools of enormous complexity with infinitely subtle applications, and reality cannot be smaller than either, nor is it likely to be simpler. Given that a single set of goals and a single reality generate the puzzle, multiple equivalent solutions that are significantly different are little more than a theoretical possibility. It is hard enough to find a single individual's set of beliefs leading to barely adequate satisfaction of a restricted set of goals; that there would be two or more incompatible ideologies resulting in maximal and equal satisfaction of everyone's goals is a consummation that can hardly be expected.

However, a different sort of problem for the claim that individual ideal sets of belief will be identical arises when we consider that different individual belief sets might best contribute to goal satisfaction just because they do differ, even if they collectively constitute a uniquely true set of beliefs. Could not a division of belief, of both principles and facts, do more for the satisfaction of the whole than the identity of all individuals' beliefs would? Given that the true belief set is really the entire *collection of individual belief sets* (see chapter 4) including a particular distribution of individuals' beliefs, a distribution that does not provide the same doxological toolkit to every social actor seems a real possibility. Production processes are known, to benefit by a division of labor; if beliefs are true because productive of the widest possible goal satisfaction, shouldn't we expect specialized individual beliefs to be part of the collection of all true beliefs? Might not one agent's specialized belief contradict another's?

The real bearer of truth is indeed the set of sets of belief of all interacting believers, and it is that system of systems of belief which best achieves goal satisfaction that is or isn't true. But there is reason to think that that system would have individuals with at least highly similar, and probably identical, individual sets of belief. Individuals' actions, although necessarily different to maximize social satisfaction, can yet be guided by the same beliefs, and should be to facilitate coordination. Although teammates need to act differently according to their position, it can only help if they have a common understanding of the facts of the game, the best strategy, and the team mission. The sole exception is the belief that situates each individual, and assigns her the part she should play in order to maximize goal satisfaction. John Perry (1979) has persuasively argued that there is no objective belief, socially shareable, equivalent to a self-identifying belief. "I am Mitchell Silver," is not the same belief as "Mitchell Silver is Mitchell Silver," and certainly not the same as "I am Barack Obama." Obama and I cannot share a self-identifying belief in our ideal systems of belief, and so the systems must vary to that extent. I do not believe that this single exception raises much of a specter of epistemological relativism, but as we will see later (chapter 3, section 1), it does introduce a deep challenge for moral objectivity.

44. Lillehammer (2007).

45. Perhaps "transcendental" is a more generous designation than "question begging" of the view offered: I begin by assuming that some beliefs can be true, and then provide an account, an explanation, of how we would know if a belief is true. If asked to justify the explanation, I have to, ultimately, either abandon it for another account, making my argument inconsistent, or employ the same explanation of justification that I am asked to justify, making the justification self-consistent but question begging. The later in this situation is the better choice, for a circle *can* stabilize and secure its members place and function, even if the circle itself is ungrounded. Although necessarily ungrounded, a theory of justification can be justified by its own lights. A pragmatic theory of justification must be useful for some goal. I mean to show its usefulness for securing moral objectivism (which is not to say that that is it only use). I accept it on that, among other, *pragmatic* bases. Self-authorization is a property of Reason; a feature, not a bug. It was fatal to Descartes' program to begin

by doubting everything (1641), which Kant, the father of transcendental arguments, realized led, not to the firm foundation of knowledge Descartes sought, but to Hume's all- encompassing skepticism. For more on the argumentative form of transcendental strategies see chapter 4, section 10, and Aikin (2017).

46. I am summarily denying correspondence theories of truth we can find in Wittgenstein (1922), Russell (1940), Kripke (1975), and Millikan (2013).

47. See chapter 4 and the appendix for a further account of this conception of justification, in particular its relation to meaning, and how it could in principle judge total utility.

48. Bear in mind that a reconciliation of perspectives does not need to pronounce all calls correct. They do, however, all need to be accounted for. The reconciliation requires we understand how the mistaken call came to be and why it persists.

49. Richard Rorty's "solidarity," (1989) is liable to be misinterpreted, by Rorty himself in careless moments (see Misak 2000, 12–13), as denying any role for nature in justification. But rather than seeing "solidarity" as a term for replacing reality's effects with social consensus, I think Rorty's "solidarity" is best understood as acknowledging all people's goals, rather than the properties of things-in–themselves, as the standard for truth. Steven Levine (2010) addresses these issue in the course of describing and contributing to the "new pragmatists'" project of salvaging truth and objectivity from Rorty's dismissal of those ideas. Levine thinks Robert Brandom's riposte to Rorty's argument fails because Brandom misperceives the basis of Rorty's view, which is not the incorrigibility of first person reports of mental states, but rather the lesson Rorty draws from Sellar's denial of any epistemological "given." For Levine's Rorty, it is the absence of sense data with epistemic status that makes objectivity a senseless ideal. Levine thinks the correct route to refuting Rorty, while accepting Sellar's doctrine, is to revive the classical pragmatist idea of thick experi- ence. I think a better approach is to accept Rorty's notion of the justificatory role of solidarity, and, *à la* Brandom, show how solidarity is both an account of objectivity and sensitive to nonepistemic effects.

50. Joel Marks suggested this formulation.

Chapter 3

Others

1. TWO METAPHYSICAL PRESUPPOSITIONS OF MORALITY

First, no one is alone. There are "others." They are "not me," but existence external to me is insufficient to constitute these others; they must also be *qualitatively identical* to me in a fundamentally important way. The others must be of my type. Without our commonality, without those external beings being of my "kind" (*our* kind) I would not be. Although the elements of which I am made could be without others, without others they would not be me. The others' being is essential to my being. I only assert that now; I will argue it shortly.

The choice of terms for our kind—"minds," "persons," "selves," "sentient beings," "subjectivities"—is less portentous than its characterization, for how the kind is characterized shapes moral philosophies. Are we those that can suffer and enjoy, or those who have preferences and interests? Are we the conscious ones or the self-conscious ones? Does the possession of intentions and projects define our set, or is it our capacity to choose and freely pursue them? Are we those with interests, or those who recognize that there are others with interests? These characterizations are at a minimum intertwined, and some may be of a piece, even synonymous. But *for now*, in keeping with pragmatism, I take the critical similarity betwixt me and the others to be that we each have goals whose achievement constitutes our individual good, and we are mutually interested in what's true. As we shall see, the metaphysical belief that there are others give rise to moral concern.

If this first metaphysical conception of others generates morality, a second creates its problematics. It is the idea that these others are *different* from me—not simply distinct entities, literally "not me," for that point just recapitulates

49

their otherness—but rather, although of the identical kind, the others are significantly different in quality. The qualitative difference takes two forms, one leading to a central metaethical issue, the other to normative problems.

Others are more or less different from me in circumstances, psychology, and culture. They have goals that are not mine, not only in being theirs, but in being dissimilar to mine. How to accommodate this diversity of goals creates one category of normative problems. Treating others specifically and concretely as we want to be treated would ignore the qualitative differences within our kind. As has been frequently noted, one should *not* always do onto others as you would have them do unto you; they may have different tastes.

Moreover, moral conflict might arise in a world of clones with precisely the same tastes. Here is a second category of normative problems that arise from others having different goals. In a world of only mocha chip ice cream lovers, there may not be enough mocha chip to go around, and even in a world of abundance, our qualitatively identical goals may be incompatible. We cannot both win the chess game we play against each other. We are different, and the satisfaction of our individual sets of goals does not automatically follow from the satisfaction of anyone's goals. The diversity of goals can lead us in different directions, their distinctness can cause us to butt heads. Normative moral theory tries to reconcile or adjudicate between uncoordinated and clashing goals.[1]

However, beyond the normative problems raised by the difference between us, there is a metaethical problem: because they are not me, I cannot have the same relationship to others or anything about them that I have to myself. Practically speaking, no one is just one among others to oneself. This is not a psychological statement about a universal bias; it is a metaphysical claim about agency. To act I must know who I am, or more precisely how I am situated in the world. Others can know as precisely as I do how MS is situated in the world, but only I can know that I am MS. "I am MS," is not a tautology, it is not the claim that "MS is MS." It is something I discover, something I could be wrong about, and it is something that most of my actions must take into account. Knowing that MS should do something gives me no reason to do that thing unless I know that I am MS. Only actions that, regardless of context, are justified in their full specificity could ignore their subjective starting point. If no one, under any circumstances, ought to torture anyone, I do not have to consider anything about myself to justifiably refuse to torture. But in many cases, only by considering my personal positioning am I enjoined to act in a particular way. If everyone should treat his or her spouse especially kindly, and everyone, including MS, knows OG is MS's spouse, still I must know that I am MS to know how I ought to treat OG. The question we must confront is whether this irreducible practical subjectivity is a morally important fact, and if it is, what does it import.

The egoist believes the relational difference each finds in his goals—not that tastes may differ or goals may conflict—but that my goals are *mine*, and yours are not mine—is so fundamental that, for practical purposes, the others' goals constitute a different species.[2] The egoist claims that in theory he fully acknowledges that there are others with goals. He protests that he is not blind to the metaphysical reality of others. However, others are of no fundamental practical reality for him, and there is no practical irrationality in ignoring them. That not all practical truths can be translated out of the subjective realm gives this view some plausibility. But it is mistaken; it implies a practical solipsism that is not a possibility for our kind.[3]

2. THE INCOHERENCE OF "SUBJECTIVE RATIONALITY"

Egoism would make pragmatism an ally. The pragmatist views justification as relative to goals; the recognition of truth depends on the satisfaction of goals. The egoist thinks there is no bar to restricting the relevant goals to her own. Reason may not require that restriction (although most egoists would argue it does), but it surely, the egoist argues, does not disallow it. The egoist would be guided by practical principles whose truth is judged by how well they serve *her* goals.

However, in a pragmatic framework, the rejection of the salience of others' goals does not merely lead, as the egoist would have it, to separate personal goods; it leads to separate personal truths. Goal satisfaction justifies beliefs as well as actions. The egoist cannot enlist a pragmatism animated only by subjective goals to justify her practical principles, unless she is prepared to deploy only subjective goals to justify factual beliefs. Pragmatism recognizes factual truth by the same standard that certifies the truth of practical principles. The egoist is not just committed to subjectivism of practical principles; she is committed to a subjectivism of all theoretical reason.[4] It is a commitment she cannot keep. There is no purely subjective rationality.

Rationality is socially grounded. There is no private rationality for reasons analogous to those that prevent private languages: both need standards of truth that an isolated subjectivity cannot provide. Even consistency, the minimal qualification for truth, is bestowed by agreement.[5] Inconsistency is not what I find inconceivable, it is what we all agree is inconceivable. Ironically, unanimity could not be achieved by an isolated subjectivity. One cannot agree with oneself because one cannot disagree with oneself. Judgment by an inner umpire without any resources for questioning the call is no judgment at all.[6]

Imagine a practical solipsist who attempted to justify all of her beliefs according to how well they satisfied her goals, and only her goals. She would have a unique standard for evaluating her practical *and* factual judgments. The justification of her belief that "the cat is on the mat," the standard that marks the belief as true, would be a private measure, as private as the measure of her belief that "cats ought not to be tortured." Others, using different standards, might judge that "the cat is on the mat" is false.[7] Their judgment that the cat is not on the mat would no more conflict with the solipsist's judgment that it was on the mat, as a judgment of others that cats ought to be tortured conflicts with the solipsist's judgment that cats ought not to be tortured. There is no adjudicating standard, and because this is the case with all of the practical solipsist's beliefs, there is no logical space in which her cat/ mat beliefs conflict with others' beliefs. All of the practical solipsist's beliefs are incommensurable with others' beliefs, and therefore others' beliefs can neither correct nor confirm them.

Nor could there be self-correction and self-confirmation. Cut-off in her own epistemic world, whenever she felt fully contented, the pragmatically minded practical solipsist's beliefs would be fully justified. A sufficient dose of heroin justifies all of her beliefs. Neither her future nor past unsatisfied goals are germane, even if accurately remembered or anticipated, because as currently contemplated they are not causing frustration. Moreover, there could be no possible grounds for believing any memory or prediction false, for if the memories and predictions were part of a belief system that currently satisfied, they would be *ipso facto* justified.[8] It is not that the practical solipsist would take each of her current beliefs to be true—we all do that—it is that her grounds for taking them true are unchallengeable, for neither others nor her past or future self provides the epistemologically challenging frustration.

But couldn't we at least attribute to the practical solipsist a moment by moment rationality: "My goals are not fully satisfied, so my beliefs not fully justified" or "I am fully satisfied so my current beliefs are justified now?" Not really. The attribution of reason to solipsism of the present applies much attenuated senses of "rationality" and "justified," ones that deprive the terms of epistemic content. There is no one else for whom the solipsist's beliefs are true, so they are not justifiable to others, including the other who is her future self. This makes her "rationality"—her sensitivity to enduringly useful beliefs, not a capacity to be moved by sound justifications, but, rather a lucky fit between her nature and the world. She is rational only in the sense that the well adapted cockroach is rational—her dispositions serve her well. With a fixed nature in a slowly changing world there can be such luck. But even that luck is better termed "good instincts" than "rationality." Reason is not *any* property which produces satisfaction. A plant may well have an "internal" structure that reliably produces behavior that meets the plant's needs. But it is not thereby rational. The imagined solipsistic "justification" completely collapses epistemological virtue with an emotional state. While pragmatism certainly connects knowledge to well-being, it is a highly mediated connection, not a simple identity. Reason is the social activity that mediates the connection by certifying truth through intersubjective goal achievement. Solipsism and good instincts might well be a superior route to personal satisfaction, but it is not the way of Reason.

Reason seeks truth, and the search for truth requires the external standard provided by others. Without knowing what constitutes finding, there can be no searching, and mutual satisfaction signals that the truth may have been found. Disagreement on particular beliefs, of course, does not preclude reasoning together, indeed it stimulates it. Nor does disagreement on particular beliefs mean that none of the disputants possesses the truth. But reasoning can occur only in the context of substantial agreement because communication can occur only in the context of substantial agreement. People who cannot agree on a sufficient number of truths cannot communicate, cannot understand what the other is saying, indeed must be skeptical that the other is saying anything at all, or even is an *other*—a truth seeking subjectivity like oneself. Reasoning and communicating alike assume a mutual interest in and capacity to recognize the truth, and they have no existence apart from that assumption. They assume others.[9]

Rationality is the achievement of goals by special means. Goals are achieved rationally by responding to truth—truth found through the satisfaction of the set of distinctive, perhaps overlapping, yet different sets of individual goals. It is a virtuous circle: our collective ability to respond to the truth helps us flourish (achieve our goals) and our flourishing justifies our belief that it is truth we are responding to. It is a social circle: no realization of a single individual's good can verify, but each individual's good is in the truth certifying set, and so each individual can be appealed to and enlisted in the quest for truth—a collective effort to satisfy the collective good. This collective good is not the good of some transcendent entity—"the collective," "the state," "society," "the universe," or "God." It is the totality of *individual* goods, just as objectivity is the totality of individual perspectives. Rationality is a collective tool whose effectiveness lies in the recognition of the epistemic value of individuality and whose purpose is the enhancement of individual goods, including the goodness of individuality.

Other social animals can collectively pursue a collective good, even a good distributed to individual members without remainder. However, they do not reason because they do not recognize the individual's separate good, separate value. The quest for truth is a way of making separate, subjective individual value a social value. It is the means whereby we rational beings pursue our individual goods collectively. Truth is the shared value—the recognition that each will measure the good by all of our goods, that each will judge reality by all of our goods.

Objective truth is not a kind of truth; it is the only kind of truth. Only objective justifications render judgments meriting the predicate "is true." Although individual subjectivities are irreducible and metaphysically necessary for rationality, isolated they cannot constitute rationality. For an isolated subjectivity that measures all things by itself, there is no truth. It may seek its good, but not through reason.

Rationality, the search for truth, needs plurality, but not a multitude; reason can be realized with just one other. As long as there are distinct sets of individual goods, reason, and truth can take shape. Reason necessarily includes all of "us," but it sets no minimum above two regarding who *we* are. However, whomever we speak with, or judge that we can speak with, we implicitly acknowledge as one of us, as a genuine other. She is among the verifiers, she has a good. By speaking with her, we presume she understands us, and that she can recognize the truth and respond to it.[10]

Bad faith and self-delusion on this matter is the perennial human sin, the inconsistency that is immorality. However culturally taboo and ideologically camouflaged, however deeply repressed, slaveholders have always known that their enslaved were truth sensitive and had their own good. Slaveholding is a willful denial of the truth, as are all the common, less dramatic, social interactions that do not treat others as of our kind. The egoist isn't really a solipsist. He builds his understanding out of the other's good, but acts as if the other's good has no reality.[11] Only saints do not do some of that, but egoists would make a doctrine of our endemic bad faith.

3. SELF, OTHER, AND WORLD

Above I called belief in others a presupposition of morality, and of course the existence of others is assumed by any moral theory. Many moral theories make an even stronger claim: others are not just the occasion for the application of morality; rather they are structural elements of the moral domain. These philosophers have argued that the moral dimension is constructed out of the historically evolved or essential nature of our relations with others. This is most pronounced in the Kantian tradition. Kant himself, in the "Kingdom of Ends" formulation of the Categorical Imperative, makes explicit, the foundational role of communal relations in our moral life. Stephen Darwall founds morality in the mutual and reflexive recognition of authority and accountability inherent in addressing another or being addressed by her. Christine Korsgaard roots morality in a practical identity that is shaped by the requirement that our reasons be public, a requirement compelled "in a deep sense, [by] our social nature."

Aspects of this line of thought can be found throughout moral philosophy.[12] Call this theme the "social metaethics" tradition. My argument is squarely in this tradition. Morality, through rationality, is grounded in truth, and truth is a social predicate. Truth is only discovered with others. But too often social metaethics gives insufficient attention to how this dyadic relationship must be mediated and valorized by a *tertium quid*: our world.[13] However, before bringing in the world let us return to the self.

A self is an individual that knows itself as such. A self experiences itself as separate and distinct from that which is not itself. This goes beyond simply having actionable knowledge of where one's body begins and ends. Body awareness is knowledge of correlations between sensations and perceptions: if that fire touches that leg then that pain occurs. Such causal knowledge can be learned without any idea of others.[14] But a self knows itself as an individual subjectivity, a possessor of unshared experiences.

The notion that one's experiences are one's own, and that there may be other sets of experiences which, just because they are other, may not be exactly similar to one's own experiences, is the notion of distinct perspectives. The knowledge that one is a distinct perspective can only arise in the company of the general concept of perspectives, which, again, is simply the possibility of others. Self-conceptualization entails conceptualizing an other.[15] One does not need to believe there are actual others (although in their absence the idea of them could not be formed). The sole survivor of a nuclear war could remain a self, but only because she retained the idea of an other.

Solipsism, understood as the belief that one is the only possible self, is incoherent, and understood as the belief that one is the only actual self, is an empirical thesis that flies in the face of all the evidence. However, not as doctrine, but as condition, a profounder solipsism emerges, or rather is sunk into, with a disappearance of the idea of others. With the loss of the idea of others comes the loss of the external world. Without others, there can be no cleavage between appearance and reality, a distinction which can only be operationally manifested through the divergence of the merely subjective and the securely intersubjective. Without others, a local phenomenalism becomes one's implicit metaphysics. It is not that to be is to be perceived, it is that the duality of being and being perceived does not arise. The solipsist neither denies nor disbelieves in an external world, she simply cannot conceive of it because there is no internal world. No inside, no outside; no subjectivity, no objectivity; no self, no external world. And internality, subjectivity, and self-hood are born through comprehension of the other.

Self and others give rise to an external world as a common space for us to live out our relationships. The world is our common referent making communication possible. It is in communication with others that we and they come into being, and our communication requires a world to be about. It is the place we meet; it is how we are present to each other. And our differing relations to

that world are what also make us distinct from one another. We are individu-
ated through the external world. Self, other, and world form a conceptual triad
in which each concept exists only in relation to the two others. I am not the
world, because you see the world differently, and you are not me for the same
reason. Without you I merge into the world, and both world and I disappear.
But without the world, you would never appear.[16]

The world is the generator of true belief, and so, without others, there
would be no truth. Without truth there can be no rationality, and therefore no
moral truth or practical reason. All of these losses are a consequent of losing
the other's primal co-creator, the self. The possibility of the other is a condition of selfhood, reason, and morality.

None of this depends on actually arriving at the truth. The common search
for truth creates the community of rational beings—cooperators for whom
justifying beliefs is the project which coordinates action, spreads knowledge,
and enables individuals mutually to recognize themselves through others. In
humans, all that is procured from our natural aspiration to respond to reasons,
even if we never achieve full rationality. The sincere quest for truth makes the
rational community, not truth's complete realization.

The relationship with the other and the world enables the self-constituting
phenomenon of distancing. What turns a mind into a self is it's consideration
of itself as a mind, as merely a possible perspective on the world. A mind that
understands it is neither the entire world nor a necessarily exact, complete
representation of the world is a self. A perspective may mislead, so assessing
its reliability is always in order. And so we observe the observer and thereby
create a perspective on our perspective. Every newly created perspective can
itself be put in perspective. This ever-present potential for taking another step
back, for distancing oneself from any given mental content, makes selves. It
also forms rationality, the critical faculty of seeking truth. Of every belief, we
have the possibility of asking "Is it true," of every sensation or desire "is it
good?" Only rational beings can ask such questions, and only those who can
ask them are rational beings.[17]

This distancing implicitly operates in all communication between rational
beings. We make claims which the other can affirm or deny. By presenting
claims for assessment, we acknowledge the possibilities of acceptance or
rejection, and that acknowledgment separates us from the claims themselves.
Others can disbelieve what we believe, casting doubt on our beliefs for us too.
Through the act of communicating them, we put distance between ourselves
and our claims. We "put them out there," and in doing so transcend them.
Because distancing constitutes one's selfhood, selfhood is not so much a state
achieved as it is a capacity to step back, to further assess, to question. It is the
other who elicits the question, and the world gives the questioning meaning
by validating answers.

NOTES

1. In the appendix, I discuss how justified beliefs, that is, beliefs that lead to maximal goal achievement, would respond to inconsistent goals (whether intra or intersubjective).

2. It is not only egoists that find the "whose goal" question morally significant. The large literature that sees a fundamental moral divide between agent relative reasons and agent neutral reasons (e.g., Williams 1981, 1985) is, I believe, impressed by the same distinction that drives some philosophers to egoism.

3. Of course, the egoist allows that others' goals should be taken into tactical account. But they are not goals for him, just objects, like the others whose goals they are, that need to be navigated around on his way to satisfying his goals. *Mutatis mutandis*, all those who claim it is irrational to be motivated by others' goals, even those with goals that aim at others' welfare, although not egoists, shares the egoist's practical solipsism.

4. Is this only a problem for the egoist if she accepts pragmatism? I think not. Rationality is a normative affair regardless of epistemological commitments. The egoist offers no good reason why an objective standard is dispensable for judging practice but not belief. Even If the egoist accepts a correspondence theory of truth, and believes there are facts which make beliefs true, he cannot ground the principle "one ought to believe what is true" let alone "one ought to measure the good by one's own good" as corresponding to some external reality. Even the correspondence theory cannot make an uncompanioned subjectivity rational.

5. See chapter 4 and chapter 5, section 2 for fuller discussions of consistency.

6. Korsgaard (1996, 136–140) has also noted the ethical implications of this Wittgensteinian point.

7. It is not that her believing "the cat is on the mat," made it true, but that, if that belief was ultimately most useful to her, regardless of its utility for others, it would be true for her. However, assuming it was not coincidently the belief that best served others' goals, it would not be true for them.

8. Nagel (1970) discusses the profound structural similarity of prudence and morality, both requiring standards that go beyond the phenomenal self.

9. This assumption can be sustained in their absence, although it might not be possible had they never been present. See also Davidson (1967, 1973).

10. Darwall's Second Personism (2006) is only one form this essential point has taken in the history of moral thought.

11. What of beings that have a good, but are not themselves rational? Can we rationally ignore their goods because they do not share with us the pursuit of truth? Nonhuman animals are the most prominent case: most of us believe that animals have distinct goods—and we can recognize what those goods are. But it does not appear that they can recognize that we have such a goods. Hence, their hybrid moral status. If we acknowledge they have a good, reason requires we care for them, although because they cannot acknowledge others' goods, they are not rational and have no moral duties. However, unlike slaves, at least in theory, it is possible to deny that

animals have goods, ignore their well-being, and remain fully rational. But only if one can *consistently* treat animals and form beliefs about animals as one treats and believes about rocks. More on animals in chapter 7, section 4.

12. Kant (1785), Darwall (2006), Korsgaard (1996, 135). Similar themes are discoverable in social contract theory, for example, Hobbes (1651), which rests on recognizing that others are able and motivated to keep agreements, in Hegel's dialectic, where morality gives conceptual stability to identity (1807), in Nietztsche's genealogy (1887), wherein the other directed emotion of resentment gives birth to morals, in the openness of Martin Buber's I—thou relationship (1923), and in Levinas' call and response (1999), and in any of the many moral philosophers labeled "constructivists" (some constructivist metaethicists are discussed in chapter 4, sections 8 and 9).

13. Marx (1844) is the most significant exception to this lack of attention. His argument against idealism is that it takes as fundamental a play of concepts from which reality emerges, whereas he argued it was the other way around: being determined consciousness. Now, my account might appear closer to Hegelian idealism in that I see the *concept* of the World as emerging in the interplay of self and other. But, like Marx (1859) and Dewey (1932), I assume a reality, that while not given to us or known to us apart from our social lives, affects the conditions under which our social lives are lived. Although being determines consciousness, I argue that consciousness determines what is known of being.

14. Cf. Strawson's (1959) account of persons. Also see Levine's (2019) pragmatically informed account of self-formation (which downplays the role of others that I emphasize in this chapter).

15. Cf. Dewey (1932, 227) "the human being is an individual because of and in relations with others. Otherwise, he is an individual only as a stick of wood is, namely, as spatially and numerically separate."

16. An earlier version of this argument can be found in Silver (1980). For a classic step by step account of how this might develop see Mead (1913).

17. Cf. Korsgaard (1996, 93).

Chapter 4

Meaning, Morality, and Social Agreement

1. MEANING AND TRUTH

Truth and meaning are not the same thing. Meaningful things—sentences and beliefs—can be false. Truth and meaning, however, are difficult to disentangle, for meaningless things cannot be true, and the truth value of a belief or sentence depends on its meaning. The possibility of true moral principles entails the possibility of meaningful moral principles. A prominent mode of moral skepticism is based on the denial that moral propositions have meaning. That skepticism relies on arguments which resemble the amoralist arguments that deny truth to moral principles because they correspond to no entities; the "moral meanings" skeptic denies moral meaning because moral statements have no referents.

A defender of moral objectivism and moral cognitivism—the view that moral principles can be true and known—must show that they can be meaningful. Unfortunately, as was the case with vindicating morality's possible truth, vindicating its meaning requires an excursion beyond ethics into a general theory of meaning.[1]

2. MEANING AS INFERENCE RELATIONS

I will present an inference theory of meaning as a semantics that can make morality meaningful. I do not believe my metaethical position depends on any highly specified inference theory of meaning. While there are noninferentialist theories of meaning that are incompatible with the truth of moral principles (because, unless Platonic semantics is true, these theories render moral language meaningless by denying principles the referents they need

59

to be meaningful), there may also be noninferentialist theories that allow for meaningful moral language. Still, one wants an example of a credible theory of meaning that supports the notion of moral truth, and so I *sketch* one, a broad, minimally detailed inference theory, that allows meaningful moral language. There are many versions, and many objections to an inference theory of meaning. Here, I give one version and generically reply to a few generic objections.[2]

First some jargon I will employ: by a "social system" I mean a group of individuals who have trafficked or ever will traffic in assertions in a common community. This need not be direct commerce. If Becky speaks to Nicole, and Nicole to Lydia, whether or not Becky or Lydia ever met, ever corresponded, ever lived during the same time or were in the same place, still they are part of the same social system. If what anthropologists tell us is true, and all modern humans are descended from mitochondrial Eve, assuming she and her offspring were linguistically competent and had the idea of true and false sentences or beliefs, then all linguistically competent humans have been part of the same social system. The most isolated, "uncontacted" clan of hunters and gathers, the most august emperors of the Tang dynasty, and the most cloistered seventeenth-century Carmelite nuns, are all members of the same social system, if only because they have spoken with those who have spoken with those . . . who have spoken with mitochondrial Eve. For the vast majority of humans, there are much closer connections than this common matriarch. Still she suffices to unite humanity in a unitary quest for truth. There may be other social systems, but by definition, as soon as we communicate with them we merge into a single social system.[3]

By "belief system," or "system of belief," I will mean the synchronous beliefs of an individual in a social system. Right now you and I have, presumably quite similar, but certainly different, belief systems. Tomorrow your belief system will be highly similar to today's belief system, but not identical, so it too will be a distinct belief system. A belief system is someone's collection of beliefs at a point in time.

I term the collection of all contemporaneous individual's belief systems in a social system a "social system of beliefs" (SSB). When there is a single belief change of a single individual, although it is slight, both her belief system and the entire SSB are changed.

For simplicity's sake, we can think of a belief system, an attribute of an individual, and a particular belief, an attribute of a belief system, as having truth value, as indeed we all do in all nonphilosophizing common parlance. However, ultimately, truth should be understood to be a social property distributed across the individual minds of a social system's current living members. Only social systems of belief can be true. But we should accept a belief as true if it appears in some justified social system of beliefs (TSSB).[4] A TSSB is justified because it is the optimal set of beliefs, optimally arranged, in a social system. Optimality is judged by the achievement of goals of all members of the social system—past, present, and future.

In sum, a belief belongs to a belief system, a belief system belongs to an individual, collections of belief systems constitute an SSB, SSBs are properties of a temporal slice of a social system, and a social system is the totality of individuals with connecting interlocutors. Social systems of belief can be true or false, and loosely speaking, so can beliefs and belief systems insofar as they are components of a justified social system of belief. Neither a belief nor belief system can be true without regard to the SSB that houses it. True beliefs do not make a true system of beliefs, nor do true systems of beliefs make TSSBs. Rather a TSSB makes them both. A TSSB is what is ultimately justified and its components' justification come from being part of that justified whole.

3. BELIEFS

A belief is a structured region of a belief system. We can be neutral regarding the ontological nature of the belief system—soul substance, mental stuff, behavioral dispositions, brain state—whatever. The only requirement is that the belief system be complex and consist of differentiable regions which themselves have structural complexity. I take the predicate "is true" as primitive, and as I have just said, applying in the first instance to SSBs, and derivatively to belief systems and particular beliefs that are components of a TSSB; individual beliefs we may consider true if they are, or could be, parts of a fully justified belief system. False belief systems, nonetheless, can be more or less similar to a fully justified belief systems. More of this anon.

The meaning of a belief consists in its inferential relations to other beliefs. To claim that one belief, or a set of beliefs "imply" a belief, is to claim that if the "premise" beliefs were in a true belief system, the denial of the "conclusion" belief would not be in that system. (A belief's denial is any other belief that cannot be in the same true belief system regardless of any other beliefs in the system.) If it is, then the system is not a true belief system. My belief that the cat is on the mat implies that the mat has a cat on it. The denial of "the mat has a cat on it," is "the mat does not have a cat on it." To claim that the "the cat is on the mat implies that the mat has a cat on it" is to claim that no TSSB will contain both "the cat is on the mat," and "the mat does not have a cat on it."[5] Obviously, many of the inferential relationships between beliefs will depend on the other beliefs brought into consideration. The meaning of a belief consists of the totality of its inferential relations. Isolated from all other beliefs, a belief is meaningless.

False beliefs, that is, beliefs that could not appear in any true system of beliefs, can still have meaning. Consider belief 1, "No cat has ever been on any mat," and belief 2, "No mat has ever had any cat on it." Although, given our experience of cats and mats, neither would appear in a true belief system (i.e. they are both false), what would appear in a true belief system is belief 3, "If (counter factually) belief 1 were in a true belief system, the denial of belief 2 would not be in that system." Belief 3 is a belief that creates an inference relation between belief 1 and belief 2. If I have belief 3, I do not need to have belief 1 or belief 2 to understand what those propositions mean. True inference-rule beliefs are structures in true belief systems that give the meanings of false as well as true beliefs.

Strictly speaking, if a system of belief is not true, it is false, and it is highly probable that no system of belief has ever been, or ever will be true. However, among the false systems of belief there will be more or less similarity to a true system of belief. The most similar will contain many beliefs that would appear in a TSSB, and many beliefs that are more or less similar to beliefs that would appear in a TSSB. If a belief can be replaced by a belief that will make the system it is in more similar to a true system of belief, the replacement belief is "truer," than the replaced belief.[6]

Inference relations, which constitute meaning, are a matter of social agreement.[7] The validity of a given inference relation is bound to the idea of truth. Beliefs imply, allow, or deny each other because of their necessary, possible, or impossible couplings in a true belief system, and so the validity of inference relations depend on the truth of the belief system they inhabit. The justification of a belief system, that is, its claim on truth, is that it makes the widest set of goals achievable and those goals are both disclosed and certified as achieved by individuals *in community.*

Beliefs form inference relations because they work together. Insofar as they work together well, they are justified—legitimately taken to be true. Hence, the close connection between meaning and truth conditions. There is no access to meaning without access to truth,[8] no access to truth without access to goal achievement, no access to goal achievement without social intercourse, and so no access to meaning, the precipitant of inference relations, without social intercourse. As I argued in the section on objectivity, an objectively true belief system need not share all of the judgments of less objective, less true, belief systems. But it must agree with enough judgments in each "lesser" system to recognize it as a belief system that has truth value. We could feel good without others, but we would not know that a goal has, or even what it means to say it has, truly been achieved.

4. THE REALISM OF INFERENTIALISM

This view separates meaning from reference, but it does not thereby make it unworldly. The structure of a belief system will be caused by reality and its effects will be determined by reality.[9] Therefore, although the meanings of beliefs are constituted by their structural role in a belief system and, strictly speaking, are only "about" each other, these belief systems are created by mind-independent reality, and, given the pragmatic theory of justification, it is mind-independent reality which will cause them to be successful and thus justifies them. On this view neither truth nor rationality are independent of reality.

This theory can accommodate imprecise but roughly useful talk of a belief being "about" an aspect of reality. If the belief "the cat is on the mat" is part of a true belief system, the system is justified, because it achieves goals; the belief that the cat is on the mat, an element of that true belief system, contributes to goal achievement. Presumably some subsection of reality, if not necessarily wholly discrete, then at least with a localizable center of gravity, empowers the "cat is on the mat" belief to contribute to the belief system's truth. Roughly speaking, that subsection of reality is what the belief is "about." But the belief does not represent, stand for, mirror, picture, or name the part of reality it is "about." Nor is the belief an effect of that part of reality. It is simply that that part of reality has effects that account for the presence of the belief in a true belief system.[10]

Beliefs on this view may be thought of as theoretical entities attributed to individuals to explain their behavior.[11] Beliefs explain behavior because they are thought of as maps of regions of the world used by individuals to guide their actions. If we know the map someone is using, we think their past actions more intelligible and their future actions more predictable. A proposition has the form of an item on a belief map. It indicates the position of a node in a system of belief. It describes the relations of one node to other nodes, the way a subway map's icons' placement reveals a station's immediate and distant connecting stations. A proposition may or may not be instantiated as a belief (some stations don't exist), but were it to be instantiated, we understand the actions it would explain and predict because we are aware of its hypothetical position in a belief system. If we know the map someone is using, we think we can figure out why they took a certain route, and where they may try to go next.

Correspondence theories of truth are common because it is natural to think of a map as attempting to picture the terrain it is mapping. To the extent the map is a good likeness, it is an accurate, or a "true" map. But that misconceives the function of maps and how we evaluate them. Their virtue lies in their ability to get us where we want to go. They can be radically dissimilar from the regions we expect them to help us navigate. Perhaps some kind of isomorphism is required for a map to be effective, but degree of similarity does not correlate with the effectiveness of the map. A sharp, detailed photograph can make a far inferior map than a highly schematic one. The map that most looks like reality is not necessarily the best one to guide you through it.

Moreover, sometimes our "maps" are essentially instructions, which take the terrain into account but are nothing like the terrain. Some beliefs may be more like driving directions than they are like road maps. The latter don't much look like the landscape they would guide us through, and the former not at all.

These beliefs, these theoretical maps explaining behavior, although often convenient to think of in isolation, cannot help but function as a collective. A person's system of belief constitutes the map that explains her behavior, even if one part of the system is more salient for explaining a particular action. We understand that Othello killed Desdemona because he believes she has been unfaithful to him with Cassio. But the explanation of his action also presumes an infinite number of other beliefs of Othello—for example, Desdemona would die if deprived of air, he had the strength to hold the pillow over her face long enough to suffocate her, the dead stay dead, it was wrong of her to be unfaithful, she knew she was having sex with Cassio and had not mistook Cassio for Othello, his agonizing thirst for revenge would be slated by her death, her unfaithfulness dishonored him, and so forth. We posit a system of beliefs when we explain an action, even if in many cases we assume that large sections of the system are of no interest because they are ballpark standard enough not to interfere with the explanatory power of the particular belief we are highlighting. The meaning of a belief, its explanatory power, is a function of its relations with other beliefs. A proposition—a belief considered apart from its instantiation in a mind, is the belief's meaning because its relationship to other beliefs, real or potential, explains behavior, whether actual or hypothetical.

The theory on offer is a frank holism with regard to absolute justification and precise meaning, but one that leaves space for smaller units of relative justification and vague meaning. Both are to the good. It strikes me as self-evident that no belief is *fully* justified unless it is fitted into a fully justified theory of everything,[12] and no meaning is fully specified until all of the elements of its defining terms, and their defining terms in turn, have been tied together leaving no unconnected danglers. But with this ideal as our measure, we can still judge how well we think partial justifications are faring and local connections are signifying. We are forever judging what role a region of our belief system will have in a true system of belief.

Striving for rationality may not bring us to the truth, but there is value in approaching it. There are degrees of falseness, and being less false, being relatively more similar to the best system(s) of belief, is likely to be more useful than belief systems more distant from the truth.

A deontic semantics based on an inference theory of meaning, which posits no mind-independent referents to provide meaning, can still use technical machinery fully analogous to the powerful semantics of modal terms to specify truth conditions: just as necessity and possibility are usefully interpreted as what there is or isn't in possible worlds, deontic semantics can be interpreted as what is done or not done in the ideal world. Although David Lewis has argued for the reality of possible worlds,[13] the utility of possible world modal semantics doesn't require it. So too, a deontic semantics does not require some actually existing ideal world. What we put in the ideal world, just as what we put in possible worlds, depends on what best works to make sense of our inferential intuitions and linguistic goals.

Although fundamentally an attribute of belief systems and their parts, truth can also be attributed to "expressions of belief," for example, sentences. I offer and endorse no theory of belief expression, beyond claiming that insofar as nonbeliefs are justified, they are so by virtue of their relationship to justified beliefs. Propositions, "the meanings" of beliefs, are not expressions of belief, nor even quite representations of belief, but rather reifications of belief. Propositions are theoretical entities built out of other theoretical entities, beliefs, and are convenient for describing logical relations. Propositions do not exist apart from beliefs, but as abstractions of them, and as such can also carry truth value.[14]

5. THE MEANING OF MORAL LANGUAGE

David Hume observed that no statements of facts, without the addition of principles of action, can justify an action; one cannot derive "ought" from "is." Some have taken Hume's observation as underwriting their moral skepticism, even claiming to derive from it morality's nonexistence, or at least nonexistence as anything other than the name of local feelings. However, the moral skeptics make an error analogous to the one Humeans accuse some moralists of, for insofar as one cannot derive "ought" from "is," one cannot derive the falseness or nonobjectivity of principles of action from the nonderivability of "ought" from "is." Principles of actions may not have exclusively factual parentage,[15] but unless one adds the premise "only facts and their purebred offspring are capable of being true" (which, if true, cannot be true, so is not true), "ought's" nonderivability from "is" does not undermine the possibility of objectively true principles of action.

We have already seen how principles of action are susceptible to objective justification. However, the Humean point does raise a metaethical concern: what do moral terms, which make no reference to facts, mean? A principle may be true without representing any *thing*, but it cannot be true if it does not mean anything.

Once again, as is the case with justification, we require no special theoretical apparatus to explain how moral statements are meaningful.[16] A statement's meaning is given by its logic—what does it imply and from what is it entailed. Hume's point goes to moral statements' meanings, not their truth. It tells us what we already know: moral statements are different from factual claims, and their immediate, literal meanings depend on their inference relations to other moral statements. The *meaning* of the claim "one ought not to torture cats," has not to do with the cat's placement on the mat or any other facts, although some of those facts will be relevant to its justification. The meaning comes from its relation to statements such as "torturing cats is wrong," "causing any suffering is not right" "torturing is unjustifiable," and statements such as "one should cause extreme pain," "cat suffering is good," and "there is an absolute duty to bring pain to felines." Roughly speaking, the first category of statements implies and is implied by the claim that one ought not to torture cats, and the second sort of statement implies its denial. Those inference relations constitute the principle's meaning.[17] Principles of action's meanings are no more mysterious than the meanings of nonmoral statements, which are also constituted by their inference relationships. Although we find practical principle's meaning in a different region of language than factual statements, we find it in the same way.[18]

Lacking a route from the language of the factual, the more radical moral denigrators refuse to travel in the region of language where moral terms live. They argue that it is a fantasy land unanchored to the factual. Few of the radicals, however, acknowledge the full implications of their radicalism. Prudential "oughts" are no more inferable from "is" than are moral "oughts." Indeed, even theoretical "oughts" must be discarded: one cannot infer from the overwhelming evidence that the cat is on the mat, the complete absence of evidence contrary to the cat's bemattedness, the self-conscious knowledge of all the relevant cat-on-the-mat evidence, the universal happiness and the personal salvation that will result from one's belief that the cat is on the mat, and the *truth* that the cat is on the mat, that one *ought* to believe the cat is on the mat. "Ought's" nonderivability from "is," if fatal to the principle commanding kindness to cats, is equally fatal to the principle of ever commanding belief in cats. To give up rational moral imperatives because they do not offer facts is to abandon all rational imperatives, all recommendations, all commands, hypothetical as well as categorical. From no set of facts can we infer the hypothetical imperative "Given the evidence, you ought to believe that the cat is on the mat." Although we can infer from certain facts that, given the evidence, your disbelief will be false, absolutely nothing about what you *ought* to believe follows from the falsity of your belief.[19] "You ought to believe what is true," is no more a description of what *is*, than "You ought not to torture cats."

The moral skeptic who is willing to bite this particular bullet can only appear, or pretend, to speak our language. She cannot mean what most of us mean by such statements as "you must find the defendant guilty," "try the risotto, it's delicious," "I recommend you see the new Scorsese," "don't hit me," "pass the salt," "stop beating the cat," and so forth. These become, if meaningful at all, descriptions with meanings quite different from their standard normative sense: "the defendant is guilty," "you will like the asparagus and the new Scorsese," "I want the salt and not to be hit," "the cat is being hurt, and you and I do not like cat suffering." The skeptic is not actually making any requests, recommendations or demands. Indeed, she cannot do anything with language other than describe how things are. She denies practical reason and rational agency. She is still capable of acting in accordance with reason (not from her perspective, but from the perspective of acceptors of practical reason), but she cannot think of herself as acting rationally. Her denial of the existence of sound justifications of action, denies the existence of the cause of rational action. Since in her view the cause is nonexistent, so must be the effect. It is no small thing to deny one's rationality. Amoralism grounded in skepticism of moral semantics is even more burdensome than moral relativism. The latter only imposes a kind of alienation from one's principles, the former fails to acknowledge them altogether.

I think the skeptic's denial of rational capacity is self-denial. She may sincerely fancy herself immune to the power of justifications, because she thinks sound justifications don't exist. But they do, and she may be influenced by them, and when she is, she acts rationally, a living counterexample to her theoretical views. A susceptibility to quasi-rationality is sufficient to be listed among the rational. However, a being who was genuinely *immune* to the motivational efficacy of justifications for belief and action, sound or otherwise, would not be a person. It is one thing to never act rationally, but to be totally incapable of rationality is to lack the most significant properties of personhood, for humans are justifying animals. Many of the other animal types declared to be uniquely human—the political, social, religious, free, and, of course, moral animal—are based in the capacity to provide and request justifications. We know we are in the presence of our personal peers when we argue with them.[20]

6. THE NATURE AND SIGNIFICANCE OF THE NONDERIVABILITY OF OUGHT FROM IS

With the machinery developed in sections 2–4 we can further analyze "ought" statements' logical relations to factual claims. A review of the terminology developed in those sections is in order before firing-up the engine: a "social system" is a set of intercommunicating individuals. The communication need not be direct or contemporaneous. All linguistically competent humans comprise one social system. A "belief system," or "system of belief," are the beliefs held by an individual at any given time. The beliefs of all contemporaneous individuals in a social system I term a "social system of beliefs" (SSB). Strictly speaking, only SSBs have truth value, that is, can be true or false. If an SSB is fully justified, and so should be accounted true, it is a "true social system of beliefs" (TSSB). A TSSB is an ideal in which the individuals in a social system could not achieve a superior SSB for achieving their goals.

Derivability of one proposition from another (propositions being the "meanings" of beliefs) is the incompatibility of the *denial* of the second proposition with the assertion of the first proposition. In other words, when we have concluded that X and *not-Y* cannot both be true, we have declared that Y can be derived from X.[21] So to maintain that no "ought" statement can be derived from any "is" statement is to say that the denial of any set of "ought" statements, is compatible with any set of "is" statements.[22] For example, we cannot absolutely rule out the possibility that the two propositions "the cat is suffering from being tortured by P and no one's goals are advanced by the torture" and "the cat ought to be tortured by P" would both be true, and since we cannot rule out that combination as part of the most justifiable set of beliefs, we cannot derive "P ought not torture the cat" from "the cat is suffering from being tortured by P and no one's goals are advanced by the torture."

However, all that tells us is that our level of certainty of the compatibility of any given "is" belief and any given "ought" is insufficient, or at least insufficiently consensual, to be enshrined in language. The nonderivability of "ought" from "is" is completely a matter of social epistemology, and tells us nothing about the metaphysics of morals.

I do not contest the epistemic status conferred on "is-ought" compatibilities by our social system of belief—the beliefs of anyone, any group, with whom we have communicated or will communicate, however indirectly. While I do think that "P ought to torture the cat," and "the cat is suffering from being tortured by P and no one's goals are advanced by the torture," do not both appear in any true system of belief, I recognize that the society we are part of thinks they just might, as, indeed, might any is-ought combination. So no derivation of ought from is, as things stand.

However, it is worth noting that subsections of our social system— particular epochs, religions, cultures, or ideological communities—have enshrined is-ought derivability into their languages, and that we denizens of the contemporary world, in our use of certain "thick" concepts come close to doing so too.[23] A thick concept is one which most literally is only descriptive, but is very tightly associated with specific evaluations. The statement "If you do X it will be a cruel, selfish, dishonest, cowardly, short-sighted, anti-social, and ultimately a self-destructive act, not that I am saying you shouldn't do it," sounds like a joke because it both implicitly acknowledges but formally denies the derivability of ought from is. All of the adjectives can be given strictly descriptive content—they are "is" statements.[24] But, normally, when no normative comment is appended, we do intend that when an act is so described one should infer that it ought not to be done. To claim an act is cruel, selfish, dishonest, cowardly, short-sighted, anti-social, and ultimately a self-destructive act, is to say that it ought not be done. However, we recognize that it doesn't say it to all with whom we might communicate with, including those whom we would concede are competent English speakers, or competent speakers of languages into which English is translatable. And so ought cannot be derived from is.

The nonderivability of ought from is tells us something interesting about our certainty in the relationship between descriptive and normative statements, but tells us little, if anything, about the relative justifiability of either. One cannot derive "Elizabeth II is the current Queen of England," from "the Universe in about 14 Billion years old," but that shakes my confidence in neither, nor tells me that scientific statements are more likely true than historical ones. Some are, some aren't. I would be more amazed to learn that I am wrong about the identity of the current Queen of England than that I am wrong about the age of the Universe (I believe both based on the testimony of others), but more amazed to learn that water is not made of hydrogen and oxygen than that there actually was a survivor at the Alamo. It is not the category of statement that generally makes for confidence, (unless there is a good reason to discount an entire category—e.g., horoscope predictions). Nor need a category of statements seek its credibility in its relation to an epistemically more privileged category. There are moral statements that we all believe more justified than many historical and scientific statements. If we could derive "Lee Harvey Oswald assassinated JFK unaided" and "there are multiple universes" from "treat others respectfully," the two first statements would be on much firmer footing.

It is unlikely, that we will ever be able to derive "ought" from "is," because it is unlikely we will ever achieve a TSSB, or get close to achieving one. In a very large jigsaw puzzle, it becomes epistemically certain that adjacent pieces do or do not belong together, but till we get near completion we, have no way of seeing how the pieces at the bottom of the puzzle connect with the configuration of pieces at the top. Although part of the same whole, it appears to us that the arrangement of pieces at either end can remain what they are without regard for each other.

And why are "ought" statements and "is" statements at different ends of the puzzle, or more literally, as of yet and likely forever inferentially unlinked? It is because the beliefs they represent elicit different kinds of responses. "Is" statements inform the tactics of an action, "ought" the strategy, or perhaps even the mission. It is to be expected that many tactics will be cheek by jowl with certain other tactics, in some cases, so obviously coupled that all agree

they must go together, one implies the other. But strategies' tactical requirements are far more disputable, and more to the point, it is seemingly impossible to discover a mission from any incomplete set of tactics, however large
the incomplete set may be.

The meaning of statements that employ moral terms such as "ought," and
the circumstances in which they are true, are, like all statements, determined
by a consensus of a linguistic community. Whether the nonnormative statement "humans suffer," is true, depends in part on what we mean by "humans"
and "suffer." It is true, if it is, by virtue of its meaning and how the world
is. In the pragmatic theory of justification, if the world is such that holding "humans suffer" to be true ultimately is part of that set of beliefs which
achieves the widest set of goals, it is an objectively justified belief. The
belief "one ought to mitigate human suffering," is objectively justifiable, if
it is, in the same manner; it too must be part of a belief system that achieves
goals. Our extensive agreement on a wide range of beliefs is partially due
to the overlap of goals. The commonality of the goals is a product of common circumstance and the recognition of the achievement of others' goals as
legitimate measures of truth. It is what makes individuals a community. Of
course, a TSSB could be, and likely would be, unable to lead us to perfect
satisfaction for all,[25] which is why we will never be certain all of our beliefs
are justified, even if they were.

If all our beliefs were genuinely justified they would contribute to our goal
achievement as well as any beliefs could. But how do we know goals have
been achieved? A goal realization's most salient feature is sincere acknowledgment it has been achieved by the person whose goal it is. Similarly, the
optimality of an SSB, and hence its justifiability, would be most marked by
universal social acceptance that no principles of thought or action would
render greater satisfaction. Perfect goal achievement would be most certified,
although not absolutely guaranteed, through acceptance by everyone who can
communicate her goals to us, that she believes her goals could not be better
achieved by an alternative SSB. However, that consensus is unlikely to happen. Are we bereft of any rational course till then?

7. JUSTIFIED ENOUGH

Given that final and full justification is never to be had, a criterion for ultimate justification is only a philosophical bauble if we've no way of judging
an actual belief's credibility. Full rationality is an unrealizable ideal, so our
practical rationality would lie inert if it we were unmoved except in the presence of what we considered fully justified judgments. If imperfect justifications made all our judgments equally irrational, as finite creatures, nothing we

believe or do could claim to be more rational than any alternative. Thus we want criteria for judging whether a proposition is justified *enough* to act on. In the next chapter, we will see that Reason can motivate; what we need to investigate is which inconclusive signs of Reason *should* motivate.

In instances where we can suspend belief and delay action "justified enough," may be a high bar. Where indefinite agnosticism has no cost, "enough" might be roughly equivalent to fully justified, and as fully justified never happens, there is never enough justification to act on some propositions. There are times, however, in which commitment to a practical course is unavoidable,[26] and although some of those times any choice is as (un)justified as any other, often Reason can point the more likely way, or at least discourage some roads. How so? What determines rationality this side of epistemological perfection?

I have said that of two beliefs, the first is "more justified" than the second if it resembles a belief in a TSSB more than the second does.[27] But that is both insufficiently informative and misleading. Misleading because whole systems are the bearers of truth value; insofar as similarity justifies, it is system to system similarity. Insufficiently informative because I've yet to provide means of judging similarity?

To judge whether a social system of belief is more similar to a an ideal SSB than an alternative social system of belief, we must assess the conditions which give rise to it—namely are they conditions that promote objectivity. Are many, well attended, detailed perspectives brought into play, and are many goals, from a large range of sources, used to evaluate the effects of the SSB or at least those regions of the SSB that have been most influential in the formation of the judgments under consideration? The more the conditions of belief formation enable objectivity, the more we can presume (without ever knowing) that the resultant SSB resembles a TSSB. As women's perspectives and judgments, for example, have gained influence in shaping our beliefs, increased confidence that our SSB more resembles a TSSB is justified.

This makes epistemology inescapably ethical. How we attend to others' views is the mark of our SSB's reliability. The social dynamics of inquiry and deliberation vouch for the system's likely degree of validity. A SSB forged through uncensored, open discussion—discussions that are transparent and comparatively unhobbled by prejudice or systematic exclusion of perspectives, should be supposed more similar to a TSSB, than a SSB poorer in those objectivity-making features. Science's credibility rests largely on its formal devotion to this ethos, and, relative to most other human institutions, its implementation. Science's comparative record of delivering the goods reinforces the sense that weighing evidence and arguments from all sources leads to the most effective, and therefore the most likely true, beliefs.

Conditions of formation, however, are not, or not directly, how an *individual* claim ought to be assessed. Individual claims should be judged by their compatibility with the other members of the relatively most justifiable SSB. We judge yardsticks by the way they are produced, but we judge particular lengths by our yardsticks. Where two claims fit into a relatively justified SSB equally well we have a balance of evidence. What counts as fitting in with a SSB? Here we can invoke W. V. O. Quine's web of belief:[28] How many and how central are the beliefs that would have to change to accept a belief? Beliefs that live peacefully with the long established and most densely connected beliefs are more credible than those whose acceptance entails major renovations of the SSB. Nonetheless, a belief might be warranted even if it deeply disrupted an existing SSB, but that would be because it helped generate an alternative SSB that was more objective than the replaced SSB.

8. RATIONALIST PRAGMATISM IN COMPARATIVE CONTEXT

I call the view developed here "Rationalist Pragmatism" (RP). Some of the finer points of RP, in particular the role that social consensus plays in determining and justifying moral truth, can be brought into better focus by comparing it to similar positions.

RP shares many elements with a family of theories termed "constructivist," but there are too many versions of contructivist metaethics, and too many proposed criteria for qualifying as constructivist, to declare unreservedly whether Rational Pragmatism is of the kind. Carol Bagnoli defines metaethical constructivism as "the view that insofar as there are normative truths, they are not fixed by normative facts that are independent of what rational agents would agree to under some specified conditions of choice."[29]

Under that description, RP comes awfully close, but does not quite qualify as a constructivism. RP does deny "normative facts" floating free of what rational agents decide, and social agreement does play a central role in the theory. However, in RP, it is not rational agents agreement "under some specified conditions of choice," that "fixes" normative truth; instead social agreement provides the standard for judging whether a normative claim is true, and social agreement under specified conditions of social deliberation constitutes the best evidence for particular normative claims. But, for a pragmatist, this is not anything special about normativity—it is the case with all claims.[30] Rational agents "get things right" including moral norms, not because rational procedures stipulate correctness, but rather because correctness of belief stipulates rationality; if deliberation doesn't get things right, doesn't guide us effectively, it has not been, according to the standard of rationality we accept, fully rational. Social consensus defines rationality, but what meets that definition, in principle is an empirical question—albeit, in moral cases an empirical question in which social consensus is by far the most compelling evidence.[31] So if constructivism merely means that we "construct" the work-space and tools to build and evaluate norms, then RP is a constructivism. But if constructivism entails that social consensus stipulates which norms are correct, RP is not a constructivism.

Getting things right, in thought or deed, is having the best possible thoughts and acting the best possible way. Our thoughts and actions are tools, and while we can be mistaken on how well they work for us relative to other possible tools, only we have the authority to pronounce on what counts as effective or to declare them perfected for *our* purposes. Our recognition does not create reality's effects, but it is the sole means by which some of these effects, namely our beliefs and actions, are evaluated. Social agreement does not create truth, factual or moral, unaided by reality. Social agreement is not sufficient for "fixing," truth. Everyone can agree that our collective beliefs, moral and factual, are true, and that consensus can hold till doomsday, and yet those beliefs may not be true. We remain irremediably fallible. Social consensus is insufficient for establishing truth because we could be mistaken about whether our current beliefs are the best we could have for achieving our goals. Since even the best set of beliefs will leave quite a few goals unachieved, there is no way of knowing for sure whether we could do better with different beliefs, or whether this is, epistemically speaking, as good as it gets.

However, social agreement does set the standard for recognizing truth, and pragmatism claims that standard is effectiveness. Moreover, until everyone agrees that they are true, it is near certain that our beliefs are not all true. And if our collective beliefs aren't true, none among us has completely true beliefs. So, besides being formally necessary for their being any justification at all, social consensus is practically necessary for justifying specific beliefs; whether our beliefs meet the standard of truth must be judged by how they acquit themselves from the perspective of *all parties that share the same standard of truth*, and if all parties are not in agreement, confidence that the beliefs are nonetheless justified is inappropriate. This is particularly so when we consider that an important goal of rational beings is to be rational. As long as we remain in disagreement our goal of being rational is thrown in practical doubt. Social consensus creates the standard of truth,[32] and social consensus would surely be a feature were we ever to possess the true theory of everything.[33]

For David Copp, the fundamental metaethical question is whether morality can peacefully coexist with our naturalist *weltanschauung*, and he thinks the preferred answer is "yes," for we hope that the ontology science offers is compatible with normativity; we loathe to think normativity unreal but equally dislike recognizing realities not encompassed by science. Theories that reconcile scientific naturalism with the existence of norms that are more than mere local conventions, Copp calls compatibilist, and their theoretical task is accounting for this compatibility.[34] Some metaethicists hold that it can't be done; they are of the schools I've called "the adversaries,"[35] nihilists or relativists of various types. Others declare nature and norms compatible by keeping them completely separate: there are natural facts and normative facts, and they cannot conflict because they exist in nonintersecting realms. But for Copp, this is hardly a genuine compatibility, for our naturalism is voracious, and claims all reality as its domain. A true compatibilist solution would account for normativity in naturalist terms.

Copp's suggested solution, "pluralist teleology" takes norms to be tools for solving generic human problems that are "affected by [human] actions and choices."[36] Pluralist because such generic human problems are of many types, teleological because norms are understood in relation to what they aim to achieve. A true norm, or "real" norm if you will, is part of the ideal code—the code that would best "ameliorate" the problem.

Here we are presented with a normativity that is entirely natural—generic human problems and their effective amelioration. Of course, Copp assumes that the description of a generic problem implies standards for evaluating the effectiveness of a solution. Without that assumption, we could not identify the ideal tools because their ideality can only be established by an evaluation of their effects. But if we allow that the status of "problem" is naturally given, we should grant the same to solution. If tuberculosis' *problematic nature* is natural, so is what counts as its most effective cure. Similarly, if social strife is natural, so are the rules whose adherence most promotes social harmony. In other words, a natural social consensus that something is a problem provides a natural social consensus about what counts as the best solution.

Rational Pragmatism is quite similar to pluralist-teleology. It too provides real norms without positing nonnatural entities, and so is compatibilist. In RP norms, as in pluralist-teleology, are tools, and as in pluralist teleology the tools are ultimately judged against hypothetical but fully natural phenomena, problem-solving for pluralist teleology, goal achievement for RP. Both theories are tied to an ideal but naturalistically understandable state—best solutions for pluralist-teleology, and maximal goal achievement for RP.

However, although very like pluralist-teleology, Rational Pragmatism better meets the criteria for Copp's preferred compatibilist metaethics. RP is clearer about the standard of normative correctness, for it is not a pluralism of norms. All norms are measured by a single norm—truthfulness—and truthfulness is judged by the completely natural phenomenon of goal achievement.

RP's goal achievement is more forthrightly naturalistic than "amelioration" of generic problems. The constituent goals that are raw materials of the truth-norm in RP are actual human goals in all their variety. The natural subjectivity of goals is granted, and they are turned into justified beliefs (including practical principles) by the equally natural phenomenon of intersubjective assessment of goal achievement.

Furthermore, RP has a better account of the universal "bindingness" of morality—the notion that morality's standard(s) apply to all agents. In pluralist-teleology, a norm is justified because it solves a problem, and the solution is widely valued because the problem is endemic to the human condition. But its applicability to any individual depends on her personally valuing the solution. We know enough about people to know that even the most widespread values, including staying alive, are not universal. In RP, regardless of what she may value, a person's status as rational, as potentially recognizing truth and acting accordingly, binds her to morality. This is not to claim that rationality is a more reliable spur to moral compliance than widespread human values. But it is definitive of our personhood, and even when it doesn't move us, Reason calls us. Our irrational actions remain unjustified whether or not we care about practical justification. Signing up to the practice of affirming and denying—judging—makes you subject to judgment. You have heard it said "judge not lest ye be judged," but verily I say unto you "ye cannot help but judge, and so cannot avoid judgment." Unless ye be not of our kind.

For Copp, a genuine compatibilist solution would account for normativity in naturalist terms, but the compatibility is no less if our knowledge of factual *truth* is accounted for in normative terms. Whether "facts" account for norms or norms for "facts," the result is existential comity. RP explains knowledge, our possession of "factual" as well as moral truth, as generated by norms, but this does not imply that RP takes normativity to be ontologically fundamental. Reality and nature contain no norms independent of rational beings, and require no rational being to exist; RP is no idealism. But the *truth* about nature does need us.

9. BUT IS IT PRAGMATISM?

To what extent is RP a traditional pragmatism or a traditional rationalism? While its pragmatism is standard, its rationalism is too removed from the views of the classic rationalists to be grouped among them. The raw ingredients of RP are pragmatic, although its final flavor is rationalist. Pragmatism provides the epistemology, semantics, and structure of the entire enterprise. But it is by creating the space for Reason that pragmatism leads to morality. In grounding terminology, Reason grounds morality, but Reason is grounded in pragmatic considerations, which are normative. The view is rationalist because respect for truth is the source and shaper of morality, but more fundamentally it is pragmatic because our good justifies our knowledge.

However, there is cause to wonder whether this view really is more pragmatist than it is rationalist. Robert Brandom is a prominent advocate of a kindred position which, like RP, views norms and reason as ineluctably social. Brandom too claims a pragmatist skeleton with rationalist sinews, saying that his pragmatism is "joined to a kind of philosophical rationalism,"[37] Daniel Dennett, however, suggests Brandom's views are more rationalist, if not idealist, than pragmatist. If Dennett is right, RP must be distinguished from Brandom's "pragmatism . . . joined to . . . rationalism," or RP must give up its claim to be a fundamentally pragmatist view. It is not merely an issue of which philosophical label is affixed to the RP packaging; the realism of RP is at issue; if it is not standing on its pragmatist feet, RP fails to make contact with reality. So is Dennett right, and if he is, does RP escape the idealism he finds lurking in Brandom's "pragmatism?"

Dennett embraces the essential role that the "other" (in Brandom's terms "community") plays in the making of rationality, but he believes that the correctness of reason-making norms find their resting place in "predictive utility."[38] Surely, he is right that both a nonregressive explanation of normativity and pragmatism demand as much. Dennett, in a courteously diplomatic spirit (Brandom call it "statesman like,") asks Brandom to look upon his push for grounding norms in utility as a friendly amendment. But his characterization of the disagreement reveals the weighty stakes: "roughly, it's the difference [in whether you characterize irrationality as . . .] being stupid [or] being naughty."[39] Dennett thinks that if normativity is to be pragmatically grounded, ultimately it must do work, it must be *good* for something. Replacing "utility" with "community," as he claims Brandom does, turns irrationality into an arbitrary *faux pas*. For his part, Brandom rehearses all the areas of agreement betwixt himself and Dennett and hopes that their "approaches can be seen as complementary,"[40] but he "resists" the central thrust of Dennett's "amendment," namely that "we can illuminate the issue of what language is by asking what it is for."

Mutually accommodating as they are, more can be done to close the Dennett–Brandom gap between utility and community by nudging each toward RP. Dennett argues that conditions for creating norms *are made by nature*, which has no norms, only effects. Brandom argues that conditions for creating norms are made by nature, *which has no norms*, only effects. The difference of emphases indicates each philosopher's concern. Both agree that normativity (and hence Reason) is a manifestation of a necessarily communal dynamic. But, because nonhuman nature is normless, for Dennett, nature is where we must find the noncircular *explanation* of normativity.

But just because nature *is* normless, for Brandom, our understanding of what normativity *is* need not go there. Dennett is struck by the natural endowment of subnormative "design" work that made normativity possible. Brandom presumes the subnormative work (or something pretty similar) but thinks the genesis of normativity is irrelevant to what normativity is.

Dennett is right that Reason must be good for something, but here he loses sight of what he well knows: whether something is good or useful is *always* a normative question; our norms must be good for something, but only norms can say for what. Nature's "purposes" may have created normativity, and respecting nature's ongoing demands allows for ongoing normativity, but only a community can say what normativity, or anything else, is *good for*. This is squarely within the main line of pragmatist thought, which is at pains to stress that our goals evolve as much as our techniques for pursuing them. We have for millennia extended our goals beyond surviving long enough to pass on our genes.[41] There is no good or utility outside of community sustained norms, only events of various kinds.

However, Brandom undermines his pragmatist street cred when he reduces a norm-sustaining community to assertion making communicants who need have no practical cooperative endeavors. He thereby loses the external world, the locus of assertions' truth values. It is not that nature provides the goods to make good our claims, but it provides the arena and raw material. The community alone, *à la* Brandom, verifies and valorizes, but, *à la* Dennett, it imposes these norms onto something that *happens in nature*. For RP the relevant community is the "social system," comprised of all connected communicants regardless of degrees of separation, and nature is where they meet to establish facts and vindicate norms.

Brandom's characterization of his view as "pragmatism . . . joined to . . . rationalism," is also a fair description of Jurgen Habermas' "Discourse Ethics," and in many ways RP mirrors Habermas' moral theory. Both views incorporate the Hegelian notion that selves are socially constituted and that the justifiability of moral claims depends on others and their goals.[42] Both RP and Discourse Ethics tie the rationality of belief to the social conditions of its formation and maintenance, with a special emphasis on the dynamics of interpersonal discourse: truth is approached by multiplying the perspectives, equalizing the power, and promoting the autonomy of the interlocutors. Habermas, as I and all orthodox pragmatists do, rejects any correspondence analysis of "truth," and roots his moral realism in the practical effects reality attaches to a set of beliefs.

However, Habermas, does not sufficiently free himself of a sharp fact-value distinction which is foreign to a thoroughgoing pragmatism, and thereby compromises his moral cognitivism, and casts doubts on his moral realism. He holds that, because different types of interests are involved, the norms of discourse that lead to valid empirical claims are fundamentally and qualitatively different from those that lead to valid moral claims. But this is tantamount to equivocating on "validity"; if beliefs about the wrongness of torturing cats are not justified by the same fundamental logic that justifies beliefs about cat biology, we are left without any grounds for thinking factual and moral beliefs are "true" in the same sense. And if the "truth" of morality is essentially different from factual "truth," moral truth will be classified as only metaphorically "true," if not as altogether *ersatz*.[43]

In contrast to Habermas' Discourse Ethics, RP makes no categorical epistemological distinction between normative and factual justifications. Of course, methods of inquiry and relevant evidence vary with the nature of a claim being judged. But the "empirical," label does not denote unified, sharply defined means or criteria of verification. Abstract, unobservable principles, for example, Occam's Razor, play a justifying part in empirical as well normative propositions. Sensory perceptions of all sorts help justify normative as well as empirical claims. Think of the ways we go about justifying claims such as "the salt is on the table," "Felix is a cat," "Vitamin C is essential to health," "Christianity contributed to the collapse of the Roman Empire," "Polish is an Indo-European language," "there was a conspiracy to assassinate Lincoln," "deficit spending will trigger inflation," "anatomically modern humans walked out of Africa 100,000 years ago," and "light is both a wave and a particle." All are empirical propositions, but modes of verification differ radically.[44] So too with normative claims: "you should not hit your brother," "it was wrong to invade Iraq," "Lincoln was a greater President than Madison," "one should believe in natural selection," "neither a borrower nor lender be," "engineering is a nobler profession than college teaching," "a wise person holds no grudges," "Beethoven symphonies are beautiful," and "*Per Se* merits its 3 star Michelin rating," all of which we classify as "normative." The "factual" versus the "normative" quality of a claim is merely a place along a continuum, and hardly the only continuum on which we can locate propositions. There are continua within the normative, such as aesthetic and moral, within the empirical (psychological and physical), and continua that intersect them both (e.g., historical and sociological). Just as we might judge something as *more* of a normative question than an empirical one, we might judge it to be more of an aesthetic than a moral question, more a physical than a psychological question, or more an historical than sociological one. The evidence that is adduced for a claim, and how that evidence is gathered, depends on the claim's location in our belief structure, but the logic with which the evidence is deployed, and the status of truth the evidence aims to establish are the same for all claims: we deduce, calculate probabilities, and judge whether the claim ought to be believed.

None of which is to say there are no generally useful distinctions to be made between facts and values, normative and factual statements, or aesthetic and moral judgments; only that the distinctions are neither metaphysical nor logical. The distinctions are practical; factual beliefs tend to be general tools useful for serving the broadest range of interests, making agreement about relevant evidence less plagued by the multiplicity of goals that certify relevance. Normative statements tend to allude to less fully shared goals, making evidence of their utility more difficult to assess, which often, but hardly always, makes them more controversial. The wrongfulness of chattel slavery and the literary merit of Shakespeare, normative propositions, have long been less controversial than the effects of tax cuts on job growth, or meat consumption on cardiac disease, empirical issues. There are insufficient pragmatist grounds to embrace a deeply principled distinction between means of justifying empirical and moral truth, and Habermas weakens his moral objectivism by doing so. One wonders whether concerns with the nature of the meaning of moral statements plays a part in Habermas' assigning them their own special mode of justification.

10. RATIONALIST PRAGMATISM AND
TRANSCENDENTAL ARGUMENTS

Cheryl Misak's moral epistemology anticipated many of this book's core claims and central arguments.[45] For Misak, as in RP, the key to moral truth is the rejection of the correspondence notion of truth and the embrace of a pragmatic conception. Prominent among the many elements that RP shares with Misak's pragmatism are (1) sets of beliefs are the bearers of truth; (2) sensory perception is not the only kind of evidence;[46] and (3) "Epistemic holism"—the idea that an individual belief's truth value cannot be judged in isolation from other beliefs. Most importantly, these elements are similarly deployed by Misak and me to vindicate moral objectivism through pragmatist epistemology. Nonetheless, there are differences in conception that make a difference.

The first difference comes in the characterization of "the core of the pragmatic conception of truth."[47] Misak gives a number of formulations: truth is that which "best accounts for experience," or is belief that would "stand up to the evidence and reasons," or belief which would "fit with experience and arguments," or belief which further "inquiry could not improve."[48] Although not all the same, each description makes truth-seeking an activity judged exclusively by its capacity to explain. Especially, as Misak emphasizes in *Truth and the Ends of Inquiry*, its capacity to explain experience.[49] These characterizations fail to highlight pragmatism's practical lodestar—the purposes of truth-seeking. Or rather they narrow truth-seeking to too few purposes. The mark of truth I've commended is "goal achievement"; beliefs are judged by how well they guide our actions, which in turn is judged by how well they enable us to achieve our goals. The regulative ideal of truth at play here is "no beliefs will do better at helping us achieve our ends," rather than "no further evidence will change our minds."

The problem with Misak's descriptions is that they confine the purpose of pursuing truth to explaining and understanding. These are, I believe, important human purposes, and often final purposes. But they are not our sole purposes. Beliefs are much broader tools, and their virtue must be judged against all human purposes.[50] The "goal achievement" standard does not characterize justified belief, as Misak fears it may, as a measure of some psychologically rewarding state, such as "most consoling." That would be as confining as "best accounts for the evidence."[51]

At times, Misak edges toward the broadening captured by "goal achievement." She speaks of true belief as meeting "expectations," as accounting for experience and "interests," as "never lead[ing] to disappointment," as "satisfying" the aims of inquiry and *other aims*.[52] But these characterizations do not ever clearly embrace *all* of our aims as the measure of beliefs. This hedging makes her pragmatic conception of justification more palatable to epistemic traditionalists who think of justified belief as disinterested knowledge, but it doesn't make full use of all of pragmatism's resources to illuminate and strengthen our moral and political practice.

A second difference regards epistemic holism. Although she calls her holism "radical holism,"[53] I think it not radical enough. Misak's holism appears to take an individuals' set of beliefs as the bearer of truth rather than the community as a whole. And even when she suggests that we take the set of an entire community's beliefs as the truth bearers,[54] too often the community she has in mind is a subset of the human community, such as contemporary Xhosas or Albertans, rather than all knowers. This reticent holism also compromises moral cognitivism.

RP, by making the truth bearer the set of beliefs of all contemporaneous communicating persons, and making the measure of justification that belief set's performance in achieving the goals of all past, present, and future members of that community, conceives a comprehensive holism along multiple dimensions. This better enables RP to grapple with some puzzles that bedevil defenders of moral objectivism.

Misak raises three categories of such puzzles: under-determination, regret, and tragic choice. Each raises doubts about the claim that moral judgments are truth apt. If, once all the evidence is in, the truth remains indeterminate, why believe there is a truth to be known? If one has done the truly right thing, and thereby avoided doing wrong, why are there situations that seem to make *regret* inescapable no matter what is done? And if doing the right thing is knowable, why are there situations in which every choice seems *tragically* wrong? A noncognitivist who takes moral beliefs as manifestations of subjective feelings finds none of this puzzling. Feelings don't have right answers and need not be coherent. However, for a cognitivist upholder of objectivity, conceding that some moral judgments are neither true nor false is an embarrassment. Hence, the challenge to objectivist morality posed by under-determination, regret, and tragic choice.

Misak handles the under-determination problem as well and in the same way as Rational Pragmatism would.[55] She notes that many normative judgments appear underdetermined by evidence because their framing is too general. "What is the best sort of life," admits of contrary answers, but not because of under-determination. The question of whether Mary's life, with her talents, interests, inclinations, history, and social setting, should pursue an athletic life may be fully determined by the evidence, and the similar question that substitutes Jane and *her* circumstances, might be differently but equally well answered in favor of a philosophical life. These are not matters of under-determination regardless of the evidence, they are matters of under-specified questions. Specification resolves the conflict.

Regret is feeling bad even though you believe you've made the right choice. Misak chalks it up to value pluralism; the best actions still leave valuable alternative actions undone. Misak's analysis is sound, but by using "goal achievement" as the standard of rightness we can deepen the analysis of regret. A social system of beliefs that maximized goal achievement would still leave many goals unrealized. We cannot get everything we want, and the want of getting some things make us feel bad.[56] The "goal achievement" standard makes explicit that even acting in accord with unequivocally true judgments can entail serious losses.

However, it is with tragic cases, where remorse is in order, that RP is most helpful to the objectivist cause. Misak accepts the possibility of moral tragedy—situations in which no matter what is done, a wrong is done, situations wherein the apparent tautology "Doing X is not both morally permissible and morally impermissible" is false. Her acceptance of tragic cases is a step back from moral cognitivism, for it leaves some moral questions with no truth to be known.[57]

The phenomenology of tragic cases are compelling, but they should not drive the epistemic analysis. With the *effectiveness-at-goal-achievement* as our standard of justification, we can explain the strong paradoxical intuition that a right action is wrong, a true judgment false. Sometimes doing the right thing involves a *type* of act so terrible that it is best to believe that no decent person could perform it, or having performed it he should be wracked with guilt. For instance, let's assume some ticking-clock hypothetical—a city with a million people blown to smithereens unless the bomb setter is tortured to reveal the bomb's whereabouts—*does* justify torture. Torture in this instance, *ex hypothesi*, is the right thing to do. Still, beliefs that the torture be *treated* as wrongful may also be true. The totality of goals may best be met by judging that you ought to do something that you ought to hate yourself for having done. Tragic cases are cases where one should feel remorseful and feel the need to expatiate sin, even though the right thing was done. There is nothing paradoxical about this; our goals may best be met by believing torture was the right thing to do, and believing we ought to be unable to go on living with ourselves for having tortured, or only live with unending remorse.[58] Specification, awareness of lost value, and horror at being dutiful when duty entails a horrific act, explain in objectivist terms the whiff of subjectivism clinging to seemingly contrary yet correct judgments, to actions that cause regret, and to tragic choices demanding remorse.

RP can go a step further in avoiding embarrassments to objectivism. Its form of holism and standard of justification can give an objectivist account of the simultaneous full justification of outright "contradictory" beliefs, for the individual beliefs are not, strictly speaking, truth bearers. "One should *never* torture," and "one should torture this person for this purpose at this time," might *both* appear in a true social system of belief, if that is the set of beliefs that will best achieve the community's goals. Truth could encompass both beliefs, not because truth toggles, but because it is not measurable at the level of individual belief. The teamwork of beliefs at times might demand a division of labor that pits individual beliefs against each other to achieve the fully justified set of beliefs. My believing executing murderers is unjustified and your believing that executing murderers is justified, might better maximize goal achievement than us both believing either one. For reasons I discussed,[59] if this occurs at all it would be very rare, and its theoretical possibility is never reason to abandon efforts to reconcile contradictory judgments. But the perennial failure of a particular reconciliation is not cause to doubt objectivism as conceived by RP.

Allowing that at times the relevant epistemic community is less than all rational beings in mutual contact also weakens moral objectivism. If some truths in principle are recognizable only by Xhosa, some only by Albertans, but others are recognizable by everyone, the truths of limited availability are second-rate truths.[60] Of course, Xhosa and Albertans weave different goals into the common fabric on which truth is measured and provide different angles for the measuring, including perspectives that may be difficult if not impossible to convey to those with a different history or in a different social setting.[61] But none of that amounts to claiming that the same specified proposition is true when believed by the Xhosa and false when believed by the

Albertans.[62] Of course, the same "division of labor" that allowed for individuals to have contradictory beliefs can allow social groups to contain them.[63] That, however, it is not because there are cases in which truth is relative to the group, but rather because the particular groups' beliefs contribute to but don't determine justification. All competent humans constitute our community of verifiers, and no truth is justified if not measured against the goals of that entire community.

Misak's skepticism toward any "transcendental" defense of moral objectivism is the most striking difference between her approach and RP. She defines a transcendental argument as one which purports to show that something "is a necessary condition for the very possibility of some undeniable fact [or capacity we have]."[64] She also associates transcendental arguments as trafficking in noncontingent, metaphysical claims. She'll none of that.[65]

RP has a fair amount of that. I begin with the metaphysical assumption that there are selves and argue that selves presuppose others, an external world, and practical engagement with those others in that external world. The practical engagement of self and others (not as multiple organisms, but as multiple *selves*), in turn, presupposes truth and rationality.

Although "transcendental," this argument does not make truth, reason, or morality necessary beings independent of history. There is surely a natural history that brings this cluster of person-constituting concepts into being, and it is as contingent as any series of historical events. Selfhood and reason are constitutive of who we are, but *that* we are is utterly contingent. Nor does the metaphysical assumption of selfhood have further metaphysical implications; it has phenomenological and logical entailments. We conceive of ourselves as selves, and so we must conceive of an external world and the possibility of other selves. Whether there actually are others or an external world is another matter. But to fail to act as if there are is to lose objectivity, truth, and selfhood.

This view is in line with Scott Aikin's general defense of transcendental arguments,[66] which concludes that they can establish what we must believe, but not what must be case. This he thinks imposes modesty on transcendental arguments—after all it asserts that they can establish no absolute metaphysical claims—but not too much modesty (what he calls "self-effacing"), because they needn't merely explain belief, or excuse belief, but can actually justify belief.

I won't reproduce Aikin's arguments for the potential cogency and limitations of transcendental arguments, which I find persuasive. However, I think he mischaracterizes his conclusion as permitting transcendental arguments only *modest* results. Aikin demonstrates that successful transcendental arguments *justify* beliefs, show that rejecting the beliefs are irrational, and that the beliefs ought to be *accepted* as true. That their truth ought not to be understood along the lines of the mistaken epistemology of correspondence theory, or that the belief in their truth is not infallible, are hardly grounds for modesty. The inability to defeat a global skepticism, that itself assumes a correspondence theory, is only humbling to those who buy into a correspondence rooted epistemology—which, Aikin and Misak, as pragmatists, do not.

Although providing a strong Kantian component, this "transcendentalism" does not undermine or supersede RP's pragmatism. Not only does a pragmatic metric continue to evaluate the truth of social systems of belief, pragmatism also grounds and motivates the transcendental argument. I have argued that explanation and comprehension are not the sole purposes of belief, nonetheless, they have become for us deep-rooted purposes of belief. Like all human goals, they are historically evolved, contingent, and subject to change. But philosophical puzzlement is as real a human problem as hunger, albeit of less urgency and lower priority. Some theoretical problems are of concern only to a tiny coterie, and their particular resolution, or lack of resolution, are without significant consequence. But some theoretical problems, even if technically formulated and tackled, engage problems that at some level are widely felt. Among the most pressing of these problems is the difficulty of understanding our moral lives and our entrenched sense that some things are right and some things are wrong. If a transcendental argument offers a more satisfying solution to that problem than an alternative theory, it answers to a real need. The truth of our metaphysical assumptions, like any other truth, must be judged by how well they do their job of explaining morality in a way that is compatible with other beliefs that seem to do their jobs well. And, as both Misak and I believe, a true metaethics will have favorable moral and political consequence of value beyond the intrinsic good of philosophical understanding. Pragmatism wedded to rationalism is not a submissive spouse forced to take its partners surname.

Ultimately moral skepticism is based on doubts about rational agency. "Error theorists," amoralist deniers of morality's existence, appear to ground their denial in a straightforward ontological claim: there is no being, no *thing*, on which to base morality. But it is only because this ontology is seen as disempowering practical reason that the amoralist judges morality to be illusory. Moral action is impossible, she concludes, because there is no morality to move us. But, because skepticism about rational *action* is the immediate source of moral skepticism, such skepticism need not be grounded semantically or ontologically. A moral judgment, even if allowed meaningful, true and about an independent reality, would do little for morality if it was unable to move us.

NOTES

1. It is an area of keen interest to philosophers and other students of language, but its technical details makes discussion of it tedious to many readers. However, in my effort to uphold morality in the face of the major sources of skepticism, I cannot avoid the task. But this chapter (except, to some extent, sections 1, 5, and 7) are relatively heavy sledding. If you are content to grant the meaningfulness of moral statements' without slogging through a general meaning theory, and instead go directly to the issue of whether moral judgments can move us, the remainder of this chapter can be left unread without losing the main thread, and so you may choose to skip prose soaked in jargon and technical distinctions that will strike some readers as mind-numbing pettifogging.

2. The version I provide is roughly similar to the inference theory of Robert Brandom's (1994), but despite the common features (e.g., holism, pragmatism), there are significant differences, and my sketch in any case would not qualify as even a summary account of Brandom's sophisticated, detailed theory. Wanderer (2008) provides a useful introduction to Brandom's inferentialism.

3. This possibility of other social systems, with individuals whose goals none of us have or will ever hear of, is a concession I make to relativism. If there are rational beings on a distant galaxy with whom our kind never interacts, they may have different fully justified beliefs.

4. Note I do not say "if and only if"; I am not giving an essentialist account of truth. I am claiming all justified beliefs should be *taken* to be true, but make no claims about the possibility of truths that are unjustified, or truth in and of itself, apart from justification (if there be any such thing). I call a justified social system of belief a "*T*SSB" rather than a "*J*SSB" to emphasize that when it is fully justified, rationality *requires* we take a belief to be *true*. There is no practical point to questioning the truth of a fully justified belief, that is, a belief that is a member of a fully justified social system of belief—a TSSB.

5. Subject to the caveat regarding a possible "division of labor" among beliefs in a TSSB discussed in note 43 of chapter 2, section 6, chapter 5, section 2, and this chapter, notes 33 and 63, as well as pages 82–83.

6. For discussion of "similarity" to true beliefs, see section 7 of this chapter.

7. This way of putting it appears to align me with Brandom (2010) in the dispute with Dennett (2010), that the latter cleverly characterizes as a disagreement over whether semantic mistakes are stupid or transgressive. But I think the disagreement evaporates when we consider that falsehoods are known as such because they would ultimately be transgressive, but secure their transgressivity because they are "stupid." I doubt that Dennett or Brandom would disagree, although each would emphasize a different stage of the making of errors. A fuller discussion of Brandom and Dennett on this issue appears in section 9 of this chapter. For a fuller accounting on the role of social agreement in justification see section 7 of chapter 2 and section 8 of this chapter.

8. A main lesson I take from Davidson's semantics (1967).

9. There is a plausible evolutionary story to account for these relations, but the fact of the relations is independent of its etiology. See Dennett and Brandom in Wanderer (2010).

10. I take this view to be compatible with Millikan's naturalistic semantics (1990), even though her naturalistic account of representations might seem more at home in a full blown correspondence-theory-of-truth semantics, as Millikan herself believes it does. In this I think her wrong. Millikan argues (to translate her views about sentences into beliefs) that a belief's truth conditions are fixed by the circumstances that led to the reproductive success of those holding that belief. When believed in dissimilar circumstances the belief is false. Hence, truth is a matter of a belief's corresponding to the circumstances that are similar to the original circumstances that made the holding of that belief serve a biological purpose. I find Millikan's detailed, naturalistic account of the genesis of "truth" compelling, but believe its apparent support for truth as correspondence disappears when we consider how purposes and meaning can change in tandem. Suppose "Run!" was repeatedly uttered by some individuals whenever there was a saber-toothed tiger behind a conspecific in their presence. Members of a community that responded to that "Run!" vocalization by speedily running straight ahead, without looking back, more successfully survived and reproduced than those not disposed to run. "Run!" meant "there is a saber-toothed tiger behind you," a proposition which, when believed, sometimes induced running. But running can be useful in a host of circumstances, and if it was sometimes used when other dangerous animals were present, that use and response might too favor survival. Indeed through a series of transformations, every one of which keeps the circumstances which commonly produce "Run!" aligned with the utility of the common response to its production, "Run!" can come to be commonly uttered when someone believes that a business' stock shares are overvalued, and typically elicit the response from hearers of "Run!" of putting in a sell order. There is no reason to think the sentence "Run!" in the presence of an overpriced stock is false because there are no saber-toothed tigers around. Millikan is correct in believing that reality contributes to making things true, and does so by making them generally useful. But reality and utility change, and the standard of justification is utility over time for all belief holders in communication. Although evolutionary utility is the original ground of utility, and perhaps must remain an element for judging truth, purposes other than survival get to weigh in on truth too. We can take the crux of Millikan's semantics without following her to truth as correspondence. Indeed, her brand of realism more comfortably leads to a pragmatic view of truth. In addition, I think a Millikanian evolutionary story of inference establishment is easily told. I also take an inference theory of meaning to be compatible with Gricean accounts (Grice 1957); speaker intentions are as amenable to be analyzed in terms of inferential relations as any other belief is.

11. See Dennett (1987).

12. Which is not to say that no belief is true until we have fitted it into a fully justified SSB. Presumably, many of our current beliefs will turn out to be fully justified by their presence in a TSSB.

13. Lewis (1986).

14. Even as a sketch of a theory of meaning this is radically incomplete. Besides not detailing all of the aspects it sketches, it offers no account of the meaning of sentences that make no assertions, for example, questions, nor does it explain how words contribute to meaning. On the latter point, I think it clear that words can help determine meaning without themselves being meaningful. Many things have properties by virtue of their constituents' nature and organization, without the constituents or the relations having the property. How words contribute to meaning does not affect my argument. I believe that sentences which make no assertions can be parsed by relating them to associated propositions, for example, "Where's Waldo?" is related to "I would like you to locate Waldo and inform me of his whereabouts." [See Wanderer's (2008, 20) take on the centrality of assertion to all language in his account of Brandom]. However, the inference theory of meaning for my purposes only requires that non-truth apt expressions can be handled; it is not wedded to any particular handling. For how an inferentialist might handle the compositional contribution of moral terms to meaning see Chrisman (2016, 2018).

15. A "fact" here means a true belief of a certain kind, rather than the bit of reality which makes the belief true by rendering it effective. What kind of true beliefs are "facts" and how are they to be distinguished from true nonfactual, normative beliefs? It is a matter of degree: factual true beliefs are those which cannot be ignored without frustrating a high number of goals to which the belief is relevant. Almost all goals involving Tabby require the agent with the goal to know Tabby is on the mat, and so it is a fact—but fewer goals related to Tabby must have the agent consider that Tabby ought not to be tortured. Hence, the torture prohibition is a norm. Hume's nonderivability point shows us that semantic relations are most influenced by immediate, obvious, nearby inferences, and that at a far enough remove, where there is no friction, a belief can move any which way without causing a stir in the distant belief; "facts" and "norms" easily wriggle free from each other.

16. Which is not to say that moral statements as a class do not have functions or features unique to it that are worth investigating (see Sellars, 1966). It is only to say that members of the class are *ultimately* made meaningful through the same type of relations, inferential, that make all statements meaningful. Nor is the denial of a the need for a special theoretical apparatus to explain the meaningfulness of normative terms a denial that, like other classes of expression, they present technical semantical challenges regarding how they contribute to the meaning of the expressions in which they are embedded. Matthew Chrisman (2016, 2018) provides detailed technical models for understanding how normative terms, and in particular the various uses of "ought," contribute to meaning in an inferentialist framework. But at the highest (i.e., most abstract) theoretical level, moral propositions are incorporated into semantic theory on the same bases as other meaningful statements.

17. A fuller account of the inference theory of meaning I am embracing is given in the previous section.

18. However, the two regions are still in the same field, which is probably why so many are tempted to find a semantic route from "is" to "ought." In some linguistic traditions, normative elements might be so strongly tied to descriptions of institutions and practices that one can find "is" to "ought" inferences. Indeed a theoretical

commitment regarding the nature of morality can allow an "is" to ought" inference by implicitly defining "ought" in terms of an "is," for example, in some versions of Divine Command Theory "ought" simply means "commanded by God." But those, like myself, who are struck by the clarity and distinctness of Hume's point, are not, or are no longer, native speakers of such tongues, and find the "meaning" of our moral terms in their relations to other moral terms. Nonetheless, the moral and descriptive linguistic regions, however distant and without current connecting routes of certain directions, do not occupy separate linguistic universes. An inference theory of meaning, shares the holism of the pragmatic account of justification being proffered. In theory, the full meaning of any expression is only given by its relation to every other expression in the language (which in turn depends on all of that linguistic community's social relations. But in practice, we think of a term's meaning as determined by the immediate obvious inferences it affords (those inferences are what constitutes its literal meanings), and here, without importing moral doctrine, there is no going from "is" to "ought." But, even Humeans will accept Kant's, "ought" implies "can," creating meaning relations betwixt moral and descriptive terms, (assuming "can" is a function of what "is") showing that descriptive and moral propositions have meaningful relations. More on the reasons for the current nonderivability of "ought" from "is" in section 6 of this chapter.

19. It is illegitimate for "ought" skeptics to throw a desire to be rational into the antecedent of a hypothetical imperative, *à la*, "if you want to be rational, given the evidence, you ought to believe that the cat is on the mat," because rationality's definition involves what one ought to believe, or ought to do, rendering that statement "If you believe what you ought to given the evidence, you ought to believe the cat is on the mat." Hardly a derivation of "ought" from "is." But even allowing a desire for an innocent "rationality" in the antecedent, by supposing a purely descriptive definition of rationality (belief that is likely to be true, action that is likely to attain universal well-being), the "ought" skeptic is still left without even hypothetical imperatives, for "if you want to be rational, given the evidence, you ought to believe that the cat is on the mat?" does not follow from your desire to be rational, and the likelihood, given the evidence, that the cat is on the mat. You still need the premise, "You ought to satisfy your desire to be rational." There is no getting to an ought, any sort of ought whatsoever, without starting from an ought.

20. It is worth placing this point in the context of the explanation/justification distinction. We *explain* the behavior of nonhuman animals and computers, we do not justify them (although we may justify their trainers and programmers.) Nor do we try to influence them by the correctness of our arguments. We employ all sorts of mechanisms to cause cats to go on mats, and computers to search out bargains, but we do not attempt to cause their behavior by appealing to what they ought to do. Once we think a being causally sensitive to justifications as such, we have acknowledged her personhood. That is why refusing to give or accept reasons to or from someone is a great insult. Miranda Fricker (2007) has explored the related insult of failing to credit someone's testimony. But to deny that they can be moved by reasons is a still greater insult. It is an insult usually given in bad faith; the slave that the master refuses to bandy reasons with, will be quickly appealed to on rational grounds when power relations change. Our refusal to argue with even the cleverest of computers or animals is

neither insincere nor (supposing we are right about their insensitivity to justifications) insulting. We do not appeal to their reason, even when the cat or (more commonly) the computer has the whip hand. Of course, there is nothing in principle that prevents evolution or cybernetics from instilling rationality in nonhuman forms.

21. See section 3 of this chapter.

22. These compatibility/incompatibility relationships are discussed in Section 3 of this chapter and in chapter 5, section 2.

23. See Williams (1985).

24. For instance, "cruel" can be an adjective for any act done for the primary purpose of inflicting suffering, "cowardly" any act motivated by a fear whose quantity would fail to motivate most others.

25. See the appendix and chapter 5, section 4 on this issue.

26. Cf. James (1896) on forced choices.

27. See section 2 of this chapter.

28. Quine (1960).

29. Bagnoli (2013).

30. Cf. Korsgaard (1996, 45).

31. Darwall (2006) thinks constructivism is what Korsgaard (1996) calls "procedural normative realism" but not what she defines as substantive realism. Korsgaard would classify RP as a procedural moral realism because it holds there are correct answers to moral questions (1996, 35), but it is less clear whether she would think it is also a substantive realism (a subset of procedural realism for her) which requires the correctness of the answers not be determined by the procedures, but rather by "moral facts." RP holds that agreement on standards (a procedure?) and the actual effects (aspects of reality, although not by themselves "moral facts") both contribute to justification. Rawls (1980), who introduced the notion of metaethical constructivism as an interpretation of Kant, seems to have a conception of it that would include RP: for Rawls constructivism holds that there is no moral truth (he says "facts") that is "prior and independent." Moral Truth can only be "identified" and "ascertained" by persons who are free and equal. Moreover, Rawls emphasizes the crucial role of a conception of persons as social in moral philosophy (1980, 555). James (1891, 186) thinks "final" moral truth cannot be had until the "last man has had his experience and said his say." All of which RP avers. But of course, RP is constructivist in this sense about *all* truth.

32. This should not be interpreted as claiming there are no natural causes why the pragmatic standard of justification was created. See the discussion of the Dennett–Brandom (2010) exchange in section 9 of this chapter.

33. Explaining that social consensus is practically necessary for fully establishing particular truths requires a more complicated story than telling of consensus' insufficiency for that task. I have argued (chapter 2, sections 4–6, and this chapter's sections 1–4) that truth is to be judged along pragmatic lines; the set of beliefs "that work best," are those we ought to consider true. The set of beliefs that I have termed a social system of beliefs derives its objectivity from its working best for everyone, which is not to say that another set of beliefs might not work out better for a given individual or limited group of individuals, but no set would serve the entire world of persons better.

Suppose there is a dissenter to the otherwise consensus view that our beliefs are the best possible beliefs. Is her dissenting belief part of the best possible set? If it is we have a situation in which the best possible set of beliefs includes the belief that the set of which it is an element is not the best possible set of beliefs. Yet because it is in that set, the dissenter's dissent is as justified as everyone else's contrary consent. In that case, the true social system of belief would include the beliefs that it is and it isn't the true social system of belief. While the partial self-referential nature of these apparently contradictory beliefs (partial because they refer not to themselves but to the set they are a part of) puts us in mind of Russell's paradox (1903), the existence of these contrasting beliefs in a TSSB is not an outright paradox, for the best possible set of communal beliefs might contain *individuals* having contrary beliefs. But the problem deepens when we consider that having true beliefs is a goal of all rational beings insofar as they are being rational. Rational beings are moved by reasons, and, when being rational, seek reasons for their actions. Rationality incorporates the quest for justification. If there is not universal consensus, someone has a belief that our collective beliefs are fully justified, and someone believes they are not. But all of our experience has led us to believe that particular beliefs expressible as direct contradictions will not both be in a TSSB. If I believe that collectively we have the best set of beliefs, and you do not, all of our experience will lead us to conclude that one of us has a false belief. But *that* belief, the belief that someone has a false belief, *ex hypothesi* is false (because it appears in a TSSB) and true (also because it appears in a TSSB), and that is an outright paradox. So, to avoid paradox, a lack of social consensus as to whether our social system possesses a TSSB, must be taken to indicate that the perfect epistemological state has *not* been achieved. If all of the experience that has led us to our current logical forms is correct, to avoid paradox, social consensus that a TSSB has been achieved will be a property of a TSSB. In a TSSB, it is theoretically possible for an individual to believe P and another individual to believe not P, especially if they remain ignorant of each other's beliefs. But to hold on to the central belief that *for all X, not(X and not X),* it is more likely that the relevant P belief, shared by all individuals in a social system with a TSSB will be that *person Z should act as if they believed P were true,* and *person Q should act as if they believed P were not true.* And in a social system with a TSSB, all should believe that they are in a social system with a TSSB.

34. Copp (2015).
35. Chapter 1, section 4.
36. Copp (2015, 64).
37. Brandom (2010, 301).
38. Dennett (2010, 50–51).
39. Dennett admits this is a severely simplified characterization (2010, 50).
40. Brandom (2010, 307).
41. Brandom makes this point (2010, 308), Dennett has made the same point (1995, 2003).
42. Habermas (1998) uses the terms "validity" and "interests" for what I am calling "justifiability" and "goal achievement."

43. Misak (2000, 36–37) makes a similar point, as does James (1891, 208).

44. Cf. Misak (2000, 87).

45. Misak (2000). In addition to sharing many of its positions, the present book, like Misak's work, is motivated by the felt need to answer moral nihilists and subjectivists. Misak uses Carl Schmitt as the representative adversary, (Misak 2000, Chapter One) a rhetorically shrewd choice, for unlike many contemporary philosophical amoralists, Schmitt uses his theoretical freedom from morality to endorse fascism. Arguing against theoretical nihilists of humane conviction obscures the potential stakes in metaethical discussions, but no one would accuse Schmitt of humane convictions. Leaving moral nihilists unrefuted harms the essentially liberal morality that Misak and I support, and more to the point, hold true. Indeed, our common argument is that our support is rational. We think our moral convictions true not because we (or the Gods) support them, we support them because we think they are true.

46. Indeed, I claim the sensory inputs is not evidence at all, only the judgments they cause.

47. Misak (2000, 48). [All page references to Misak based on the ebook editions]. She seems to not distinguish as I do (chapter 2, section 1), following Kirkham (1992), between an extensional or essentialist theory of truth and a theory of justification (recognizing truth). For her a fully justified belief is true, and a true proposition is one that is so justified. Misak (2004, 35) says that Peirce, although not defining "truth," is interested in a pragmatic elucidation of the concept of truth that seems very much an extensional theory. She seems to support this Peircean extensionalism. I, however, remain agnostic on whether justification equals truth. Some might think agnosticism here betrays a covert lingering attachment to correspondence, for what more could there to be to truth beyond full justification? I don't know what more there could be, hence my agnosticism, but I don't take it to be a rhetorical question. "Fully justified," or "invulnerable to counter evidence" *may* be extensionally equivalent to "is true" but they are not synonymous, even though there could be no *evidence* separating the two. It may be of no apparent practical use to assert "X appears and forever will appear to all inquirers to be justified, although X is false," but I understand the sentence. Nor is "should be taken to be true" synonymous with "is true." We justify beliefs as true, not as justified. Truth may be knowable without being philosophically definable. Nonetheless, this is not the difference that I am concerned with above.

48. Misak (2000, 97, 130). In *Truth and the End of Inquiry* (2004), Misak seems to be endorsing Peirce's stress on the power experience has because of independence of the will. Experience is "recalcitrant" (2004, 83) and experience ultimately impinges truth upon us (2004, 26, 134). It is experience that holds in check our human standards (Misak 2011, 273). Levine (2019) further develops this idea that experiences (which for him *à la* Dewey, are historically shaped phenomena) are the final arbiter of justification and source of objective truth. Of course, I am not denying that experience plays a role in justifying belief, but that role should be understood as playing a part in goal achievement.

49. Misak (2004).

50. Sometimes pragmatists hold that just because ethical beliefs are tools that are not tied to explanations/predictions, that is, they are not truth apt. Andrew Sepeille

(2017) claims correctness doesn't apply to such tools. But why not? Is not the tool that best does the job the *correct* tool. Aren't we admonished to get the "right" tool for the task at hand? If the task of our SSB is to provide a common basis for acting so as to achieve our goals, there will be a good, better, and, in theory, a best tool. Our beliefs are justified when they are the best tool.

51. Misak (2000, 48). An additional problem with a purely "best accounts for the evidence "standard is describing what is meant by "a good accounting," or a "good fit," or "best explanation." Under one interpretation these might simply mean "provides the best predictions," and so would be close to "best guide for achieving goals," albeit still not quite the same thing. But if it is more like "sates curiosity," it becomes a kind of psychologically rewarding standard Misak would abjure.

52. Misak (2000, 58). Misak (2004) provides a good deal of evidence that Peirce had at times something like goal achievement as the measure of justification. She quotes him as saying that he seeks knowledge so he "can avoid disappointments and disasters," (2004, 88). Belief is meant to guide action and action is "satisfactory" when it is "congruous to the aim of action," (2004, 84). Misak herself most clearly hints at accepting a goal-achievement-like standard of justification when she says, "belief is a habit for future action, and we can evaluate that action as being successful or not" (2018, 418), and "what would serve us well is true" (2018, 420). But whether the measure she has in mind for "successful" action and good service includes all of our aims is unclear. Because beliefs are action guiders, one would think the standard for evaluating beliefs would be all the aims of action. Misak may hesitate to embrace goal achievement explicitly and unreservedly as the measure of justification for fear it leads to a purely subjective standard of truth, a kind of "cognitive hedonism" (2004, 84).

53. Misak (2000, 86).

54. Misak (2000, 131).

55. Misak (2000, 136–138).

56. In most cases, that feeling is magnified by the nagging doubt as to whether our choices really did maximize goal achievement—maybe the goal foregone could have been had along with the goal procured, or if not, was in fact the more weighty goal? Still, regret as sorrow for the value left unrealized is apt, even if we are not plagued by suspicions that an alternative act would have been better.

57. Misak (2004, 185–189) mitigates the weight of these concessions to moral noncognitivism by claiming that there are also instances when there are no best beliefs—no truth—about factual matters. Hence, the failure of bivalence—the objectivist doctrine that propositions are either true or false but not both—creates no special trouble for morality. While this is similar to the overall scheme of this book, an approach Lillehammer (2007) labels a "companions in guilt" strategy, and I call a "fellowship in truth," view (see chapter 6, section 7), Misak's use of it concedes too much by diluting objectivity's bivalence in all domains to keep moral objectivity on a par with the factually objective. The standard of goal achievement maintains bivalence across all propositional domains.

58. When confronted with these (highly artificial) ticking-clock hypotheticals, whose trickle down effects I believe empower real world torturers who hear ticking-clocks whenever their fears combine with their power, I am inclined to ask whether

the torturers are willing to be severely punished for torturing; if the consequences of not torturing are dire enough to justify torture, I hold them to be dire enough to make self-sacrifice a duty. If you perceive a moral duty to torture to save the world, than the prospect of life in prison should not deter you from this world saving duty. If it does deter you, I judge that not enough was really at stake to justify torture.

59. Chapter 2, section 6, note 43.

60. This is an error analogous to one Misak (2000, 36–37) and I (this chapter, section 9) find in Habermas' equivocal use of "true" in moral and nonmoral contexts.

61. Moreover, the judgments each group makes may so little affect the other group that each is indifferent to the others' judgments, at least on some issues.

62. Misak (2000, 131; 2004, 189) suggests it does.

63. Misak (2004, 190) seems to be open to a view similar to this "division of labor" view; she allows that rather than viewing a tragic choice as indicating there is no (or multiple incompatible) right choices in the matter, a disjunction of choices for the entire community of inquirers might be the correct principle. So even if Xhosa in circumstances C should do X and Albertans in C should do Y, it is true that everyone should do {X or Y} in C. It is not relativism, nor a violation of bivalence—in morality the idea that an action is right or wrong but not both—that it may be right for Albertans to do X and Xhosa to do Y, because their cultural location might have different effects relative to the *same standard* of overall goal achievement. Another way of saying this is that being Xhosa in C and being Albertan in C are different circumstances, because Xhosa doing X in C will have different outcomes than Albertans doing X in C.

64. Misak (2000, 137). However, Misak does offer such transcendental arguments to support certain practices: "scientific method is more than a good strategy, we cannot help but generally adopt it" (2004, 84).

65. Misak (2000, 36). While that is Misak's official position, she flirts with claims that put truth seeking at the center of humanity in a way that smacks of a transcendental argument: our humanity is somehow "bound up with that of others (2000, 46)." Still, she is reluctant to argue that our relationship with others constitutes our humanity or in any way necessitates morality. In response to Karl Otto-Apel's (1999) and Habermas' "transcendental," arguments, which make the acceptance of certain moral principles the precondition of communication, Misak asserts that the facts refute their claims. I think Misak believes that the facts would also refute any argument that a commitment to acting rationally (and hence morally) was constitutive of our personhood. For her, one's commitment to finding truth with others is optional, a commitment one *undertakes* (2000, 46). But here I think Misak confuses a practical commitment to reason, which makes one a person, with a full or perfect enactment of rationality, and/or conscious acknowledgment of one's rationality, which is indeed optional. Claiming you are indifferent to truth, a willingness to ignore inconvenient truths, and an unwillingness or inability to pursue the truth in some circumstance are not an indifference to truth. Most people do much of the former frequently; no sane, intact person does the latter.

66. Aikin (2017).

Chapter 5

Morality's Motivational Powers

1. DESIRES AND MOTIVES

Whether and how moral judgments motivate are topics of philosophical debate, but it is a bit puzzling that this is so. Although action may be mysterious,[1] and so motivation, that which causes action, may be mysterious, why would one think that moral judgments are especially mysterious motives? That there are moral judgments nearly everyone concedes: moral nihilists say they are all false, moral relativists (of an extremist stripe) that they are all true, moral cognitivists that some are true and some are false, and moral expressivists that they are neither true nor false. But none deny that moral judgments occur, and in general what occurs may cause other things to occur. Of course, the capacity to cause some things is not the capacity to cause all things. At issue is whether the causal powers of moral judgments extend to causing *actions*, thereby qualifying moral judgments to be motives.

One would think this is an empirical question: we could identify moral judgments, identify actions, and note if they correlate in such ways as to justify supposing a causal relationship. Casual study gives little ground for skepticism of a causal relationship between moral judgments and actions. It is a commonplace observation that people often appear to act in concert with their sincere moral judgments, and act differently when those judgments change. The denial of a causal relationship, the claim that this correlation does not reflect causation, is hardly justified by the absence of perfect correlation, for few contend that moral judgments are always dominant. The debate regarding moral judgments' motivational force is not about whether we can resist moral judgments, but about whether the judgments exert any practical force at all.

The denial that moral judgments have any force comes from a theory of motivation and a conception of moral judgments which together render the judgments ineligible to be motives. The theory of motivation asserts that desire is a necessary ingredient of motivation, and the conception of moral judgments claims that judgments are beliefs, not desires, and do not by themselves generate desires. It follows that moral judgments by themselves cannot be motives. No matter what I *believe* about the ice cream—it is delicious, nutritious, and the smooth, sweet, creamy stuff on my tongue will bring me joy—without a *desire* to eat it, a desire for nutrition, gustatory pleasure and joy, I leave it melting in the bowl.

That moral judgments are beliefs I grant. If moral judgments can be true, and sets of beliefs and their derivatives are the bearers of truth (both views I have adopted), then judgments are indeed beliefs. However, the claim that desire is required for or constitutive of motivation is either a stipulated definition of "motive" which tells us nothing of its nature, or is an empirical claim for which no evidence is provided.

States of mind are the salient causes of actions, for an event would likely not qualify as an action were it not, at least in part, caused by mind. *Whatever* the action-causing state of mind is, that is the action's "motive."[2] We are free to use "desire" as a synonym for "motive," and in common English it is sometimes so used. But not always; I have gone to many a meeting I sincerely and idiomatically asserted I had "no desire" to attend, but my attendance was my action, and I certainly had motives for attending. English frequently distinguishes "desires" from "motives." The desire theory of motivation cannot disempower moral judgments on the thin lexicographical grounds of "desire" and "motive's" partial interchangeability.[3]

The primary source of the desire theory of motivation, David Hume, was making a substantial claim about human nature when he declared Reason to be a slave of passion:[4] For him, Reason—judgment—is about the truth, and its role in action is to help steer, not to power or set final destination. Passion, for the Humean, is a distinguishable state of mind from reasoned belief. Were it not, it would be senseless to say who was master and who servant. And for Humeans, passion has to be understood not simply as *whatever* happened to cause action (i.e. motive), otherwise the Humean claim is reduced to a dull tautology—our actions are always performed in the service of whatever motivated them. The Humean conception of passions must be more than motive, and different from belief. The mastership of this other-than-belief breeds the desire theory of motivation, for desire does not *mean* motive and *is* not belief. Desires, like Humean passions, are neither true nor false. So the heart of the desire theory is the claim that we are unmoved by mere truth. Not merely that we are unmoved by what "is," (unless what is contains a desire we are subject to) but that we are unmoved by our judgments of what is, and what there ought to be.

What reasons are there to believe that the state of minds that cause action cannot be beliefs, but must be desires? Beliefs and desires are the theoretical posits of what philosophers have come to call "folk psychology."[5] On the one hand, "folk psychology" is a demeaning term, suggesting that scientific psychology has, or will have, better terms to describe the mind, and "beliefs" and "desires" will not be descriptive of any real, or heuristically useful types. If this demeaning line is embraced, there is certainly no reason to subscribe to the desire theory of motivation, because we have no reason to think there *are* desires.

However, folk psychology, or at least its vocabulary, has its champions. They believe our common terms for the contents of mind are the best, most explanatory psychological entities currently available, and they think it unlikely this vocabulary will soon, if ever, be replaced.[6] Without attributing beliefs and desires (and "feelings," "attitudes," "tastes" "values," and the like), we would be at a near total loss to explain, predict, or understand (if there is more to understanding than explaining/predicting) almost all human behavior, most particularly human action.

If folk psychology is our best vocabulary for discussing human action, then the desire theory of motivation cannot be dismissed because it invokes desires. However, to be justified, it would require a folk psychology rooted argument, supplemented perhaps by more rigorous, systematic observations.

But this it wholly lacks. Evidence of desire—verbal confessions, known personal and general human needs, facial or bodily expressions of certain emotive types—often do precede action. But often they do not. Actions not in service of a known need, calmly done, preceded and performed without grimace or glee, are ubiquitous. If the desire theory advocate says that a desire can be known to be present because the action took place, she is clearly arguing in a circle.[7] Given the total absence of a noncircular argument that has any empirical evidence for the desire theory of motivation, there is reason to believe that what seems to happen sometimes does happen: people do things because they judge that it is the right thing to do.[8]

Even if the desire theory of motivation were correct and moral judgments, as beliefs, unaccompanied by desire, were incapable of motivating, all moral judgments could *still* be empowered if we posit a natural desire, or at least inter-culturally ubiquitous desire, to act in accordance with one's moral judgments. This is essentially what Hume did by positing natural sympathy as the basis of morality.[9] Some have thought that this approach removes morality from the domain of rationality, but that does not follow unless you also believe that the litmus test for practical rationality is that practical reasons *qua* reasons must be *directly* motivating. If practical rationality is, as I have argued, a motivational *sensitivity* to reasons, it may be the case that a desire of a certain kind that makes one sensitive to moral reasons is a prerequisite of practical rationality. But, whether mere sincere belief in (true) moral principles makes one sensitive to their motivational force, or a widespread set of general desires makes one sensitive to them, it is the *sensitivity* to reasons itself, not its cause, that is the hallmark of practical rationality. What is important is that you are reliably moved by moral reasons because you believe them true. How their truth moves you, the mechanism of practical rationality, is a separate issue from its existence.[10]

And practical rationality, even within a Humean framework, must have some *mechanism* for sensitivity to reasons. If practice is made rational by employing Reason, there cannot be motives only for outcomes, there must also be motives to use effective means of obtaining outcomes. A passion for ice cream by itself cannot motivate anything other than a wish for ice cream. Action ensues only when one is motivated to employ definite means to acquire ice cream: I can search the forest for abandoned freezers full of Breyers, entreat the ice cream fairy to deliver Häagen Dazs, petition the Lord for Friendly's, cry into the void for Sealtest, pound rocks together till they turn into Toscannis', or go to the store and buy Ben & Jerry's. My choice of tactics is an action, and if only passions motivate, my choice of tactics needs to be determined by a passion. Going to the store to buy ice cream must be based on *the passion to employ reason* in service to my other passions. A Humean who denied a passion for Reason would also be forswearing the possibility of practical reason. Reason would become a slave that passion could never put to work.

2. CONSISTENCY, RATIONALITY, AND CONSENSUS

Ralph Waldo Emerson's quip, "foolish consistency is the hobgoblin of little minds,"[11] is properly invoked in defense of an expansive broadmindedness, but too often mischievously cited in defense of blatant irrationality. A "foolish consistency" is foolish not because it is consistent, but because its consistency is stubbornly local. Its foolishness derives from its *inconsistency* within a wider context. Boiling all food is a foolish consistency that aspires to homogeneity in the tiny category of cooking techniques. Preparing all foods so as to best bring out their flavor and nutritional values is a more robust consistency displaying loyalty to the larger category of best-metho ds-for-promoting-health-and-gustatory-pleasure. There is always the possibility of new discoveries that render a current consistency foolish: should there be a God that offered salvation to all and only those that exclusively ate deep-fried food, consistency to the principle of prioritizing salvation might require the unwavering immersion of all edibles in hot oil. Consistency is never foolish, only maintaining a small consistency at the expense of a larger, more serviceable one. Rather than foolish, consistency is a central notion of rationality.[12]

Before arguing for consistency's centrality to rationality, the claim that rationality is never foolish also needs defense. That the rational and the foolish are antonyms strikes me as tautological, but to some ears, ears sympathetic to the foolishness-of-consistency claim, complete rationality connotes robotic inflexibility that dismisses emotion, intuition, value, ambivalence, and unexplained but undeniable human realities. But any such dismissal confines rationality; consistency is the core of Reason, and Reason is stunted to the extent any phenomena are left unreconciled. If, for example, all evidence presented at a criminal trial does not appear consistent with the defendant's innocence, and yet a jury member has a gut feeling that the defendant is innocent, Reason is not fully mollified until the feeling and evidence are rendered coherent. Perhaps the defendant is guilty and *felt* to be not guilty because he resembles the beloved brother of the jury member; guilt and gut feeling of innocence are rendered consistent. Or perhaps, the feeling has been caused by vaguely, unconsciously remembered tendencies of the prosecutor to fabricate evidence; evidence of guilt and innocence are made consistent. Rationality does not dismiss misfits; it explains how they fit into a clearer, fuller picture.

Consistency is a *sine qua non* of Reason, but as full consistency is unattained this side of omniscience, Reason for limited beings is an ideal we can only move toward. Controversy arises with choice of routes to the ideal; if inconsistency of some sort must be endured, the inconsistencies that are most tolerable are left in place.[13] The relative tolerability of an inconsistency depends on the constitution and purposes of whoever is doing the tolerating. Ultimately, just as a completed science would be free of any observed anomalies, full rationality would require thoroughgoing coherence of all belief *and* action. Full rationality is an aspiration achieved when one becomes God.

Recognizing consistency is very similar, but not the same, as recognizing truth. Consistency does not ask whether a belief is true, but whether, given other beliefs, it might be true. I have argued earlier that a belief system is justified to the extent it serves all goals. There could be no better justification of a system of belief than that it best achieves all actual goals, that is, any goal that is or will be in a social system. We hope to get ever closer to that belief system, but we know it will remain, in its fullness, beyond our grasp. But we have come to agree that *no matter what goals may arise or evolve, and no matter how reality affects the efficacy of beliefs, a true belief system will not contain certain combinations of beliefs;* without knowing whether a belief will be in a true belief system, we have judged that certain combinations of beliefs disqualify a system of beliefs as a candidate for truth. This agreement, this *common judgment* of what a true belief system cannot contain, determines inconsistency. Inconsistency is known when beliefs, or expressions of belief, are shown to be in violation of this consensus. To declare a group of beliefs inconsistent is to claim that we have ruled out their common membership in a true system, even without claiming to know the set of goals that will prove the actual measure of truth, or the beliefs that will best serve them.[14]

On what basis might such an agreement be reached? What persuades us that certain combinations of beliefs are suboptimal under all imaginable circumstances? It can only be experience. Experience has taught that the combinations of certain belief-types is never justifiable, for such combinations, sooner or later, always have proven dysfunctional. The lessons of the past, whether culturally transmitted or naturally selected, have bequeathed the agreements we call "logic." We have embedded these agreements, which are born of universal experience of dysfunctional belief ensembles, into the structure of our beliefs and the very marrow of our languages.[15]

Competency to express beliefs in a language[16] requires acquiescing in the language's structural incorporation of this consensus on the pervasive and ultimate disutility of certain combinations of beliefs. Language is a tool to navigate and manipulate the world with others, and breaks down without common understanding of how the world basically works, and of how beliefs and expressions of belief relate to the world's invariances. Logic—inference relations—reflects a linguistic community's exceptionless experience of the minimal requirements of useful beliefs, deviance from which is unimaginable, unexpressible, "incoherent."[17] In formal languages, these disallowed combinations are stipulated. In natural languages, the permissible combinations crystalize experience as meaning.[18] Languages are translatable, and speakers of different languages find the same formalizations useful, because all humans have experienced some of the same fundamental utilities. Beings that had insufficiently common experiences of utility, would have different logics, and would not acknowledge enough common truth to communicate. Truth, whatever else it might be, is what is good to believe, and meaning is a linguistic community's agreement on the necessary forms of good belief.

Were we in possession of the system of beliefs that best satisfied all actual goals, the distinction between true beliefs and consistent ones would be without value; if we knew ultimate truth, then knowing what might be true but was not would afford us nothing. But we do not have complete, final knowledge, so knowing what might be in the running is very valuable. We've only our best current theories, and at the core of all of our theories, the part of each of them which retains our highest confidence, the aspects whose revision we would find most disorienting, is "logic," the beliefs which grant or withhold consistency. Consistency is the heart of rationality because rationality seeks to admit only truth and consistency rigorously screens the applicants. The strongest epistemic condemnation is "inconsistent," the label we apply to the hopelessly false.

Theoretical consistency, consistency within belief, is the core of theoretical reason, and practical consistency, consistency between belief and action, is central to practical reason. Practical inconsistency occurs whenever theoretical reason delivers a practical judgment—a belief that something ought to be done—and yet it is not done. To judge that one ought never to eat cookies, and still eat cookies, is to be practically inconsistent. Practical inconsistency is not theoretical inconsistency; all of one's beliefs may cohere, indeed may actually be true, but remain motivationally inert. The fault in practical inconsistency is not a violation of logic, but rather a breach between what is believed and what is done.[19]

Nor is practical consistency the whole of practical reason; to be practically reasonable is to act *because* of a sound judgment, and one's action may accord with a sound judgment without being motivated by it. Yet just as theoretical inconsistency guarantees theoretical irrationality, so too practical inconsistency ensures practical irrationality. To be practically reasonable is to be motivated by a sound judgment, and action inconsistent with a judgment cannot, and therefore is not, motivated by that judgment. If it is true that I ought to never eat cookies, then my cookie eating is irrational. Practical inconsistency demonstrates practical irrationality, but its absence does not establish practical reason. Motivational sensitivity to judgment constitutes a *capacity* for practical rationality, and actually being moved by *sound* judgment realizes it. Only if my cookie abstinence is caused by my true belief that I ought not to eat them, and not because I am too cheap to buy them, is my cookie rejection rational.

Reason, theoretical or practical, is the affinity for truth. Theoretical reason discovers truth, and practical reason extends truth into the extra-mental world. Practical reason puts to work what theoretical reason declares most workable. And what theoretical reason has pronounced most workable has by social consensus been enshrined in thought and language as logic, the measure of "consistency."

3. REASON AND INSTINCT

Our rationality serves us by revealing truth, but it is not our only serviceable capacity. Useful responses, not only in terms of species survival but also measured by individual contentment, can be generated by mechanisms in which beliefs play no role at all. No beliefs close our eyes in a sandstorm or remove our hands from a flame. More complex threats and opportunities might also be well met by belief-free "going with one's gut." Such responses are not all biologically embedded reflexes. Experience that never congeals into belief can also cause responses sensitive to reality. You need believe nothing, either true or false, to hit a baseball well or ride a bike skillfully.[20] Indeed, even the most propitious choice of a spouse or a career may be made "instinctually," without opinion, let alone conviction, determining choice. Sometimes it is just chemistry, and sometimes, maybe even usually, chemistry works better than philosophy.

Instincts might even perform well socially. The ant colony is the standard dispositive evidence here. Ants require no beliefs to respond effectively as a coordinated set of individuals to collective need. And, insofar as we can attribute well-being to individual ants, their instincts might conduce more toward each ant's good than any rational capacity could. Beliefs, even when true, might be a relatively bulky and unsubtle way of responding to reality.

However, it is only beliefs, and their derivatives, that are *justified*. We might be better off in a world devoid of justifications, with many desires satisfied, many pleasures had, many harms avoided. The attempt to guide action by belief may, all things considered, be counter to our individual and collective well-being. But whatever good is to be had through justification are unobtainable by instinct. Furthermore, there is no avoiding justificatory process. We have eaten of the apple, and are no longer beasts that want discourse of reason. We may evolve to some other life form that neither makes nor evaluates assertions. But should that happen, our descendants would be of a radically different type, and we have no standing to judge whether it is better to be them than us.

However, we ought not to resign ourselves to rationality solely because it constitutes who we are. We have some reason to believe it is useful, not just inevitable for us. While rationality might be, in Stephen Gould's term, a spandrel,[21] that is, a nonadaptive side effect of an adaptation, or rationality may even be just a random development unrelated to any adaptation, that notion seems implausible. Reason is a complex, developed capacity, which, were it to be nonadaptive, would be the product of coincidence. Astounding coincidences do occur, but should not be assumed when better explanations are at hand. Therefore, although lacking the details, we should conclude that rationality is an adaptation, and so at least useful insofar species survival is among our goals.

However, there is a more direct argument for the utility of Reason. One of our goals, for many of us a central goal, is to be justified in word and deed. We have come to attach intrinsic value to believing what is true and doing what is good. The best instincts in the world could never afford us the happiness derived from believing ourselves knowing and virtuous.[22] Reason may be the ultimate bootstrapping phenomenon: its value is grounded, at least in part, in its valuing itself. Although one can question the comparative size of the reward, and wonder if those not of our kind are playing a game with richer prizes (although who would be evaluating the relative prize sizes is a vexed question), truly, virtue is its own reward, and so is truth.[23]

None of which denies that justification's *origins* reside in its extrinsic rewards, nor that a substantial portion of justification's current value remains instrumental. Moreover, we can give instinct its due and even acknowledge its probable superiority in certain realms. However, all of this is compatible with Reason being an intrinsic good and the source of moral goodness.

4. IS REASON A SIGNIFICANT MOTIVATOR?

The goodness of being moved by Reason would be of small worth if it were an exceedingly rare event. The most precious gemstone is of little value if it is barely visible. It is not news that people often act irrationally, and earlier I remarked the ubiquity of pseudo-rationality, where justifications serve only to disguise or decorate operative motives. However, recently both psychologists and experimental philosophers have suggested that rational action is so rare that it indeed is analogous to the invisibly tiny diamond; hardly worth attending to when contemplating human agency.[24]

The frequency of rational action is an empirical question. Once we have established that people can act both from reason and without or against reason, the proportions of each are a matter for historians, biologists, and social scientists. The evidence will be difficult to interpret, and I do not think our current theories or data are sufficiently advanced to pronounce with great authority. Still I want to push back a little against the fashionable (and it may turn out justified) view that Reason is a very marginal player in human affairs.

The first thing to note is that only if we have a sense of what it is to act rationally in given circumstances could we conclude that people usually don't. Nor is this sense of the rational an extraordinary faculty confined to a handful of geniuses. The wide *acceptance* of experimental results pointing to irrationality shows that the ability to recognize irrationality is broadly distributed. Believing that we can distinguish rational behavior from non or irrational behavior is no evidence that that knowledge is frequently effective, but it eliminates an important barrier to rational action; we are not barred from often being moved by Reason because we can seldom recognize it.[25]

The literature on the motivational force of Reason quite naturally, aspires to be interesting. Documenting the innumerable quotidian acts of practical reason is not interesting, so they go unnoted. I see it is raining, I put on my boots. You cut your finger, you get a band aid. Julia is having guests for dinner, she buys groceries to cook. Maria's car needs to warm-up on cold days, so she warms it up on the present cold day. A nurse judges that the administration of a medication is more time-sensitive than writing a note in the medical chart, so he gives the medication before writing the note. Socrates knows that all men are mortal, and that he is a man, so he buys a burial plot at Forest Lawn. We see our cat in terrible pain so we take him to the vet. These aren't instincts or habits, they are taken for granted acts of practical reason. Few will publish papers to prove the existence of these rational acts.

These simple acts of reason run through our daily life as certainly as instinct and habit, and many habits are acquired by making reasoned responses automatic in repeated situations. Reason as the driver of human behavior hardly appears a black swan once we register its familiar feats which don't impress because they are so common. We too easily ignore how very smart even a stupid human being is. It is our basic expectation that people are rational that gives the literature demonstrating irrationality its punch: we are less rational than we thought. But that still leaves us plenty rational.

The rationality shortfall suggested by experiments is of three types, corresponding to what I have called quasi-, pseudo-, and nonrationality. Quasi-rationality is an unsuccessful attempt to be guided by good reasoning; we are responding to justifications we mistakenly think are sound. In pseudo-rationality we represent ourselves as responding to a justification, and we may or may not believe we are doing so, but the purported justification plays no actual motivational role. Nonrationality makes no pretense that Reason impels the action.

I have argued that short of omniscience we are fated to a degree of quasi-rationality. Still, minimizing the degree is and ought to be a perennial goal. It is good to discover when our reasoning is faulty, and especially useful to learn we are prone to particular errors. For instance, we often handle probability poorly. But probabilistic reasoning is a sophisticated skill developed through education. It is not that we are unmoved by the odds, just that we often miscalculate them. In simple situations requiring understanding the odds, I speculate people are pretty good at producing action guided by reason. If you compel people to play Russian roulette and offer them a choice of pistols, one with five bullets and one empty chamber, the other with five empty chambers and one bullet, I'd bet you'd find people are an overwhelmingly rational species. And whatever impression one gets from the literature, I think my wager would be rational, and most people would make the same bet. The literature that brings to light rationality's failures are important because they increase the possibility of reform, but unless they are compared to rationality's successes, we can draw no conclusions about the relative frequency of acts that *good* reasoning motivates.

Perhaps, even after acquiring a genuine understanding and belief in the true odds, people ignore them in determining their actions. But much of the "people-are-not-rational" literature only shows that our natural rational faculties, if left uneducated, are flummoxed in certain types of circumstances. Overrating our rational skills is not evidence that we are indifferent to Reason, nor is overrating a sign of low absolute achievement. I think Brahms is overrated (I know—you disagree—evidence to me that he is overrated), but

I still judge his achievement *very* great and *very* beautiful. Perhaps human-ity's rationality has been overrated, but that doesn't make it negligible.

The more damning charges don't allege we are poor reasoners, but rather that our apparent reasoning is mostly fraudulent—mere pseudo-rationality. There are two kinds of pseudo-rationality: first, we have motives of which we are too embarrassed or ashamed to admit to ourselves or others, motives we hide behind impotent justifications. Call this "bad-faith" pseudo-rationality." Then there are acts which we honestly think are reasoned, but that are other-wise motivated: "innocent pseudo-rationality."

Bad faith pseudo-rationality often doesn't testify to Reason's motivational weakness, but rather its being harnessed to unacknowledged purposes. The self-deluded person is frequently moved by justifications, just not the ones he tells himself are at work. He tells himself he is dieting for health, but it really is out of vanity. The argument that dieting leads to weight loss, which leads to health, is doing no motivational work. But the argument that dieting leads to weight loss, which leads to a slim figure, is efficacious, and is just as much an argument. So too for outright phoniness: the justification urged for a dona-tion—that it will benefit the poor who should be benefited—may not spur the solicitation, but the request for a donation is still activated by an argument; it is a different argument, whose conclusion is the requester will be able to raise his own salary. Bad faith, the abuse of Reason, is not evidence of its frailty or rarity. It only is evidence of its capacity to conceal its purposes.

Much of the "people-are-not-rational" literature purports to uncover inno-cent pseudo-rationality. People's choices, which they mean to be reasoned, are shown to be frequently influenced by "irrelevant" factors: they judge the defendant's guilt by the color of his jacket, their answers to a pollster questions depend on the order in which they are asked. Sometimes the high correlation between sociological profiles and cultural and political prefer-ences is cited as evidence of innocent pseudo-rationality.[26] "If arguments determine belief, why do they produce one set of judgments in Oklahoma and another in Massachusetts?" Location does not seem relevant to judging fair tax schemes, but apparently it is relevant to the formation of belief about tax schemes; opinion and location correlate strongly, and as no apparent *reason* makes location relevant, it must be nonreasons forming the judgments. In addition, the stability of practical judgments, rationalized by ever-changing justifications, appears to indicate that the justifications are not motivating the judgments. If the justifications motivationally engaged, certainly their outputs would vary with the justifications. The outputs' constancy shows they are being put out by something other than the inconstant justifications. So goes a line of thought supporting the "people-are-not-rational" theses.

Relevancy depends on the particular argument being evaluated, and argu-ments that constitute the justifications of practical judgments are replete with hidden premises that constitute the argument. Before we can judge relevancy we must be sure we are judging the operative, not merely the explicitly articulated, justification. A justification may vary with location if different hidden premises are assumed in New England (e.g., income is largely a function of luck) from those which are assumed in Oklahoma (God helps those who help themselves?). Location may be producing different premises rather than nonreasoned judgments. The irrelevant location correlation can be simply an effect of highly relevant hidden premises.

Changing justifications may be an effect of trial and error introspection. We presume, perhaps wrongly but not necessarily so, that our beliefs are justifiable and caused by their justifications, even if we are unsure of the motivating justification. We try out candidate-justifications to discover the real motivator. The fact that it took some thought and exploration of dry holes to bring a justification forth is not proof that it wasn't in motivational play prior to its conscious discovery. I believe that there is objective right and wrong, but it takes investigation to find my beliefs constituting the justification that might actually cause that conviction. It is different sort of work from searching for the best argument, if "best argument" simply means the one most convincing to others, rather than the argument that employs my actual beliefs as premises. Reason is no more immediately available for conscious articulation than emotions.

Jonathan Haidt contends that reasoning is mostly *post hoc* partisan advocacy for judgments reflecting nonreasoned intuitions.[27] He illustrates his thesis with the following case: respondents are asked to assess the morality of an incident of sibling incest in which no harm befalls the brother and sister lovers or any third party. The respondents judge the incest wrong, but when their arguments for its wrongness are refuted, they stick with their judgment. Haidt concludes that their judgments were formed by intuitions, a sort of moral perception, and proffered reasons are tassels hung on judgments to make them look good.

But the case's description fails to consider unrefuted arguments that may have been doing work. Perhaps the respondents were rule-utilitarians who judged the hypothetical harmless act of incest as artificial or highly atypical, and so, although *ex hypothesi* harmless, wrong because such acts are almost always harmful. Or maybe they are epistemically modest conservatives—"in long established and multiple cultural traditions incest is morally impermissible, and just because I cannot explain its wrongness in this hypothetical case, I hold it is wrong because it is more likely I am missing something than that humanity has been universally mistaken." Haidt is too quick to conclude that there is no good argument for his respondents' beliefs.[28]

Haidt might rejoin that because these arguments were not offered, they could not have been the bases of the judgment that the incest was wrong.

But it is a mistake to think rational processes must be fully conscious. Much philosophical work consists of excavating the real reasons that justify *and cause* our beliefs. In many cases that may only be finding justifications for beliefs otherwise motivated, but often it is discovering the motivations whose complexity and subtlety have made them not readily accessible to consciousness. But obscured Reason is still Reason. Such cases are not pseudo, but rather not-easily-articulated-semi-conscious rationality.

Furthermore, Haidt's metaphor that *post hoc* reasoning is akin to defense lawyer evidence-spinning, rather than disinterested judicial reasoning, is not always the best metaphor for reasoning subsequent to initial belief. An alternative metaphor likens moral reasoning to jury deliberations in a criminal trial. Our moral intuitions, are comparable to a juror's beginning hunch. That hunch may arise from personal or social bias, or any other nonrational cause. Or it may be based on the thinnest and weakest of reasons. It is almost certainly always there. The idealized juror who forms no tentative opinions before jury deliberations is a regulative ideal that no one believes actually exists. Mr. Spock and Jack Webb as jurors are idealizations intended to prevent inevitable tentative opinions from becoming entrenched, but that such opinions exist is tacitly understood. In fact, before the evidence is weighed in deliberations, where in theory they are supposed to be weighed for the first time, a straw vote, which presumes some opinions have already been formed, is often (according to the movies at least) taken. Yet the fact that the jurors come to the trial, and then to the deliberations, with opinions, more or less strongly held, does not mean the deliberations are otiose. The deliberations are intended to override biases and unfounded beliefs, to defeat the weak arguments, to come up with the best theory of the case. And opinions are changed. Sometimes jurors enter deliberations in complete agreement, but often they don't. Yet disagreement only results in hung juries on occasion. Dissenters are persuaded, and initial majorities can come around to the initial minority's viewpoint. Even many hung juries, I suspect, would converge on a verdict if time to deliberate were truly limitless (although in fairness I should note that many a jury consensus is forged by the desire to be done and get home). Of course, consensus jury verdicts may be mistaken, and sometimes mistaken because shared biases shaped the deliberations. Still, requiring group deliberation, imposing norms meant to discount biases, expecting jurors to justify their positions to other jurors, each juror having formal equality to speak and vote—these are all procedures designed to align verdicts with true guilt and innocence. And some verdicts are the result of deliberations, not baked-in-advanced prejudices.

Hardly perfect, but I believe the analogy to moral belief is telling. We start moral reasoning with "intuitions" from many sources, some reputable, some scandalous, many simply under-supported by reasons. When moral disagreement, or life's circumstances, challenge our views, our norms require engagement in moral deliberations in quest of social consensus. Sometimes we are a hung society. Social prejudices and class interests surely distort the deliberations and results, and imperfect reasoning and incomplete evidence doom our moral "verdicts," even those widely shared, as unlikely to be precisely true. But the process remains rational—the best procedure for getting to the truth. Fortunately, our moral discourse, unlike jury deliberations, is unending; we can constantly revisit our verdicts as new evidence comes in, biases are exposed, and faulty reasoning is corrected. Nor are we constrained to a crude choice of guilty or not guilty. We can refine the degrees and admixture of right and wrong with as exquisite a discernment as human intelligence will bear. The causes of initial moral beliefs are not identical with the causes that sustain moral beliefs, nor the motives that ultimately enact them. Demonstrating that belief was prior to justification does not prove that the justification is motivational make-up rather than motivational muscle.

Like jury deliberations, it is essential that moral reasoning is social. No individual juror can be counted on to reach a correct verdict, and no moral reasoner a true judgment. The rationality, the truth-tracking, is a social effect. This is the case with the rational practice *par excellence*, science. Like moral beliefs and juror's inclinations, the sources of scientific hypotheses, may be anything—dreams, hunches, cultural inheritances, innate beliefs, emotional associations, and social biases. The nonrational origins of a scientific hypothesis does not make the process of explaining or confirming it nonrational.[29] Just like moralists, scientists often are tenaciously attached to their hypotheses. Some not well-tested hypotheses stick around a long time as scientific dogma or common "knowledge." But appropriately accepted scientific propositions are tested and remain forever open to retesting and reinterpretation. So too properly accepted moral beliefs. Moral discourse in philosophy seminars, law journals, editorials, TV talk shows, social media, bars, religious fellowships, and kitchens test moral beliefs. Moral reasoning is not the only test of moral belief, it is not a sufficient test, but it is a crucial test. Our moral beliefs tend to lose their grip if they do not make sense, if they do not cohere with our other beliefs whose truth we would not happily abandon. And the coherence, the "making sense," is ultimately a social phenomenon.

At bottom rationality is predicated of communities, and individuals are better or worse functioning elements of the community's rationality. Scientific rationality consists in the practices and norms of scientific communities, and the beliefs that emerge from those practices. Individual scientists embody scientific rationality in so far as they are good members of the scientific community. Their willingness to provide the best defenses for their views, their willingness to entertain multiple theories to support their hunches, their efforts to probe their theories for their deepest, perhaps unsuspected, implications, the inspiration they find in gut feelings—none of these make them pseudo-scientists. Indeed, the vigorous clash of theories contribute to scientific advance and requires scientists to do their utmost to champion their sincere beliefs. It is the willingness to put those beliefs in the arena so that they may be assessed by the community in light of communal logic and experience that makes good scientists. Good scientists test their beliefs and try to conform their beliefs to the test results, but they know that the test is not subjective. Everyone's observations, perceptual and logical, must be considered. In this fashion, we believe science approaches truth.

So too morality. Moral convictions may be stubbornly held and defended, and moralists ingeniously argue for their beliefs; their creative dialectics may be in service to social bias, neurological idiosyncrasy, flawed education, or limited experience. However, if a person seeks to justify her moral judgments to others, if she holds herself responsible for considering counter arguments, if she listens seriously to other viewpoints, and if she ultimately proves motivationally sensitive to the justifications that are the current survivors of that social process, then her moral practice is as rational as any scientist's empirical claims. She is a good member of the moral community.

I do not deny that psychologists, economists, and experimental philosophers have demonstrated that rationality is in many circumstances more quasi then commonly thought, and they have exposed innocent pseudo-rationality where we had thought rationality reigned. Although we've known about bad faith pseudo-rationality forever—Shakespeare, Voltaire, Jane Austen, Marx, Freud, Nietzsche, and Sartre are only some of the most prominent analysts of the phenomenon—the recent academic findings have certainly added quantitative empirical data and structural details. I have argued that I do not believe a convincing case has been made that practical reason or moral reason is insubstantial, and that there are good grounds for thinking practical rationality practically important, but I do not doubt that quasi reasoning, pseudo-rationality, and other nonrational impulses loom large in human thought and action.

The most distressing cases of rationality's impotence or abuse are a farrago of bad faith and innocent pseudo-rationality: the "justifications" offered in defense of social domination. Sometimes these "justifications" are pure rationalizations of non-rationally caused judgments, judgments caused by biases of class, race, sex, or other social identities. Pernicious, but "innocent," in that the agent believes his rationalizations are justifications and the actual cause of his beliefs. However, I think more often bad faith, not necessarily quite conscious, is at work. The advantaged group member is moved by reasons of self-interest, is acting "rationally" only insofar as the goals of his action exclude the interests of outside and subordinate groups. Candid admission that certain others are discounted may be socially unacceptable or not

comport with one's self-image. So the motivating justification is replaced by
a more acceptable, but inert, justification.

This points to the largest failures of practical reason in the moral realm, the
failure to believe that others, especially others' whose social identity is alien,
are as real as we are, with goals that are as objectively valuable. This is less
a failure of reason than a failure of perception, or more precisely metaphysical imagination. Reason's power is not at fault. Oppressors are impervious to
logic, they are ill-informed. Of course, they theoretically acknowledge others'
reality, and possess that ontological information abstractly. But their practical reasoning is not infused with a lively, vivid, sense of others and others'
ends. The oppressors' acts are not without strategy, but it is a strategy with a
stunted mission because it is blind to the full reality of others. It is the sort of
bad faith captured by the quip that you can count on a person's ignorance if
his salary depends on it. Moral judgment suffers metaphysical myopia when
contaminated by self-interest, an infection few of us completely escape.

NOTES

1. The discussion above presumes we have enough of an intuitive grasp of what
counts as an "action" to continue to employ the unanalyzed term. In light of the large
and contested philosophical literature on action, that presumption wants a prima facie
defense. It seems to me that some of the action literature is written in a pre-Wittgen-
stinian, (1953) essentialist, natural-kindist spirit, as though certain movements of the
human body were actions, other weren't, and we might discover the necessary and
sufficient properties that would separate the groups cleanly. Once again, I have a pragmatic take: actions are those human activities for which we hold people responsible.
These behaviors tend to have certain properties: they serve a purpose, the person performing them knows the purpose they serve and knows how this behavior will achieve
that purpose, we believe holding the person responsible for the behavior will encour-
age/deter similar behavior by the person or others in the future, we believe that some
people in similar circumstances would have behaved otherwise, we believe that the
behavior flowed from relatively settled parts of the persons character, we feel that had
different beliefs been in play the behavior would have changed. The list is not exhaustive. I doubt that any item on it, even were the list exhaustive, is necessary or sufficient
for an event to count as an action, with the exception of some very general properties
such as being a behavior affected by the person's mental state. What we find useful to
hold people responsible for will depend on circumstances. Nonetheless, we are familiar
enough with the list to recognize what will count as actions when we see them.

2. Our concern here is not with identifying action, which we *presume* we can
recognize. Our problem is simply figuring out the nature of its causes.

3. If the lexicographical grounds seem somewhat thicker, and the stipulated
definition seems something more than arbitrary, that is because actions aim at goals,
so motives cause goal seeking, and it is always appropriate to name goal seeking

as desire. But this tells us only that whatever a motive is it can be called a desire, it doesn't tell us about the nature of motives.

4. He famously said reason "is, and ought to be" a slave of passion, making both a factual and normative claim about the reason/passion relationship Hume (1739).

5. See Stich (1983).

6. See Dennett (1987), where he argues that we must employ these mentalistic terms in our most explanatory and predictive theories of our own and other's humans behavior.

7. There is a difference between this uninformative circle that defines "action," "motive," and "desire" so as to demonstrate that all "actions" are caused by "desires," and the circle that characterizes all theories of (including pragmatism's) justification. The former circle's toggling smallness deprives it of any explanatory power; it organizes no realm of ideas, reveals no connections, unearths no presuppositions, highlights no implications. It is analogous to a two word dictionary that tells us that Zrpx means Njgyl and Njgyl means Zrpx; not helpful. Although the Oxford English Dictionary defines each entry in terms of other entries, the amplitude of its circularity is richly informative. I take a good theory of justification, although in the final analysis only justifiable in its own terms, pays its way in its ability to organize and clarify related concepts. See Darwall (2006, 12) on terms only definable inside a closed set of terms. I am grateful to Hadass Silver for pointing out the need for this note.

8. Nagel (1970) and Parfit (2011, 108–109) provide related arguments against the view that only desires motivate. *A priori* arguments that beliefs cannot motivate tend to assume a correspondence theory of truth restricting belief's role to inertly mirroring or "fitting" the world, and claiming this passive status deprives them of the capacity to motivate. But we have rejected the correspondence theory, and if beliefs are more like dispositions to act in certain ways in certain circumstances rather than being like pictures of reality, a "direction of fit" argument loses much of its purchase. Even if we accepted a correspondence theory, functioning to mirror or fit the world would not clearly render beliefs inert. A mirror image may only be able to contain what it reflects, but what it contains retains causal capacities.

9. Hume (1739). Natural sympathy enables the Humean moralist to counter the Humean egoist. Both accept the "only passions motivate" thesis. The egoists thinks it clear that, in a Freudian spirit, all human energy has its origin in in a voracious, solipsistic id. Hume himself was somewhat less cynical about human nature, providing himself with a theoretical basis for morality within his theory of motivation. Sympathy, like any other moral foundation, is rooted in nonsolipsism's demands or promptings.

10. Dewey (1932, 187) says that the "thought of the object" can transform the impulse that led to the thought into a "different desire." Although he believed a thought "impotent" without desire, he also believed it capable of forming desires. I take this to indicate that Dewey believed Reason could motivate.

11. Emerson (1841).

12. Although the aspiration for consistency and reason is never foolish, paralysis in their absence can be. Sometimes we judge that *something* must be done [William James' forced choice, (1896)], and doing something is therefore rationally required.

However, it is often the case that we have no decisive reason to do any particular thing, or, what's worse, anything we do will be inconsistent with one or another practical judgment we hold. In such cases, whether and however we act we are doomed to inconsistency and irrationality at some level. It is not foolish to acknowledge that inconsistency and enact it. But that is not the same as embracing it.

13. So, in the case of strong trial evidence precluding innocence and a gut feeling of innocence, the rational response might be to vote to convict, not because the gut feeling is necessarily irrelevant, or even necessarily of less weight than the evidence presented, but because we suppose that it is *likely* explained by something other than actual innocence. The tension between gut feeling and innocence is more tolerable than the conflict between trial evidence and innocence.

14. Cf. Susan Haack's (1993) "foudherentist" epistemology. Haack compares knowledge to a crossword puzzle. If the answers do not fit together, we know they cannot all be correct. This comports with a consistency requirement for beliefs. But fittingness is insufficient for a crossword answer's correctness. It must also be an answer to the clue given for the word. The pragmatists' analogue for the crossword's clues is effectiveness. Effective beliefs that fit together are justified. But, ultimately what counts as fitting together is also a judgment of effectiveness.

15. That this agreement can change with different experiences I take to be Quine's (1951) main criticism of the analytic/synthetic distinction.

16. Language, of course, also expresses aspects of mind not well categorized as beliefs.

17. Of course, we can be playful with language, make jokes, write poetry, talk nonsense—and partially ignore its logic and distort its meaning. But the fun of the play is parasitic on its paradigmatic literal use, and when it is not the "language" being played with is no longer functioning as a language.

18. The difficulty of communicating across scientific paradigms, of talking about how the world works, Kuhn (1962) explains as significantly due to a change of meanings, and Davidson (1973) has argued that too much disagreement regarding what is true makes shared meaning, and hence communication, impossible.

19. One might suppose that practical inconsistency could also stem from actions at cross purposes. While that is a form of inconsistency, in such cases at least one of the actions must be inconsistent with a judgment, so that the primary source of practical inconsistency is a conflict between belief and action. Two conflicting judgments, for example, "Mitchell Silver ought to eat cookies" and "Mitchell Silver ought not to eat cookies" are theoretically inconsistent, but do not constitute practical inconsistency—although if both are believed by the same person, they inevitably lead to one. Although theoretical and practical inconsistency are not the same, our *recognition* of practical inconsistency depends on finding a theoretical inconsistency The breach between belief and action occurs whenever the propositional content of an action's description is theoretically inconsistent with the propositional content of the description of the act being enjoined by the practical judgment. So, "Mitchell Silver ought not to eat cookies," is a judgment which prescribes the act described as "Mitchell Silver not eating cookies." But if I *do* eat cookies, *that* act is described as "Mitchell Silver eating cookies" The two descriptions, "Mitchell Silver eating cookies," and "Mitchell Silver not eating cookies," are theoretically inconsistent. An action is not

the same as the description of itself, and that is why practical inconsistency is not a form of theoretical inconsistency. Nonetheless, we recognize practical inconsistency by recognizing a theoretical one. Arguments over whether actions are practically inconsistent reduce to arguments over how these actions are properly described.

20. Cf. Dewey's (1932) similar, but different, notion of habits. Beliefs can help cultivate a habit, but the habit is not activated by a judgment.

21. Gould (1979).

22. Joel Kupperman (2006) sees these opinions in Confucius and Plato.

23. This discussion is a variant of two topics in Mill's *Utilitarianism* (1861a). First is Mill's treatment of how instrumental values, such as justice, can come to have intrinsic value. Second is the issue of qualitative difference in kinds of pleasures of equivalent intensity and fecundity. Above I am suggesting that rationality, an instrument for effective response to reality has come to be valued for itself (perhaps just a philosopher's bias), and further, even if Reason does not bring home the bacon as well as a well-honed instinct to pursue the odor of pigs, the pleasure of righteously eating vegan bacon might be more valuable than the pleasures of savoring the pig's flesh. Similarly the satisfaction the Wright brothers had reasoning themselves into the air a few hundred feet at Kitty Hawk may have gone deeper than whatever satisfaction the unbelieving eagle gets from soaring for miles.

24. For a sampling of this suggestiveness, see Kahneman (2011), Haidt (2001), and Schwitzgebel (2015).

25. A similar point should be made for the closely related issue of whether we can trust moral intuitions. Anderson (2015) argues that our intuitions are biased by social position and context. She is quite right about that, and we know it because we have come to intuitions we trust more. Anderson acknowledges as much: she "does not reject intuitions. They are the basic material of moral thinking; we have no way around them" (2015, 40). Anderson's main point is that we have come to those better intuitions not through moral argument alone. True, but the question here is what role does argument play in endorsing our newer intuitions and making us feel they are more trustworthy than the old ones.

26. Buckwalter and Stich (2014), Machery et al. (2004), show gender's and culture's influences on judgment, respectively, both presumably irrelevant to the judgment being made.

27. Haidt (2001, 2012).

28. Haidt doesn't question the correctness of the respondent's intuition, just its defensibility. But it may be indefensible and deserve to be dropped. Although the idea of sibling incest feels as "yucky" to me as it is to most people, because I find no compelling reasons to disapprove of it in the case described, I am inclined to think it would not be wrong. And I think many people would, with time to reflect and opportunity to thoroughly discuss the case, come to see that their disapproval is personal disgust and not a sound moral judgment.

29. Of course, justificatory practices in science have nonrational dimensions (Kuhn 1962), but only the most radical skeptics would deny that science is a model of rationality. Certainly, those social scientists questioning humans' daily rationality or moral beliefs rational basis are not skeptics about science although they could find analogous results in that domain.

Chapter 6

No Double Standards

1. THE FUNDAMENTAL PRINCIPLE OF MORALITY

I have argued that morality is grounded in justified beliefs; to act rightly is to act in accordance with a justified belief that prescribes the act. If the belief that you ought not to be cruel is justified, then it is immoral to act cruelly.

We cannot be certain that any of our beliefs, whether normative or descriptive, are justified. This all-pervading fallibilism encompasses our most basic moral principles. However, I will argue that there are moral principles that are about as well supported as any beliefs we hold.[1] For example, if we define cruelty as intentionally causing suffering solely for the pleasure of witnessing suffering, then "don't be cruel," is as justified a belief as anything offered by contemporary physicists or historians. Its truth is at least as firmly embedded in our belief system as are some of the most well established beliefs. It is not simply that "don't be cruel," is more psychologically compelling than "the speed of light cannot be exceeded," or "Washington was the first President of the United States"; it is also epistemically superior. It is easy to imagine new empirical findings that would, and should, undermine beliefs about Washington or velocity. New observations, calculations, and theoretical frameworks could provide reasons to abandon current doctrine about speed limits. Unexpected newly discovered documents explaining some formerly inexplicable findings in American history, could give us reasons to believe there was a conspiracy to suppress knowledge of the brief pre-Washington administration of Aaron Burr. But what would make us doubt the truth of the belief that one ought not to be cruel?

Of course "don't be cruel" isn't psychologically compelling to all, and so it might be easy to imagine universal abandonment of the "don't be cruel" belief in a dystopian fantasy. However, it is hard to imagine *good reasons*

115

for rejecting the prohibition on cruelty. Epistemic virtue is different from psychological tenacity. Because endorsing sadism would create such an upheaval of our social system of beliefs, we are hard pressed to imagine that a true social system of belief, a system justified by how well it met the goals of all, could approve or be indifferent to cruelty.[2] The endorsement of sadism would cause an upheaval because of its relationship to even more central, more networked beliefs. Our reasons for these core moral beliefs rival our reasons for our most secure empirical beliefs. Those moral beliefs constitute our fundamental moral principles.

Unsurprisingly, these fundamental moral beliefs are variant principles of equality. I believe the best formulation of the most central principle is *"double standards are wrong."* The equality of Utilitarianism—all happiness counts equally, the equality of Kantianism—the same law applies to all, indeed the equality of traditional religious moral theory—love others as you love yourself, are readily understood as forbidding applying varying standards of value or rightness.[3]

2. DOUBLE STANDARDS AND CONSISTENCY

The prohibition on double standards is securely embedded in our SSB partly because of its connection to our core commitment to consistency. Our most central belief is *"not (X and not X)."* It is universally agreed that a TSSB will not contain contradictory beliefs, or at least not within an individual believer. All double standards violate this commitment to consistency.

Perhaps this point will be readily conceded. The very phrase "double standards" connotes inconsistency. Controversy surrounds not the acceptability of double standards, but rather its analysis: what does and does not count as dealing in double standards? However, before analyzing the nature of double standards, let us make explicit their inconsistent essence.

Suppose I judge that someone is a "genius" not because of any work of art she produced, or scientific discovery she made, or her wit, or keen insights, but solely because she scored above 160 on an IQ test. If I fail to judge that someone else, who also scored above 160 on an IQ test, is a genius, then I believe both that scoring above 160 makes one a genius and scoring above 160 does not make one a genius. This combination of beliefs is inconsistent— that is, we believe the combination cannot appear in a TSSB. The straightforward, unqualified application of double standards always leads to an instance of the statement form "X causes (defines, creates, leads to) Y and X does not cause (define, create, lead to) Y." The very syntax of our thought commits us to rejecting such statements.

Having rejected double standards, we must inquire into when different standards are indeed double. Indulging in "double" standards is the inappropriate, arbitrary use of different standards. There are always causes for using double standards, but never reasons. However, the use of merely *different* standards is more often than not quite rational. Different standards are in order when making different kinds of judgments: there is no inconsistency in using a different standard to judge ice cream than one uses to judge pizza. False accusations of double standards often arise because it is not always clear what kind of judgment is being made. These charges may be refuted by clarifying the nature of a judgment. Perhaps I am not judging genius, but judging whether someone ought to be admired for her intelligence. I may think that everyone who scores 160 is a genius, but not all geniuses should be admired for their intelligence. We sometimes carelessly say we are judging one thing (e.g., genius) when we are actually judging something else (whose intelligence merits admiration) for which the first is only a fairly reliable indicator. The carelessness opens us to the charge of employing double standards. Jill is being judged admirably intelligent and the evidence cited is her genius IQ. Jack, although also of genius IQ, doesn't possess Jill's imagination, and so is not judged admirably intelligent. The appearance of double standards is seen through once we realize we were conflating judgments about genius with judgments about admirable intelligence. Once the property being judged is in focus we see that different standards were in play because different things were being judged.

Moreover, apparently dissimilar applications of a standard may not be inconsistent when the standard is spelled out. A standard of genius may actually be "one is a genius if one scores 160 on an IQ test without cheating, or using performance enhancing drugs, or taking a recently recalibrated test, etc." In such circumstances, two people can both score 160 on an IQ test and yet you can consistently hold that one is a genius and the other is not, for the "IQ of 160 genius" standard implicitly assumes facts, such as "the score reflects no cheating," which may not obtain. Most standards come with an implied *ceteris paribus* clause. Rationality requires that we note how *ceteris* is not *paribus* whenever we arrive at dissimilar judgments.

The single set of standards that rationality demands must be particularized for the property being judged. A standard for judging health will be different from a standard for judging wealth, and a standard for the health of a dog different from the standard for the health of a bird. But consistency requires that we believe only a single fully spelled out standard for judging any specified property.

Consider judging the wealth of women. Suppose we argue that a woman's wealth can be judged by the money in her bank account. We then judge that Fatima is wealthy because she has $23,000 in the bank. Heidi also has $23,000 banked, but she we judge not wealthy. We appear inconsistent, but if our actual standard is money in the bank minus debts, and Heidi had $14,000 in debt and Fatima is debt-free, there is no inconsistency. Or maybe we are judging Fatima's wealth not simply under the heading "woman," but as an Afghani woman, and Afghani women need

$10,000 in the bank to be wealthy, whereas Swiss women, such as Heidi, require $100,000. Again no inconsistency. However, if I claim that every woman's wealth, without regard to any further description of the woman, is to be judged only by her bank account total, without regard to any other asset or liability, then my conclusion that Fatima is wealthy and Heidi is not wealthy, after acknowledging their equal bank account totals, is irrational. If we find ourselves inclined to make different judgments about different objects or events, although they appear to measure the same against our single set of standards for making that kind of judgment, we have more standard-spelling-out to do, or the objects are not being judged as the same kind, but rather as belonging to different categories of the kind—or we are guilty of irrational bias.

Does this imply that favoring one's family and friends is irrational? That depends on whether a single standard is motivating the "favoring," and whether that single standard is consistent with one's other standards. Suppose I am in a position to offer a job to a stranger or a cousin, both of whom seem to be able to do the job adequately, although the evidence suggests that the stranger will be somewhat better. Obviously, it is irrational to hold both that "jobs should be given to the most qualified candidate," and "jobs should be offered to relatives so long as they are almost as good as the best candidate." Nothing on the surface is irrational in preferring the latter principle to the former. However, whichever standard is used, it must be consistent with other principles, some of which will be of a more general nature. So a utilitarian, committed to the principle that one should maximize happiness, were she to use the nepotistic standard, would need to believe that preferring relatives in employment best serves the overall happiness, a Kantian, committed to universalization, that she would think it just if she lost a job to an employer's cousin under similar circumstances.

Some of the *prima facie* most likely general standards for action may be difficult to square with the nepotistic principle. But even if nepotism (or an opposing strict meritocratic principle) found a home in a coherent set of standards, only one criterion of practical reason will have been met. Coherence alone does not justify. Ultimately, rationality requires we act in accordance with justified belief. Coherence with other principles makes a principle a candidate for truth, but to be anointed true the principle would have to be found in a TSSB.

3. DOUBLE STANDARDS AND
THE REALITY OF OTHERS

Robust belief in the reality of others is the second element grounding morality. The first element, our commitment to consistency—the idea that a belief and its denial cannot both be true, combined with the belief in the reality of others, yields the belief that all ought to be treated by the same standards. The "reality of others," means not only that they exist, but that they really possess the properties that inform our own goals: their suffering and joy, their pride and shame, their fear and hope—all are as real as our own.

Single standards in the absence of a belief in the equal reality of others does not generate morality, because consistency does not demand that the same standard be used for different types of judgment, and, if others are of a relevantly different kind, a different standard is in order. For instance, judging how to respond to real suffering is not the same as judging how to respond to apparent suffering. If your suffering is only apparent and mine is real, then I can in Reason be unmoved by your travails while motivated by my own. And, of course, I do experience my suffering differently then I experience your suffering. The enormous qualitative difference between your emotions, sensations, and perceptions, and my emotions, sensations, and perceptions as they *appear in my experience* can easily deceive me into judging that there is an ontological difference in our actual emotions, sensations, and perceptions, a difference which justifies the application of a different standard of action to your suffering and my suffering, your joy and my joy. Practical reason entails the fundamental principle of morality only if, for the purposes of at least some of my actions, others belong to the same kind as I do. Their subjectivity must be relevantly similar to mine. Were that not the case, consistency would give moral concern no purchase in reality. If your tooth pain is only apparent, or somehow less real than my own, no standard that commends alleviating my real pain applies to your merely apparent pain. Apparent pain is very different from real pain and they need not be judged by the same standards. Solipsism makes acting egoistically seem practically rational. The deepest cause of practically rejecting the fundamental principle of morality is a failure to fully escape solipsism, wherein, broadly speaking, one believes that one's own motivating experiences are more real than others' are. Rarely is solipsism a conscious belief, explicitly deployed to rationalize treating others by different standards than one would apply to oneself. Double standards betray either inconsistent or solipsistic modes of belief, and blatant inconsistency is so antithetical to our cognitive structure, we seldom enact it. Rather, I believe that residual infant solipsism is the most common cause of immorality. For once the reality of others is fully acknowledged, consistency, the minimal threshold of truth, makes morality a corollary of practical reason.

An egoist might object that a standard such as "all agents ought to do what is good for me," abjures moral concern without denying others' reality or engaging in blatant double dealing. The problem with such a principle is that it is extremely unlikely to be justifiable. It is hardly credible that the SSB that will best serve all goals, a TSSB, will contain that principle. It is not absolutely impossible that the goals of every member of our social system will be best served if all its agents were only motivated by an infinitesimal subset of those goals, namely mine, but there is no reason to believe it.[4]

It is a more open empirical question whether a principle such as "each agent should only aim at her own well-being," might appear in a TSSB. There is some plausibility to the claim the goals of everyone in a social system would be best served if everyone was motivated solely by their own goals. Here is a single standard that fully recognizes others and suggests a mechanism for the achievement of their goals that is not wildly far-fetched. Still, although a candidate for inclusion in a TSSB, this principle of egalitarian egoism must, to be justified, defeat the many beliefs prescribing specific acts of altruism that it contradicts. It might be true, but, once we categorize others as "those with goals" the constraint of a single standard will render many of our altruistically oriented moral principles quite plausible, and a principle that contradicted them all would have to make a very strong case to be taken seriously.

4. RATIONALIST PRAGMATISM AND OTHER NORMATIVE THEORIES

The "no double standards" principle that I believe best articulates the substantive normative implication of Rationalist Pragmatism (RP) echoes a founding pronouncement of western moral theory, Aristotle's "equals ought to be treated as equals."[5] However, Aristotelean-inspired "virtue ethics" is not the theoretical tradition that RP most naturally complements or most interestingly contrasts with. Rather, the most illuminating comparisons comes from considering RP in light of the schools of thought that have dominated theoretical ethics in the English-speaking world for over a century, Kantianism and Consequentialism, and the paradigm for normative political thinking for even longer, social contract theory.

5. RATIONALIST PRAGMATISM AND KANTIANISM

There are three strong similarities between Kantianism and RP, and all of them underscore their common objectivism—their assertion that moral principles are true for all rational beings. The "categorical imperative" is Kant's term for the fundamental principle of morality, and he provides multiple formulations of it.[6] We find the first similarity between RP and Kantianism in Kant's first version of the categorical imperative—his "universalization" formulation. The "no double standards" of RP does little more than express colloquially Kant's first formulation. This "universalization" formulation admonishes us to act only according to principles we could consistently will guide everyone's actions. The only constraint on which principles one adopts are one's ability and willingness to abide their universal application: the same law for all. Similarly, the "no double standards" imperative excludes no standards other than those that cannot be equitably applied. In both cases, we have no more than a formalism that is normatively vacuous. No actual law or standard is promulgated, just an insistence that it be applicable to all.

A second similarity is highlighted by Kant's second version of the categorical imperative, in which we are enjoined to always consider others as "ends" and never merely as means. Treating others as an end could be interpreted as taking their well-being as one of your ends, but that is a shallow, or as best incomplete, interpretation. A better interpretation goes on to understand the well-being of others as allowing them to pursue and achieve their own ends. To treat others as ends is to make their ends your end, or at least their capacity to pursue their ends your end.

RP evaluates the truth of moral claims by registering the effects of beliefs on everyone's goals. Other's goals—their various ends—are centrally relevant to moral evaluation in RP because good acts accord with true judgments, which in turn are made true by their consequences for everyone's ends. Others' ends contribute to justification as much as one's own ends. Being guided by true moral judgments incorporate treating others always as ends because their ends are always elements in a judgment's justification.

A third similarity between Kantianism and RP is that both ground morality in rationality. It is our capacity to reason that makes us capable of morality, and the nature of Reason that requires it. Both views consider a failure to act morally a failure to act rationally, and both consider an insensitivity to moral judgments an insensitivity to reasons. This is the core of their common objectivism: moral error is a violation of truth, and the aspiration to be in accord with truth is the essence of Reason.

However, the differences between the two theories are significant, and it would be misleading to think of RP as a form of Kantianism. The Reason of RP is not a transcendent standard that exists prior to and independent of human life, but rather the standard created by seekers of truth out of their social and historical experience. Moreover, in RP, the rationality of morality is not unrelated to utility; on the contrary, rationality is born from the ideal of ultimate utility. The pure Kantian reduces utility to a minor role, neither central nor foundational, and often overridden, in moral life.

6. IS RATIONALIST PRAGMATISM
A CONSEQUENTIALISM?

No. Although RP ultimately grounds morality in goal achievement, goal achievement is so indirectly related to rightness, and so mediated by other concepts and considerations, that categorizing RP as a consequentialism obscures more of its nature than it reveals.

The immediate justification of an act in RP is a judgment. Regardless of the consequences of an act, if it accords with a justified judgment, it is right. The judgment will in turn be justified if it is the conclusion of a sound argument, which of course requires that the argument has true premises and valid inferences. The truth of the premises and the validity of the inference rules depend on whether they express beliefs that appear in a true social system of belief. It is only at that point, far removed from the individual act that consequences come into play. While the truth of a social system of belief does depend on the consequences of that social system of belief, the line from right to good is too attenuated to simply classify RP as a consequentialism. Insofar as consequences are justificatory in RP, they justify neither acts, nor beliefs regarding acts. Rather, consequences justify the yardsticks with which we measure justification itself. It is their inclusion in a social system of belief that makes our moral beliefs true, if they are, and our actions are right if and only if they accord with those true beliefs.

An analogy might be helpful here: games may be ultimately justified because they are fun to play. However, that does not mean that our judgments within the game are based on appraisals of fun. The victorious team in a baseball game is the team that scores the most runs, not the team whose victory generates the most fun. A team scores the most runs because the rules of baseball, when applied to the action in the game, grant it the most runs, not because it is fun to grant that team the most runs. "Fun" plays absolutely no role in judging how well a game of baseball is played, nor who has won it. Fun comes into the picture only when we consider justifying the rules of baseball. If, all things considered, different rules would make baseball more fun than the current rules do, then those different rules would be better baseball rules. But being fun to watch, or having fun while playing, does not certify one as a better baseball player. Similarly, consequences determine moral rightness no more than fun determines baseball champions.

Does the analogy not suggest that RP is a rule consequentialism? Although this is closer to the mark, rule consequentialism is not quite the right categorization of RP either. Rule consequentialism makes rightness depend on adherence to a rule, and the rule's correctness depend on the consequences of generally following *that* rule. RP's attribution of rightness depends on the truth of an individual judgment, but the truth of that judgment does not depend on the consequences of generally holding that judgment true. The judgment's justifiability depends solely on its presence in a TSSB. Of course, consequences are decisive when judging the truth of a social system of belief. But, because it is the entire social system of belief for which consequences become relevant, they are further removed from rightness than they are in typical rule consequentialisms.

Even a rule consequentialism that held that only entire moral codes, that is, moral rules considered as a set, are to be judged by consequences, although more similar to RP than a rule consequentialism that assessed the effects of isolated rules, would nonetheless still be more directly grounded in consequences than is RP. In RP, the principles used to justify a practical judgment, must be true, and so there is no justification of practice that doesn't go through theory. Rule consequentialism, in contrast, bypasses "truth" as a grounding concept for "rightness." The effectiveness, and therefore justification, of a set of rules in rule consequentialism, does not deploy the concept of truth. It thereby distances morality from the objectivity that truth confers. A rule, or a set of rules, is neither true nor false, so obeying or violating a rule cannot be cleaving to or deviating from the truth.

By anchoring morality in true belief, RP is made less vulnerable to the objection that any morality ultimately justified by consequences necessarily reduces to act consequentialism. The objection maintains that the best individual rule, or best set of rules, evaluated by their consequences, would be so elaborately crafted that the rules would account for even unique circumstances. If the rules ever allowed an action whose consequences were not for the best, then it appears that the rule itself was suboptimal and cannot be justified consequentially. If the rule *"Don't lie,"* sometimes is not for the best because truth-telling can hurt feelings, then the rule should be *"Don't lie, unless needed to avoid hurt feelings."* But if sometimes we would get better results truth-telling, in spite of hurting feelings, because the hurt feelings would make a beneficial reform of character possible, then the correct rule should be *"Don't lie, unless needed to avoid hurt feelings, except when the lying would hinder a beneficial reform of character, in which case it is ok to lie, hurt feelings be damned."* However, if the lying would so injure feeling that there is a substantial risk that someone would literally die of shame, then, in spite of possibly promoting a beneficial reform of character, we should have a rule to the effect that *lying is permissible in circumstances where truth-telling seriously risks causing death by shame, but lying is not permissible to avoid some lesser degree of hurt, if possible character building results will be defeated by the lie.* This process continues until the rules simply specify the rationales for doing that which will turn out best in every situation. Any relevantly new situation merely demonstrates that our rules were incomplete or too simple, and that they were not the best set of rules. Perfected consequentialist rules prescribe perfect individual consequentialist acts.

The standard rule consequentialist reply to the objection that rule consequentialism collapses into act consequentialism is that rules must be useful guides, capable of being taught, learned, and followed by human beings with finite capacities. This puts a serious constraint on the complexity the best rules can support. At some point, more complex rules, yielding superior results in theory, are counterproductive because their complexity undermines their capacity to guide. The best rules will prominently feature a friendly human interface, and so will deviant from the moral engineers' rules designed to get the best result from every act, but falsely presuming psychologically and cognitively unconstrained actors.

This reply gains clarity and force embedded in an RP context. If we replace rule consequentialism's moral rules, which are too easily thought of as ideal instructions whose implementation is independent of the rules' intended implementers, with shared beliefs that are elements of a social system of belief, it becomes immediately clear that beliefs are inseparable from the believers, and that the social system of beliefs' ultimate effects depends on the capacities of the believers. True moral principles, the crucial premises of moral justification, are known to be true because they are components of the best possible socially shared beliefs within the widest conception of society. Although its limits are an empirical question, surely the best belief system, the TSSB, has limits imposed by our cognitive and emotional capacities, both individual and collective. A set of rules can be anything, a set of shared beliefs must be believable.

None of this is to deny the central role consequences play in RP. RP is rooted in a pragmatic epistemology wherein truth is recognized by goal achievement, and goal achievement is a consequentialist measure. But the ethics *per se* is not consequentialist, only the larger truth of which they are a part.

7. SOCIAL CONTRACT THEORY, THE NO DOUBLE STANDARD PRINCIPLE, AND UTILITY

The paramount argument for denying the existence of morality has been metaphysical: the deniers claim that the objects needed to make morality real simply do not exist.[7] I have argued that moral truth requires of reality nothing more than what empirical truth requires. Hallvard Lillehammer calls this a "companions in guilt," strategy—a defense of morality which in effect says morality is ontologically no worse off than any other domain.[8] While RP is fairly described as assimilating moral truth on equal terms into the general alethic realm, which is the essence of the "companions in guilt" strategy, I reject the connotations of that label. It suggests that morality earns its equality of rank by the demotion of empirical knowledge. Instead, I see an elevation of morality from the degradation relativism would impose and the annihilation amoralism would pronounce. Once we understand the bases of empirical facts' epistemic status, morality's equality becomes evident and knowledge of moral truth shares the merits of empirical knowledge, rather than falling short of the fictitious virtues attributed to the empirically justified. A more accurate term than the defensive "companions in guilt," for RP's strategy would be "fellows in truth." Morality is admitted to an honored fellowship instead of having its shame diluted in a merger with "facts" brought down to morality's scandalous standing.

Whatever it is called, if successful, the "fellows in truth/companions in guilt" approach establishes that there can be objective moral truths. It does not, however, show that there are any. Some amoralists argue that the pragmatist grounds on which RP would plant morality actually produce no such growth. Such amoralists allow that moral beliefs might be true if they were ultimately useful, but they conclude that moral beliefs are not useful and so not true.[9] Thus, RP cannot vindicate moral belief merely by demonstrating the possibility of true moral beliefs, it must provide reasons to believe that there actually are some, and that means showing that some moral principles would be members of the most useful systems of belief.

Philosophers who use the notion of a "social contract" to explain the origin and nature of norms have usually been interested in political norms. In contrast, "morality," is frequently understood as guiding and evaluating personal behavior. However, it is clear that the norms of institutional and political life are the creations (perhaps unintentional and collective) of individuals and are maintained and implemented through individual actions. If political norms are distinct from personal ones, as some have argued,[10] they nonetheless still are intended to govern individual actions, albeit in limited purviews. If political norms are useful then at least a subset of moral belief is useful.

Social contract theorists have sought to ground norms in social utility. For Thomas Hobbes norms (enforced by overwhelming power) usefully release us from the horrors of perpetual, universal war. For John Locke and Jean Jacque Rousseau, although norms ("rights") are natural facts, they are unquestionably welcomed provisions, promoting, prosperity, security, liberty and all of the benefits of orderly, organized, social life. John Rawls derives fundamental principles of justice from intuitive notions of fairness, but the benefits of a just society and the harms of an unjust one are not neglected in his arguments in favor of the principles.[11]

In general, social contract theorists view norms as essential for fostering uncoerced social cooperation—cooperative behavior motivated by a sense of duty—and uncoerced social cooperation is judged to be an essential condition of the possibility of good lives. The basic social contract argument for morality's utility is that we can accomplish much together and almost nothing in fearful, distrusting social isolation. Only rules that are widely accepted, or at least followed, will create the conditions for sustained cooperation and stable security. The recognition that we are social, and that our good is in coordinated activity, is a commonplace insight, stretching from the ancient Greeks to ancient Confucians, from Adam Smith to Karl Marx, and from Christian conceptions of the Church, to the Muslim Umma and Jewish Kehillah.

Morality has the same utility afforded by the rule of law. Hobbes has most memorably imagined the deprivations and injuries of life without laws, and Rousseau, although more sympathetic to the lawless "state of nature," than Hobbes, and more concerned with the deformations of rule by corrupt law, envisions a lawful regime of equality as a better condition than the noble savagery he thought our natural one.

The rule of law, when most complete, includes equality before the law as a corollary. No one is above the law if the law is sovereign, and if the enactment of laws is in service to an arbitrary individual or class of individuals, law becomes an agent of the ruler(s) rather than the true sovereign. Of course, law is not self-generated, nor is its purpose self- perpetuation (except when religiously fetishized). Rule of law is a strategy—a very high-level strategy, but still not an end. The ends of law are the goods humans can realize under a regime of law. Equality before the law most empowers the law to achieve those ends, because equality minimizes the need to enforce obedience.

That coercing obedience to law is costlier and less effective than voluntary submission is self-evident. When coercion and voluntary adherence are mixed, as they almost always are, the proportions are often the crucial factor determining the extent of the law's utility. A law-abiding people who abide because they choose to be lawful, achieve more under and through the law than either a nation of scofflaws, or a nation of rule-following but resentful subjects. Neither the anarchy of early twenty-first-century Somalia nor the police state of North Korea has the normative structure conducive to realizing the most encompassing set of goals. Denmark comes much closer.

Morality fosters social cooperation by extending norms benign influence beyond the spheres subject to laws. There is hardly an area of life that cannot profit from social cooperation. Even projects and pleasures best pursued in solitude usually involve means produced collectively, and always require that others leave you the time and space to be alone.

As in the law, moral principles' acceptability, and therefore their utility, depends on their equal application to all. Indeed, even more so; the formal and typically more severe sanctions for lawbreaking elicit a degree of obedience even in the absence of respect for the law. The prospect of mere moral disapproval has generally limited effects on those who reject the moral principles they are inclined to violate. And, of course, a moral principle that applies an especially rigorous standard only to some is likely to be rejected by them.

Knowing that the laws are the same for all enables broad respect for the law and voluntary obedience, and similarly, moral principles that apply to all will more readily be believed by all. Belief in a moral principle does not ensure action in accordance with it, but it increases the likelihood. No Double Standards is the explicit declaration that morality judges impartially and gives no one grounds to reject it as biased against her goals. It gives confidence that moral constraints can be accepted by others, and so more probably will be accepted by others, making their behavior more reliable, more predictable, and easier to complement.

None of this proves there are justifiable moral principles. There is no *a priori* proof that any TSSB will include *explicit* moral beliefs,[12] and arguments from experience, even the most universal experience, are always defeasible. However, it is hard to imagine our good achieved without social intercourse, or social intercourse without rules of the road, or discriminatory rules of the road obeyed by many, or rules obeyed by many that are believed by none. Moral belief is almost certainly a beneficial component of social life.

Arguments for the utility of belief in moral principles are substantially similar to arguments social contract theorist give for the utility of the state: both the state and morality expand the range and intensity of social cooperation. A related similarity is that both the state that social contract theory justifies (a different state in the case of different social contract theorists) and moral principles, at least those justified on RP or Kantian grounds, are the creation of our rational capacities. It is reasonable to be obedient to the just state and reasonable to feel bound by moral truth.

For some social contract theorists, such as Hobbes and Rawls obedience to a just state (a state that keeps the peace for Hobbes, one that honors the fundamental principles of justice for Rawls), is reasonable because the state serves enlightened self-interest, even if for Rawls it is only the self-interest of one's hypothetically unbiased self. Obedience to political norms is reasonable if the norms are the consequence of an (even hypothetical) agreement with rational self-interested others. In a world where the existence of others' interests requires their tolerance to most effectively pursue one's own interests, the equal extension of tolerance is a necessary, and so reasonable, concession. For Locke and Rousseau submission to a just state is reasonable because it can be motivated by recognition of the truth of natural law and the necessary means to secure conformity with that truth or to flourish in concert with that truth.

Morality's relation to Reason in RP is less connected to utility than it is in most social contract theory. Ultimately, the rationality of morality does lie in its utility, but RP's notion of utility is not calculated by each individual as utility to self. Nor is it the undifferentiated utility of classical consequentialism. Rather it is the utility of social knowledge to each individual, the utility that possession of objective truth renders to all.[13] That the truth of morality, like all truth, is warranted by its utility judged from every truth seeking perspective is a kinship RP has with social contract theory.

However, unlike social contract theory, RP does not view rationality as prior to or separate from utility. The social contract theorist posits rationality and derives normativity from it. RP finds no rationality that isn't already normative. Once established, Reason may judge the truth of additional norms, and I have argued that moral norms, in particular the No Double Standards principle, will be found true. This normative extension is not a leap into a new realm, but rather the plausible outgrowth of the essential normativity of rationality.

I have just said that social contract theory derives normativity from rationality, but that is not quite right. It must and does include a norm as part of rationality to execute the derivation: the norm of self-interest. If it isn't intrinsically rational to pursue self-interest, there is no motor driving the state of nature into a normative political state. Sometimes this original normativity is disguised as a fact: people just do pursue self- interest, and the social contract theorist is only explaining, not justifying, the political state. However, if justification of a political order is intended, self-interest must be regarded as a normative element of social contract theories conception of rationality.

In this light, RP differs from social contract theory in the particular norm it posits as intrinsic to rationality. Instead of self-interest, RP regards an interest in truth as rationality's intrinsic norm. As the normative Eve, an interest in truth is far more fecund, especially of moral norms, than self-interest. Self-interest must consider others only as external obstacles or aids to its project; interest in the truth requires others as essential collaborators. Although only experience can determine the precise terms of the collaboration, consistency, the fruit of our broadest experience, combined with the reality we must accord others as fellow truth-seekers (the more reality accorded, the more robust the collaboration) make morality, and the No Double Standards principle in particular, an organic development of rationality's intrinsic normativity.

Even Locke and Rousseau, who, by beginning with natural law made recognizing truth the fount of social normativity, fail to make rationality intrinsically normative. Instead, they make reality normative. Our reason discovers norms, it is not their source. It might appear that in positing morality as an independent reality, natural law theorists place morality on a firmer, more reasoned footing. However, there is always room for skepticism regarding "external" reality, especially when the means of discovery is the natural light of reason, and there is disagreement among the reasonable whether any external moral reality has been illuminated by their lights.

8. RATIONALIST PRAGMATISM
AND FEMINIST THEORY

Feminist philosophers have rightly made us wary of equating morality with rationality. They have argued that the equation recognizes and valorizes self-interested calculation, abstract individualism, disinterested motives, and intrapsychic satisfaction, while ignoring or denigrating caring, concrete social relations, promptings of the heart, and mutual dependency.[14]

RP does equate morality and rationality, but it escapes the most trenchant feminist criticisms because its conception of rationality is largely built out of the same understanding of social life that informs the feminist critiques of traditional rationalist ethics. The rationalism of RP is not the rationalism of western philosophy's "Man of Reason."[15] There is no notion in RP that the flesh is something to be overcome, or natural inclinations are suspect and generally to be resisted. While natural desires are not automatically approved because natural, their biological origins are not a mark against them either.

Moreover, RP conceives of rationality as a naturally, historically developed capacity. It is not a transcendent faculty whose proper operations are divorced from the vicissitudes and particularities of our natural condition. It is not merely that Reason is compatible with nature, it itself is a product of nature. Specifically, it is an outgrowth of humans' social nature. The role sociality plays in Rational Pragmatism is its feature that most makes it compatible with major strands of feminist theory. Rather than atomized individuals who become morally entangled through agreements—"contracts"—that are motivated by our desire to advance self-interest, and structured by our capacity to recognize efficient means to that end, RP sees our moral relations emerging in tandem with our selves, both springing from an already social animal. RPs objectivity rejects the solipsism which is the metaphysical source of the self-interested presumptions of some traditional moral theory. The reality of others, not the Cartesian ego, is where morality begins. And so the reality of others is not a contingent fact that moral agents come to terms with instrumentally in pursuit of preexisting goals. While our social nature and rational faculties, like our very existence, may be contingent, others' reality is not a fact practical reason responds to, it is a necessary condition for the emergence of practical reason.

The No Double Standards principle is indeed the sort of abstract, purely formal decree that some feminist philosophers decry as inattentive to realities of actual experience.[16] However, No Double Standards clearly articulates the moral demand of liberal feminism—it is wrong to use different standards for women and men. More radical or essentialist feminist thoughts are also accommodated because the single set of standards of judgment whose existence RP posits is not an imposed male set of standards, or culled from men's self-(mis) understanding, but rather is a set of standards validated from all perspectives, including women's perspectives. Those perspectives may express women's essential nature (if there is such a thing) or merely the universal historical experience of women, or very particular historical experiences of particular groups of women, or unique experiences of just one woman. Whatever they reveal, RP is committed to taking those experiences into account as relevant to justification. This results in an objectivity that is, as any genuine objectivity must be, built as much on women's perspectives as on any other group of knowers.[17] And because the verifying perspectives are the perspectives of all actual humans, the vacuity of the No Double Standards principle as a theoretical construct, is informed by concrete experience whenever it is put into practice. That there should be no double standards is given by our metaphysical situation and Reason, but only the particular experiences, desires, beliefs, and feelings of the most inclusive conceivable community, what I have called the "social system," can determine the *content* of our universal moral principles.

9. MORALITY AND THE EMOTIONS

The idea that morality is a rational capacity has long been opposed by those who believe, as some feminist theorists do, it is an affair of the heart. David Hume provides the classic version of the view: Reason does not command us, or even incline us to care. Reason is indifferent to ends; ends are generated solely by the passions. As we saw earlier, this position leads Hume to conclude that only emotions motivate, and so if there is to be any morality at all there must be moral emotions. Hume holds that, as it happens, there are moral emotions. People are endowed by nature with sympathetic feelings. We care about each other.[18] While passion for one's own well-being is strong, it is not the sole passion. Among the passions is sympathy for others, and from that sympathy comes morality. Jesse Prinz offers a contemporary theory of morality as emotionally grounded.[19] For Prinz wrongness is a *feeling* of disapprobation. The feeling gives rise to the moral judgment, not the judgment to the feeling.[20]

Hume, Prinz, and all those who believe that morality is an emotional, and therefore nonrational, enterprise, are right that desire and sentiment are the source of most (perhaps all) values, and that without them our moral lives would be much constricted if it could exist at all. But these claims are not at odds with the rationalism of RP, rather these claims are built into RP: in RP moral truth is discovered by the effectiveness of belief at goal achievement, and goal achievement is also the measure of value realized. Although "emotion" is a complex and contested concept, without something like emotions—pleasure, pain, happiness, suffering, frustration, satisfaction, attraction, repulsion—one cannot give a plausible account of the value of a given goal achieved. Feelings give goals weight and valence. RP is not a formalism that constructs a value neutral morality—or dispenses with value as an element in determining rightness. If *no one* valued anything (and feelings are the source of most, if not all values),[21] there would be neither true nor false, neither right nor wrong. RP incorporates this doctrine.

However, the emotional beginnings of most value only preclude a rationalist morality if one believes Reason cannot regiment, discipline or rationalize value. In particular, the relevance of values (goal achievement) to any claim, normative or factual, does not make the claim ineligible for truth. Indeed, I have been arguing that assessing a belief's truth value is always *ultimately* dependent on values broadly conceived. Moreover, in a more immediate way, there are true and false beliefs about goals and the emotions that generated them, and true and false beliefs about goals' and emotions relationships to each other; propositions about goals and emotions are truth apt. That morality is a function of Reason hardly negates the significance of emotions in morality.

Humeans tend to think that we must infer a relativistic lesson from the ineluctable emotional ingredient in morality's origins: because feelings are the seeds from which so many values grow, and it is beyond dispute that desire and sentiment will vary with temperament, training, circumstances and culture, it seems clear that values will vary too. What we feel depends on who we are, and our intrapersonal complexity and interpersonal differences give rise to a variety of goals.

But a variety of goals is not tantamount to moral relativism, any more than a multiplicity of destinations forecloses the possibility of a single set of road rules, accurate maps, or the fact that some particular system of transportation will serve those various destinations better than others. Some of morality's raw materials are nonrational feelings, feelings which tend to move in competing directions. Morality is the rational processing of those feelings and other relevant facts. Morality is no more "just a feeling"[22] than the Panama Canal is just water, and the rationalism of RP need deny its emotional elements no more than the canal need deny the content of its locks. Moral principles tell us what to do with values, and although we might value moral principles, or even value acting in accordance with them, the principles themselves are not values. They are expressions of beliefs, beliefs which may be true or false.

RP does not require a *specific* emotion, like compassion, fear, disgust, vanity, or love for the moral life. Nonetheless, our moral principles should reflect the specific feelings we discover in the world. Objective morality operates on the actual needs, fears, hopes, despair, joys, and suffering of all. The perfected state of that operation is highly speculative. There is strong reason to believe that all current sets of moral principles or dispositions are a considerable distance from the objectively true, complete morality. Still, like scientists who well know that their theory will be modified by new observations, probably even modified with further reflection on the experiences we've already had, we can nonetheless say, how things look to us now,[23] hoping that it is close to, but knowing it is unlikely to be an (the) objectively true morality.

NOTES

1. Perhaps no moral belief is as secure as our basic rules of inference, whose worth has enshrined them in nearly all, if not all, human languages.

2. I said more about a social system of belief (SSB) and a true social system of belief (TSSB) in chapter 4. The first term refers to the totality of beliefs held by anyone we have been or will be in (linguistic) communication with, no matter how many intermediaries are involved. The second term refers to a SSB that serves those in communication as well as any alternative SSB.

3. "About the only general proposition that can be laid down is that the principle of equity and fairness should rule" (Dewey 1932, 297).

4. Alternatively, such an egoism could be justified if I were a "utility monster," a being whose capacity for the quality and quantity of goal achievement (see appendix) was infinite. In some interpretations of religious moralities, God is such a being, and so pleasing God becomes the supreme moral principle.

5. Aristotle (c. 340 BCE).

6. Kant (1785).

7. See Mackie (1977), who argues that morality's reality require the existence of very "queer" entities.

8. Lillehammer (2007). Many pragmatists may be taken as employing a version of this strategy. Misak (2004) takes Peirce to be doing so, and it has representatives among contemporary pragmatically inclined metaethicists such as Diana Heney (2016), and of course, Misak herself (2000).

9. Joel Marks (2013a) well exemplifies this strain of thought. Although, he accepts metaphysical objections to morality's existence, his primary objection is not that moral beliefs are false, so much as it is they are harmful.

10. See Nagel (1978).

11. Hobbes, (1651), Locke (1690), Rousseau (1762), Rawls (1971).

12. However, as I have argued in chapter 4, a TSSB must include moral attitudes, because to operate as a SSB there must be multiple selves who recognize others as

co-certifiers of truth, which means in our linguistic practice recognizing others as selves, as beings with goals who understand that you too are a being with a goal. However, whether that recognition will necessitate that a TSSB will include the No Double Standards principle, or any moral principle, as a *belief* is an empirical question, although, as I argue above, it appears highly likely.

13. For how Rationalist Pragmatism might calculate this utility see the appendix.

14. See Held (1990) for a summary indictment of traditional Western moral theory from feminist perspectives, and Gilligan (1982) for a classic source of the critique.

15. See Lloyd (1984).

16. Anderson (2010). See the Introduction for further discussion, in a somewhat different context, of ethical theory and adequate attention to actual experience.

17. Cf. Antony (1993).

18. Hume (1739). Natural "caring," especially feeling created by specific relations, is the central idea of one school of feminist ethics. See Nodding (1984).

19. Prinz (2007).

20. Marks (2013a, 2013b) derives an amoralist position from the same view. Prinz is a relativist because morals are emotions and people have different emotions. Marks holds genuine morality is by definition universal, but what we call "morality" are our very particular feelings, and so there is no real morality at all.

21. I am not claiming that only feelings are valuable, nor that to have a goal an agent must have or anticipate personal feelings upon the success or failure of that goal. I do claim that all value is measured by goal achievement, and that a state of affairs would rarely become a goal unless someone felt something about it, and what they felt about it determines its "weight." See the appendix for more details.

22. See Marks (2013b, 2016) for arguments that moral inclinations should be considered mere feelings.

23. Here, by "our" "us," and "we" I precisely mean "mine," "me," and "I." While I do think that my moral intuitions and fundamental desires are widely shared, I present no arguments for that claim. But I use "we" so that the reader can more readily disagree, if they do. If I say "here is what I feel," I make claims that are hard to deny. True, a reader could still say "well I don't feel that way," but, even though they logically amount to the same thing, I'd prefer readers simply to deny the claim "we feel that . . ." when their feelings, or intuitions about general feelings, differ from mine.

Chapter 7

Our Morality

If the previous chapters have done their job, they have established that morality exists as a part of rationality and that it requires we take others' goals into consideration in our quest to find true principles of action. They have, in other words, established what philosophers call the moral viewpoint. However, little has yet been said, beyond enjoining a consistent use of standards, of what that viewpoint imports. In this chapter, we will explore how RP's way of establishing morality suggests particular principles, virtues, and values. They are hardly surprising or unusual suggestions, and that is to the good. If a metaethics suggested a wholesale revision of our moral intuitions we would have good reason to be highly skeptical of it. However, a metaethics can contextualize and renovate common morals, giving them new life and strength, and perhaps expanded or altered meaning. On occasion a metaethics might bring forth a new moral principle or at least reprioritize accepted principles. It might also give grounds for rejecting a principle that has a place in some contemporary ideology.

1. MODELING MORALITY

The Bible tells us that we are formed in the image of God. Even for many atheists this metaphor stirs the moral imagination. That God has bequeathed us her form is meant to express an essential moral truth. But what, exactly, is it? What about us is godlike, and what is its moral import? Clearly, being "in God's image," implies there is something about humanity of the highest value. But the metaphor suggests more than that each person is of supreme value. It suggests that every person shares features with God by virtue of which she shares God's value; what gives God value is what gives us value.[1]

Ludwig Feuerbach maintained that God is made in *our* image, and by reversing the biblical trope, he provides the beginnings of an answer to the question "what about us (or God) is holy?" If what gives God value is what gives us value, then what gives us value is what gives God value. Feuerbach argues that we created God by projecting our most cherished virtues and faculties; God, made from our idealized self-image, is creative, loving, merciful, just, powerful and knowing. Feuerbach's thesis suggests that we learn what we most revere in God simply by noting what we find in God, because what we find in God are only the most cherished aspects of ourselves. But let us set aside issues of the psychology and the genealogy of religion; never mind who created whom, or why, or how.[2] What about the creation is so highly valued?

It is the "knowing" bit. Surely, the divine attributes are each esteemed, but many of the familiar ones cannot serve as the image of God; an unkind, unloving, unjust, and unmerciful person would still be a person, still in the image of God. What is the core faculty that makes us godlike? It is, at bottom, our capacity for truthfulness. The capacity for truthfulness is what we respect in ourselves and each other. Even as we stray from the truth and knowingly embrace falsehood in word or deed, as Macbeth did, yet "we still have judgment here,"[3] still shoulder the responsibility to distinguish the true from the false.

All sorts of pleasures and pains are indifferent to truth, and benign or malign impulses can exist without any notion of truth. Satisfaction, pleasure, and contentment can be achieved without truth, frustration, pain, and stress without falsehood. However, moral agency, freedom, error, virtue, vice, self-consciousness, and consciousness of others could not. And because consciousness of self and others requires the idea of truth, so does kindness, love, mercy, and justice. It is the *capacity* to recognize truth and each person's role as a verifier that makes us moral equals. It is not our virtues that make us godlike, it is rather, as another Bible tale makes plain, our capacity to be virtuous, to *know* the difference between good and evil that gives us the dignity we revere as divine. Each person we encounter, directly or indirectly, has the potential to codetermine the truth of our world. While we do not create reality together, we do create the truth.

The most plausible competing conception of our divine form is that we are loci of experience and, for moral concerns especially, enjoyers and sufferers. "The question is not 'Can they reason' nor 'Can they talk' but 'can they suffer.'"[4] Jeremy Bentham was correct to see the capacity to suffer as the property that makes one an object of moral concern, but that is a different question from what confers the value we find in others and ourselves. We can value the cessation or diminution of suffering without valuing the sufferer. Not that suffering is a completely separate matter from the proper respect we owe each other; we could not be verifiers if we were incapable of suffering and enjoyment,[5] but merely enjoying and suffering is insufficient to number us among the truth-making community. Truth makers do indeed not only suffer and enjoy but also communicate to establish truth. The members of the *community* of knowers are those who command our highest regard.

What social relations properly manifest that regard? If we value others because, like us, they can recognize the truth and can act accordingly, what practically follows? For a start, callousness is a fundamental vice. Others' truth-making capacity entails that they can suffer, and insensitivity to their suffering marks us as irrational. It constitutes blindness to reality, the secular vice equivalent to the sin of failing to acknowledge God. Cruelty is a greater fault in the same domain. Although the person acting cruelly recognizes that others have feelings, cruelty perversely, *anti*-rationally, seeks pleasure in the other's pain. Cruelty is anti-rational because it embraces inconsistency. The cruel person does not merely ignore the other's reason to avoid suffering, he makes of it a reason to induce suffering. Callousness is a failure of Reason, cruelty is an aggressive inversion of Reason. The sadist is the secular version of Milton's Satan. Satan knows there is a God but is in rebellion. The cruel find others' reasons to be free from pain their reason to inflict pain. Sensitivity and kindness are the basic moral demands, for our fellow verifiers necessarily have goals, which usually include avoiding suffering, and it is reasonable to respond to those reasons, and certainly not to take them as counter reasons.

However, it is not *qua* feeling beings that we most value others. More than feelings, others have judgment. When we ignore their views, we treat others inconsistently with their status as judging beings, just as callousness is inconsistent with their status as sentient beings. Dismissiveness is perhaps the closest analog to cruelty. It is ignorant to fail to recognize others have viewpoints, it is dismissive to acknowledge those viewpoints but fail to give them *any*, even preliminary, epistemic value.[6] Perhaps the more precise analog to cruelty would be to believe something just because another did not believe it. That sort of epistemic depravity I think rare on a personal level, but something like it may appear more broadly in racist and sexist thought—"if the inferior others believe it, it must be wrong."

Consideration is the virtue where dismissiveness is the vice. It is a complex virtue. It starts with recognizing that others in general have views, and may have a view on any particular matter. It allows for the expression of those views, which at times may require inviting their expression, or even creating the conditions for them to be comfortably expressed. Next, consideration demands that the view be understood, and the reasons for it be considered in turn. If a claim made from the other's viewpoint is initially rejected, the other's status as a verifier obliges us to explain the grounds for the rejection and be open to responses to that explanation. Finally, the rejection is never final. Although actions need to be timely, and issues become moot, the other's rejected claim always remains truth eligible. More importantly, the other, regardless of how many rejected claims he or she has accrued, must be treated as if it is possible his or her next claim might be true.

None of this is to say that a merited reputation for (in)credibility or relevant (lack of) expertise should play no role in how others' claims are to be considered. Where circumstances do not permit claims to be judged directly, tentative rejection can be reached for the reason that the person making the claim was not well situated by training, temperament, or circumstances to reach a sound judgment. But if those are the grounds for rejection, they too need to be given the same consideration we ought to give claims for which the logic and evidence are immediately accessible.

"God's image" may be the paramount metaphor for what we value in ourselves and others, but god imagery is less helpful for illuminating our ideal *relations*, for, unlike God, we are mortal and vulnerable. Regardless of how godlike in reason, faculties, and apprehension we are, even as the paragon of animals we retain our animal needs, including our primate insecurities about status. What is the apt attitude when encountering another godlike knower who is vulnerable in body and spirit? What relationship best exemplifies it?

Sisterhood is among the most common models for truly moral relationship. It is better than parent/child, for it suggests the equal status of siblings. However, like parent/child it presents love as the ideal moral bond, and that is a fault. Love ill serves as the basis of moral relations based on the principle of No Double Standards rooted in the rational imperative to believe and act truly.[7] Love is the relation of caring, and even when mutual, love need not entail any equality, nor involve a common concern for truth. I can love a tree, a dog, or a baby, and in no case need take my beloved's *judgment* into consideration, just its well-being. Love does require considering the specific nature of the beloved in order to judge of its well-being—you ought not treat a tree you love the same way you would a dog you love—and so when loving a fellow verifier a lover would respect the knower in her; being respected as a knower is part of her specific well-being, just as being well-watered is part of a tree's well-being. However, love is not the relationship that expresses what we value in all others who are fellow verifiers insofar as they are fellow verifiers. Brotherhood is deficient as the model of our ideal moral relations.

A better metaphor might be one of artistic collaborator.[8] In an ideal artistic collaboration, all parties view each party as contributing to a common creation, and the full success of one requires the success of all. While we might reject our collaborators initial proposals, or they ours, we work toward a solution we can all thoroughly endorse. Acceptance of aesthetically imperfect work might often be a practical necessity—sometimes the show must go on before all the contributing artists agree it has been perfected. But such compromises, however inevitable in our world, are nonetheless aesthetic

shortcomings. The collaboration ideally remains forever open, forever willing to entertain suggestions for further improvements from any collaborator,
and each collaborator tries to enter into the others' perspective as they form
a common vision.

Every morally charged exchange with another person might be viewed as
a collective creative act, every other as a highly esteemed fellow artist, in
which truth, rather than beauty, is the sought after outcome. Only when all are
satisfied that truth has been achieved, can the encounter be judged a complete
success. In morality, there is no audience, or rather no distinction between
audience and collaborating artist. Again, as in the real world of artistic col-
laborations, real world interpersonal relations seldom approach moral ideals,
still the model is worth bearing in mind.

Anointing consideration of the judgment of others as the cardinal virtue,
and collaboration in search of truth as the ideal interpersonal relation, may
appear to be (and may actually be) a philosopher's prejudice. However, once
truth is understood as a property of practical as well as theoretical claims, and
we realize that in daily life we assert practical claims in myriad nonverbal
ways, the scope of the virtue of consideration and the ideal of collaborative
truth seeking can be seen to cover far more than good conversational man-
ners.[9] A true practical claim is a call to action, and the search for practical
truth is a quest for agreed terms of common life. Collaboration demands that
the best way for us to be with each other is always on the agenda, and consideration acknowledges that the question is only decidable if everyone's needs,
concerns, interests and goals are attended to. Consideration and collaboration
are the ideal constituent social relations of a community of verifiers. We act
in light of what we collectively take to be the truth. Vulnerable gods meet as
equals, each a justifier, each seeking justification.

2. MORAL PRINCIPLES

Treating each other as knowers—as fellow verifiers—is perhaps less a
principle of practical reason than it is the condition of practical reason.
What fundamentally follows from our common interest in truth is the No
Double Standards principle, which requires that at the most fundamental
(or the most abstract, if you will) level, the same set of standards applies
to all. But actionable principles require content that is not provided by the
No Double Standards formal demand of consistency. For content we must
resort to our values, which are most often traceable to our needs and wants,
loves and hates. Out of such emotions our goals tend to emerge. No Double
Standards, like the Golden Rule and the Categorical Imperative, operates on
our passions. Reason turns our passions into principles. Moral principles are

in part our passions rationalized, which is to say they guide us so that our action—our attempt to realize the goals formed from our and others' passions—accords with truth.[10]

Only experience can lead us closer to true moral principles, but we've enough experience to form some educated hypotheses. Many traditional principles—for example, do not steal, keep promises—in some version seem likely to turn out true. However, there are three particularly strong contenders to be the main content providing moral principles. In each case, the principle engages our desire to be counted among the rational.

The most general principle with practical content in our morality is that we ought to reduce serious suffering. The evils of hell are much worse than the joys of heaven, the agony of defeat more intense and enduring than the thrill of victory, and a grievous loss more painful than an a bounteous gain pleasurable. And certainly what saddens is generally more recognizable and predictable than what gladdens. It is difficult to know with high confidence which meal I would find most delicious at any given moment (which is why I stare at menus too long) and even harder to say what you would find most delectable (which is why it is presumptuous to order for others), but everyone dislikes hunger, and by all reports, the pangs of prolonged real starvation would not be endured to dine at a Michelin 3 stars for an equal period.

These observations suggest two principles: *do nothing to cause serious suffering*, and *relieve serious suffering*. Certainly, as sufferers and potential sufferers, among our highest goals is the avoidance of serious suffering. Moral resentment is far more deeply felt when those in a position to alleviate our severe suffering refuse or neglect to do so, than when those who could confer a boon fail to do so. Whenever anyone cannot communicate her or his goals, it is plausible to infer that avoiding serious suffering ranks high among them. *Do nothing to cause serious suffering*, and *relieve serious suffering*, are strong candidates for inclusion in our single set of objective principles.

Obviously, *do nothing to cause serious suffering* and *relieve serious suffering* do not give clear instructions in all actual cases; they are vague. Nor can they be enacted in all applicable cases; there might be serious suffering caused no matter what one does, and there is always serious suffering one might relieve only by failing to attend to other serious suffering. In addition, these principles are subject to a powerful objection: the elimination of all serious suffering can be achieved by the sudden destruction of all sentience. Blowing up the world appears to honor the principles, and blowing up the world is wrong.[11] Does not this counterexample falsify these two reduce-serious-suffering principles?

The progression of posited principle, counterexample, refined principle, reconfigured counterexample, and so forth is typical of the dialectic of moral theory. Rationalist Pragmatism does not eliminate the heuristic value of this approach, but RP's holism does reduce its decisive status. Just as in science, no single experiment can falsify a theory,[12] counterexamples to a moral principle raise questions about its scope and value, but do not prove it false. When counterexamples to a principle harness strong intuitions and employ realistic and commonly occurring situations, we rightly conclude that the principle will not find a place in a TSSB. For many, the wrongness of blowing up the world is among the strongest of intuitions,[13] but it is hardly an intuition formed out of common experience. Opportunities to destroy all sentient being never present themselves to the overwhelming majority of us, and so its misguiding directive *in that hypothetical circumstance* is small evidence that principles aimed at avoiding suffering are not true.

However, the vagueness and indeterminateness is more worrisome. First, how much suffering constitutes "serious" suffering? Next, isn't a recommendation to reduce serious suffering always in conflict with other principles or with various potential applications of itself? Which serious suffering should I reduce with my limited resources and time? Disease, violence, injustice— the sources and modes of serious suffering are disparate and abundant, and addressing one form often involves neglecting another. Moreover, should one always reduce serious suffering even if it involves dishonesty, infidelity, and injustice? Even if true, reduce-serious-suffering principles are unlikely to be the only true principles. The reduce-serious-suffering principles don't tell you what to do in any particular situation. Does this not make them useless, and so unlikely to prove true?

No. Algorithmic guides are not the only useful ones. Vague instructions can direct us to the right general region, and less than fully determinate procedures can narrow our choices. We ought not to expect more from moral principles until we have reason to believe we are in full possession of all and only true beliefs. We shouldn't hold our breath.

The fallibility of our moral lives has two sources. Our principles may be false, and the set of them are certainly incomplete. Were they true and complete, they would include principles that identify the governing principle in every situation that ever occurs. All seeming moral dilemmas would be rationally resolvable. But we will never be sure our principles are true, and should always consider them incomplete. Being incomplete, they can at best get us to focus in the region where the right action is most probably found, and consider the options that likely include the right action. Any actual moral choice is *precisely* correct only from luck.[14]

This does not make moral choice significantly arbitrary in most cases. Ignorance of the precisely right thing to do matters little if I am choosing only among very good things to do or avoiding great evils, even if not the very greatest. There are cases where the want of decisive principles does make a moral choice significantly arbitrary because the options that remain after our current resources for moral reasoning have been exhausted are radically different in effect and character. Because reducing-suffering-principles are so central, those significantly arbitrary moral choices are experienced as tragic.

The capacity to suffer and enjoy are essential to the existence of most goals. That which can do neither may have goals, but will originate few, if any. Most goals can be traced to someone's capacity for suffering or joy, although not necessarily of the person whose goal it is. Because the truth of a moral principle (like the truth of any other belief) is known from its contribution to goal achievement, a true moral principle will not ignore, much less promote, anything which normally is a manifestation of frustration. The overwhelming tendency of suffering is goal frustration because avoiding suffering is a near universal goal. The reduce-suffering-principles could only be false in a world of individuals indifferent to suffering. Not our world.

Assuming people do not want to suffer, a principle to reduce suffering not only achieves goals, it simultaneously acknowledges that the sufferer, by virtue of being a sufferer, has at least one important feature of a verifier. Principles that promote any goals, for example, a principle that promotes stamp collecting, obviously acknowledges that those with that goal are capable of having goals, and so are eligible to be verifiers. But not all verifiers will have stamp collecting as a goal, and so refusal to promote stamp collecting does not by itself deny stamp collectors' status as a fellow verifier. Refusing to acknowledge others' interest in avoiding suffering comes much nearer the mark, for it is a goal shared by nearly all who have goals.

Do nothing to cause serious suffering, and *relieve serious suffering*, encompass many, but not all of our moral obligations, for there are some that relate to certain kinds of suffering that may not be serious, and some obligations altogether unrelated to suffering. Among the most important of moral principles that apply to suffering which may not be serious is *do not humiliate others*.

Humiliation can cause serious suffering, but a humiliating experience may be of such short duration, and the memory of it so evanescent, that we would not call the suffering it caused serious. Still, we detest any humiliation. A fleeting toothache may be more painful than a fleeting humiliating experience, but there is moral weight in the humiliation absent from the toothache. While both can result from wrongful actions or innocent circumstances, humiliation always has a social dimension. Humility may be the virtue of not thinking overly well of yourself, but feeling that others think poorly of you does not make you experience them as virtuous; it makes you feel devalued. It is a reduction of the worth of oneself, and so a threat to one's very selfhood. Its direction is depersonalization. Extended, it presages the annihilation of the humiliated self. *Do not humiliate others* is a moral principle that expresses the universal interest in being counted among those who count and deserve to be heard.

Although its implications are less clear than are those of the two reduce-suffering principles and the *do not humiliate others* principle, *enable others to formulate and achieve their goals* merits consideration as a basic rule of morality. It is not assimilable to the reduce-serious-suffering principles because not all unmet goals lead to disappointment, and not all disappointments are serious. It is an independent principle, because there are goals that don't treat of suffering. An interest in traveling may have nothing to do with avoiding suffering. *Enable others to formulate and achieve their goals* enacts the truth that others have goals which constitute objective reasons for action if our own goals do. And although we all don't always like being helped, having others enable us, at least minimally, is a prerequisite to all goal achievement. To begin with, it disbars disabling activity. Our ability to achieve goals requires others to refrain from getting in the way. More positively, to reach any goal, we need raring when young, and for goals of even slight complexity, we need social cooperation and support throughout our lives. Like the *do not humiliate others* and the reduce-serious-suffering principles, *enable others to formulate and achieve their goals*, reflects a general recognition of others as beings with goals, and commands that we put that recognition into practice.

Enable others to formulate and achieve their goals and *relieve serious suffering* are endlessly applicable, seemingly requiring an exhausting moral rigor. Peter Singer believes morality does demand we put aside all endeavors that don't have us always doing all the good we can, and insofar as Singer cuts us personal slack, it is a concession to human frailty. However, being a "moral saint" is not simply beyond most humans' abilities, it is, in many respects, unappealing. If the *enable others to formulate and achieve their goals* and *relieve serious suffering* principles entail sainthood as the universal personal ideal, there is reason to doubt their truth.[15]

In a rationalist pragmatic context insatiable moral principles that would gobble up all other projects are curbed. Reason is the guide, and moral principles are only part of Reason. Practical reason encompasses prudential reasons as well as moral reasons, and perhaps reasons—aesthetic?—that are not well characterized as either. The nominal domains of practical reason are a taxonomy of convenience. "Moral" reasons focus in on effects on others, prudential on the self. But practical reason takes all action as its purview.

It may be (I think it is) true that you ought to help others achieve their goals, and true that you ought to pursue your own goals, and true that in some situations the first principle should rule, and the second in others. This is not to fall into an intuitionism as the ultimate arbiter of practice. Reason can still reign so long as the principle used to decide between the competing principles is true. The evidence for its truth would be further experience, the same sort of evidence that supports any substantive belief. The deciding principle may be continually confirmed as the correct arbiter of similar conflicts, or experience may show it in need of modification, or perhaps prove it false.

The minimal threshold for truth is consistency, which is why, given belief in the existence of others, No Double Standards is ensconced as the best established principle of practical reason. It is far from obvious that No Double Standards would make it rationally required that everyone (maybe not even anyone) be a moral saint. I have no expectation that others give up their minor goals for my somewhat less minor goals, nor any resentment that they don't. Indeed, even were my health or life at stake so that serious suffering was in play, I would not necessarily expect someone to give up their dream of being a ballerina to rescue me. No Double Standards often leads to morality (altruistic acts), but it also limits morality. As I would not choose to be a saint, so I would not compel others to be saints. I believe having personal goals that rule out sainthood is widely shared, so I highly doubt that true moral principles mandate sainthood.

However, none of that means fairly strong, open-ended principles to reduce suffering or enable others' projects is wrong. It just means there are other right things too. Reason only rules out having different standards for oneself and others. That is what is, as best as we can tell, always wrong.

3. NO SELVES

These principles grow from the metaphysical underpinnings of rationalist pragmatism, underpinnings that not all philosophical and cultural traditions share. There are worldviews that take selves to be unreal, and the unreal is seldom taken seriously. I began with the belief that selves are real, that I am a self and that others are too. But if one believes that selves are "unreal," a very different morality, or, I'd argue, "amorality" ensues. Arguments against the cogency of amorality in the context of a metaphysics that believes there are selves do not touch claims of an amorality rooted in the denial of the existence of selves. Belief in selves—persons—is the metaphysical presupposition of morality, and within metaphysics that do not share that belief the theoretical need for and problematics of morality disappear; where there is neither self nor other there can be no objectively correct interpersonal relations.

I have not argued that there are selves. In the first chapter, I simply described what I take them to be. In chapter 3, I argued that selves, if there be such, necessarily emerge with other selves and create and are created by the world they share. The cost of truly abandoning a notion of selves—of persons—is great; truth and the external world melt away. But these are only "costs" to a believer in the reality of selves. Without selves, the dichotomies of me and the world, me and you, right and wrong, true and false, not only vanish, but their disappearance is counted a benefit.

In spite of no-self philosophical traditions, no society actually dispenses with any notion of persons in practice, and so all have normative principles meant to govern relations between persons. Nonetheless, if persons are supposed to be an illusion, things of almost no substance compared to the truly real, the resulting interpersonal principles seem likely to reflect that metaphysical stance, and not in ways that believers in persons are likely to approve.[16] The demotion of persons to insubstantial illusions must put in doubt the solidity of principles meant to guide them. At least that is so in theory. It is for historians and social scientists to say whether and how a culture's official ideological allegiance to no-self metaphysics has affected its moral practices.

4. ANIMALS

Any metaethics that did not support the intuition that animals' interests are of moral concern would be unacceptable. Rationalist Pragmatism may appear to be such a metaethics. It grounds morality in our social system. A social system is the collection of individuals that can make and respond to each other's truth claims and with whom we are, were, or will be, however indirectly, in communication.[17] Moreover, the justifiability of the claims made is judged by the collective goal achievement of the members of the social system. That is what objectivity amounts to. Together, these positions might give rise to the appearance that rationalist pragmatism cannot undergird respect for animals' interests; animals are not part of the social system, don't make truth claims, and their goals are not used as a measure of truth.[18] It could appear that, morally speaking, in rationalist pragmatism animals don't count.

However, that conclusion is wrong, and stems from confusing the grounding of morality with the scope of morality. While animals do not participate in justifying true moral principles, once justified the principles apply to them. If communicating beings judge the principle "suffering ought not to be caused without compensating goods" that principle applies to animals. Animals don't get a "say" in what is right or wrong, or indeed about truth in general, but our beliefs include them. The cow can neither question nor confirm my judgment that it is a mammal, and the cow does not participate in evaluating my belief that all mammals have kidneys. But having arrived at those judgments, if I am to be rational, I must conclude that the cow has kidneys. Animals do not validate truth, but there are truths about animals.

Some animals are capable of suffering and many do suffer at our hands. We do not need to take animals' perspective to know these truths. Animals do not have to assert that humans harm them for us to evaluate the assertion. The evidence of animal suffering at our hands is readily seen from our own perspective. To deny the evidence that we cause animals to suffer would require abandoning many highly useful general beliefs about the causes, signs, and symptoms of suffering. Moreover, we have come to accept many general beliefs about the benefits that do or do not justify a given degree of suffering. Although acceptance of these beliefs has been incremental, incomplete, and intermittent, they have proven their mettle in reducing our suffering. Any principle specifying that only some suffering requires adequate justification runs afoul of epistemic beliefs at the heart of our belief system, in particular, the principle that no distinction should be made without a relevant difference. In sum, if it is good to believe that humans can suffer, that we know humans suffer when they howl, writhe, and struggle to flee, that we ought to avoid causing humans to suffer unless the gain justifies the suffering, and that like situations ought to be treated similarly, then the only way we can be rational is to believe that we ought to avoid causing animals to suffer unless the gain justifies the degree of animal suffering.

This solution in no way makes animals of lesser moral concern than humans, it just makes them nonplayers in morality's construction. That human goals only, and not animal goals, measure the truth of moral judgments, does not diminish the protections those truths give to animals relative to humans. Of course, one could say that considering the animals goals (which we would have to attribute to them in any event) as measures of truth might result in a different morality, i.e. different moral truths. This is true. A morality shaped by a lion, a rabbit, a cow, or a lobster's perspective would undoubtedly be different from our morality. But unless and until animal beliefs become part of our social system, that morality is unavailable. Animals do not tell us how they see matters, nor contest our claims about how things stand. From our perceptions of animals, we infer things about them, the way we do with all non-communicants, from stones to stars, from insects to infants. We must apply our morality to them, in accordance with our best understanding of their nature. But that application would require a far different treatment than they now endure at our hands. And far better.

NOTES

1. Taking the metaphor seriously as a useful heuristic for illuminating our morality does not imply that our morality takes the metaphor literally. What role any belief

in God or our being in the image of God plays in the actual formation of our morality is irrelevant to the above discussion.

2. Feuerbach (1841). Marx (1844) had interesting insights into the how.

3. Act I, Scene 7. There is a dual sense of judgment at play: Macbeth will be judged, because he was capable of judging.

4. Bentham (1789).

5. At least insofar as goal achievement and frustration most frequently involves suffering or frustration.

6. See Fricker (2007) for an insightful, extensive discussion of the morality of treating, and failing to treat, others as knowers.

7. In the appendix, I'll endorse love as a tool for weighing objective value, but that is different from it serving as the standard moral relationship. A scale tells me the weight of an object, but it doesn't lift, carry, drop, fatten, reduce, or treat of the object in any way.

8. This metaphor is suggested by Lackoff and Johnson (1980) in a different context. Fesmire (2003) embraces the metaphor of moral judgment as artistic creation, albeit with less emphasis on the collaborative aspect, and more on the imaginative dimension. This leads him to develop the emotional implications rather than the cognitive ones of an ethics inspired by pragmatism.

9. Thus, Habermas' ideal speech situation (1971) is extended beyond explicitly discursive contexts into all interpersonal interactions.

10. Again, I am not saying that only passions are motives, but rather that the aim of any motive is the satisfaction of a goal, and that goals typically make reference to *someone's* desires.

11. These sorts of principle R. N. Smart calls "negative utilitarianism," and are advocated by Popper (1945). The "exploding world" objection can be found in Smart (1958).

12. See Kuhn (1962) and Quine (1953).

13. I am inclined to agree that the unanticipated and painless destruction of all sentient beings would be wrong, but it is a close call rather than a very strong intuition. It is not clear to me that knowing what we know, and knowing what he should have known, the Bible's God was correct when he looked upon his creation and declared it good.

14. My account of moral principles invites comparison to Kant's (1785) imperfect and David Ross' (1930) prima facie duties. Like those duties, true moral principles, considered in isolation, can conflict, and we are bereft of a procedure for resolving the conflict. But I think there is an important difference on this score between Kant's imperfect and Ross' prima facie (or conditional) duties, and true moral principles considered in a rationalist pragmatic context. The former duties remain eternally conflicted in some situations, and only an "intuition" underlies the rationality of the correct choice of action in those situations. In RP, the true principles only appear conflicted in some situations because our knowledge is incomplete, but there is a rationally warranted standard, although we might not possess it, which would resolve the conflict. In RP we can aspire to *reasoning* our way to the correct moral choice, not just hope we are blessed with the correct "intuition." Admittedly, often in practice

there is not much difference, but a theoretical necessity to resort to intuition encourages the premature abandonment of reason, before reason has a chance to get us close to the correct set of options.

15. Singer (1979), Wolf (1982). Singer is a utilitarian, and believes maximizing utility does require something approaching moral sainthood. The term "moral saint" is taken from Susan Wolf whose article of that name is the best discussion of the issue grappled with above. Wolf makes a strong case against moral hegemony, compellingly painting Singerian moral demands as unreasonable fanaticism. While she makes a feint at the reason endorsing solution I will argue for in the text, she shies away, fearing *any* overriding ideal will lead to a similar fanaticism. She ends up with intuitionism. But I do not see how an ideal of reason leads to an objectionable fanaticism.

16. Arthur Danto (1987) has insightfully explores the moral implications of Eastern philosophies skepticism regarding selves.

17. Thomas Pölzler points out (personal communication) that the relationships constituting a social system are not fully dialogical; past members cannot respond to future members of the social system. While this does diminish their role as verifiers relative to later members of the social system, it does not in the least diminish their *goals* as part of the standard for judging truth, nor does it eradicate their assertions as relevant perspectives that must be taken into account.

18. Korsgaard (1996) makes animal vocalizations a form of communication that does make a morally relevant address to us, but I don't think she is arguing that the animals make assertions, whose *truth* we can accept or deny.

Chapter 8

Political Implications

The basic tenets of rationalist pragmatism—that Reason discovers truth, that truth is recognized because it serves all individuals as well as any alternative set of possible beliefs, and that the experiences and goals of every perspective is relevant to verification—all these grow from the seminal belief that others exist. In this chapter, I will argue that this conceptual framework, in addition to supporting the primacy of the moral principles argued for in chapters 6 and 7, recommend liberal democracy as the most justified political constitution.

Rational Pragmatism's (RP) endorsement of liberal democracy is as politically conventional as its endorsement of the injunction to reduce suffering is morally conventional. Moreover, many of the political arguments that flow from RP metaethics recapitulate classical arguments for liberal democracy found in the utilitarian, Kantian, and social contract traditions. However, I believe that rooting those familiar arguments in RP both reveals their common ground and strengthens their grip. It also suggests why certain political positions—cosmopolitanism and what I call "socialist *values*"—are likely corollaries of liberal democracy. As in the case of RPs formulation of long widely held moral principles, recontextualization of commonplace political principles can give familiar ideas and ideals a new feel and renewed vitality.

1. DEMOCRACY AND POLITICAL EPISTEMOLOGY

Whether democracy is truly the best form of government rationalist pragmatism must concede is an empirical issue. Democracy—political accountability to the ruled—is neither necessary nor sufficient to guarantee RP's ideal: the consideration of the widest array of individuals' goals and experiences. Inquisitive, broad-minded, empathetic, psychologically perceptive autocrats could seek out and consider information from all perspectives, and demo-cratically elected officials could be, indeed commonly are, close-minded, unimaginative dogmatists who are all but blind to perspectives unlike their own. Election does not assure social sensitivity, autocratic political power does not preclude it. It must be left to historians and social scientists to deter-mine whether the preponderance of experience shows that consideration of other viewpoints is best promoted by democratic governance.[1] However, har-nessing self-interest to an interest in other's viewpoints is bound to strengthen the latter. And democracy gives politicians an interest in others' viewpoints.

I do not deny that there are genuinely public spirited officials for whom self-interest drives no policy decisions. Politicians, whether democratic or not, might well care about their constituents or subjects for purely moral rea-sons. Politicians can aspire to objective truth, and prize rationality as much as any philosopher, physicist, painter, or plumber. But for those politicians whose rationality does not transcend the limited subjective truth that guides prudence (and most of us are mired in the prudential most of the time), democracy aligns prudence with the fuller practical rationality that incorpo-rates morality. One need not be a cynic to hold that politicians are, like most people most of the time, most reliably motivated by self-interest. Although historians and political scientists must examine the record to see whether democracy has in fact inclined politicians to consider the perspectives of the governed, we can look at the basic mechanism that would make this inclina-tion utterly unsurprising.

There are two prerequisites for considering others' perspectives: knowing of the perspectives and caring about their revelations. Let us examine know-ing first. To know a perspective, a governor must be aware that it exists and have access to its contents. Both are encouraged by democratic accountabil-ity. Politicians want to stay in office. If office depends on others' approval, and their approval flows from their perspectives, at a minimum a democratic politician needs to be aware of those perspectives in order to appeal to them. To respond to what people think you must know that they are thinking. Democratic accountability makes other people s' thought integral to politics.

The effectiveness of any political appeal depends on more than mere awareness that there are perspectives to appeal to; knowledge of their con-tents is crucial. (Hence, opinion polls, focus groups, "listening tours," town halls, and so forth). Security in office for the democratic politician makes her needful of the most subtle and detailed understanding of her constituents she can obtain, for such an understanding can shape her actions and rhetoric to extend her tenure. Seeing what your voters see, and feeling what they feel is valuable ammunition in defense of democratic office.

Beyond needing to understand others, the democratic politician is moti-vated to cater to the goals others' perspectives endorse. It is not enough to say "I hear you," the democratic politician must also persuade her constituents that she will act on what she's heard. "Feeling your pain" is an effective political stance because it indicates both vivid awareness of what others are going through and a motive—as a fellow sufferer—to cure the malady. The effective democratic politician must show she cares, and ultimately the test of caring is acting as if she does care.

It may be motivated caring; their constituents' goals need not be sincerely embraced as ends by the democratic politician. The democratic politician's adoption of her constituents' goals can be, for most politicians likely are, only means to prolonging her political status. Still, if they are indispensable means, they will be cared for; we care about our necessary instruments. A violin may have no value to a violinist apart from the music she makes with it, but she will lavish care on it for the sake of the music, as a soldier will on her rifle for the sake of its lethality.[2] Acting as if caring, without really caring, may be pandering for the sake of office, but the motive of a deed only reflects on the character of the agent, not the rightness of the deed. And considering others' experience is a step toward right action, whatever the motive.

Even well-informed pandering, of course, will not always, perhaps not frequently, result in policies that serve the social good—the best realization of everyone's goals. Giving people what they say they want and mirroring what they say they see, may not be giving them what they truly seek or incorporating what they actually perceive. Individuals may misrepresent their experiences—social inhibitions prevent honesty and introspective vision is often blurry. Self-reports are hardly incorrigible accounts of one's experiences and goals. And even when they are accurate depictions of experience and desire, they may result in policy preference and political allegiances that will frustrate the most enduring and satisfying personal goals. However dangerous it is, however well suited for corrupt employ by megalomaniacs, there is surely something to the notion of "false consciousness," the idea that people often do not know what's good for them. But still, hearing it from the horse's mouth is the best place to start to learn about how things look to horses and the best place to begin to consider what might be a good life for the horse. And democracies' deficiencies at recognizing or enacting the public good must be judged against alternatives; however trite the "demo cracy-is-the-worst-form-of-government except-for-all-of-the-others" sentiment may be, it rightly reminds us that practical evaluations are necessarily comparative. Nondemocratic government by perfectly benevolent social scientists would still need to begin by inquiring into the self-reported desires of "the people," to formulate policies that serve the people. Perhaps, for a time, benevolent rulers could govern well using already accumulated knowledge of human nature and "our people," without consulting those people or listening to their self-reports. But unless the rulers' knowledge was complete, and their people and the social circumstances unchanging, they would need to resort to the people's evolving experience to continue effective beneficence. The pursuit of objective knowledge in a changing world requires unending inquiry. Democracy promotes constant study of others' experiences and goals without relying on benevolent rulers' conscientious commitment to continuous research. The democratic politician's commitment to continuous research comes from wanting to keep her job, not from wanting to do it well. The search for objective political knowledge is immensely strengthened when the love of truth is buttressed by the love of job security. Democracy makes the match.

The decisive epistemic advantage of democracy is its acknowledgment that each citizen is the final arbiter of her viewpoint, each gets to say, in the end, what turned out to be truly good for her. A definitive diagnosis of "false consciousness" can only be made retrospectively by the same consciousness. Successful paternalism is only certified by the child that has become adult. Political power exerted against the manifest will of most people, on the grounds that they don't know what's good for them, can only be ultimately vindicated by democratic endorsement. The voice of the people is not the truth, but truth cannot be known without attending to it. That democracy compels listening to the people's self-reports RP counts a virtue, that non-democratic governance fails to enlist self-interest to compel listening, RP marks a political vice.[3]

2. LIBERALISM

The epistemic virtues of a democracy lie inert if it is not a liberal democracy. Truth is not approached by aggregating perspectives and calculating a mean. Knowledge does not emerge from massing the masses' beliefs. It is public deliberation that stalks truth. Voting without public deliberation is no more likely to get things right than is a jury that neither attends the trial nor collectively reviews the proceedings. The process we put juries through gives us a degree of confidence in their verdicts, and nonjury systems too demand that judges' verdicts are reached only after a highly specified deliberative procedure. Truth is found through an intersubjective process of competing, often clashing, claims asserted from differing perspectives.[4]

A society is liberal to the extent that it institutionalizes the conditions for the dialectic of individual perspectives. This dialectic is the life of public reason. The pillars of liberalism build the edifice of public reason, or more fundamentally, dismantle historical and natural obstacles to its exercise. The right to have and express an individual perspective, the conceptual and historical beginning of liberalism, is clearly a necessary condition of discursive inter-subjectivity, as is the right to hear others' expressions. Democracy without "free speech" and "free association" loses all of its capacity to track down truth. The denial of these rights is doubly damaging to public reason: it not only prevents the creation of increasingly objective public knowledge from the interplay of subjectivities, it also stunts individual growth toward objectivity. Teamwork happens only when players play together. No playing together, no teamwork. But in addition, not playing together makes each individual, *qua* individual, less skilled as a potential team player. So too with public reasoning; it does not happen when government denies the right to political expression and publication. And when it doesn't happen, individuals fail to develop their capacities for political rationality. If political rationality is among the cardinal civic virtues, then, while democracy exploits the virtue for political knowledge, it is liberalism which develops the virtue to be exploited. Without liberalism, there is scarce public rationality for democracy to engage, and no likelihood that democracy eventually outperforms other forms of government. Illiberal societies, that disallow communication and freedom of cooperative practical association reduces individuals' intersubjective engagement, which in turn distorts subjective self-understanding, makes subjective vision myopic, and prevents the formation of objective social knowledge.

Liberalism's individualism, egalitarianism, and ideal of government neutrality also contribute to the public pursuit of truth. Individualism recognizes that each perspective contains unique and significant information, and that the ideal of objective truth requires that no perspective be discarded. Egalitarianism goes a step further on the same road; not only must each perspective be considered, none should receive a lesser hearing. The goals and perspectives of the noble and the base, the propertied and penniless, the orthodox and heretic, all count the same, all are given equal evidentiary weigh. Social standing should have no bearing on political rights and civic standing. Equality before the law as a liberal ideal includes the notion that the law be judged by its effects on all it governs, and that the same effects are given the same weight, regardless of whom they are affecting. To assess the effects, we must hear from all and give all a fair, equal, hearing.

Government neutrality is another step in this same direction. A liberal government must create a public space where the unbiased consideration of multiple perspectives can flourish. Each must be permitted to enter public discourse unhandicapped by civic structures favorable to particular viewpoints. In addition to giving everyone a turn at the microphone, and listening attentively to each speaker, the microphone itself must be so placed and engineered to give no voices undue advantages. The public arena can only be equally conducive to each perspective if it is not grooved for the smooth advancement of some viewpoints, and thereby gives others a bumpier ride.

Government neutrality is the demand that the referees, settings, and rules of public discourse do not incline to particular conclusions, but rather remain forever open to further refinements and even radical revisions of political truth.

Democracies' epistemic dependence on a liberal order is vividly illustrated by the crass blindness of illiberal democracy to minority perspectives, a blindness that causes a profound ignorance that robs democracy of any cognitive advantages over autocracy. Any majority can ignore very many minority perspectives while remaining democratically empowered, for mere democratic election only requires majority assent. Without liberal strictures, democracy enshrines ignorance by systematically disempowering minority viewpoints, and a disempowered view is readily ignored. If much of the mores and policies of the past strike us as wildly ill-informed, even downright stupid, it is because liberal principles, when taken seriously, has moved us to include more perspectives into our public deliberations. It is liberal principle that enabled us first to consider women's perspectives that led to women's civic empowerment, and their civic empowerment that revealed the truth that wife-beating ought to be a crime. Liberal attitudes opened our ears to the perspective of the disabled, teaching us the truth that public space should accommodate all. It is easy to multiply examples: since the triumph of liberalism in the West the false beliefs about every sort of ethnic, religious, sex-related, national, racialized, or phenotypical minority, while hardly eradicated, have diminished, weakened, or at least been challenged.[5] Expanding the set of perspectives eligible for public view have transformed the unthinkable into the undeniable.[6]

Political liberalism's shares these norms with scientific inquiry where their power to discover truth is more widely acknowledged. When experimental results and explanatory hypotheses are suppressed science is thwarted, when they are left unpublished, it is slowed. Science investigates, or at least acknowledges and is troubled by anomalies, it does not ignore them. Experimental and theoretical errors are eliminated by other experiments and more satisfying theories, but this contest of experiences and interpretations only works well if all experiences and interpretations are permitted in the arena. The norms of scientific exchange are liberalism applied to the quest for natural knowledge; political liberalism is the application of those norms in the quest for social knowledge.

Besides activating democracy's epistemic powers, liberalism directly achieves a marker of truth: individual dignity. The equality that liberalism (in theory) bestows on all individuals contributes to a goal we presume all to have: recognition as a person—as a being capable of formulating a judgment and asserting a claim worthy of consideration. Liberalism is then both a way to find truth and a manifestation of it; it discovers goals and realizes a central goal. Liberalism is constituted by a set of procedural norms whose enactment realizes the substantive good of individual dignity. An illiberal regime may have some virtues, but it is necessarily flawed, and the flaw is no mere mote; however, contented, considered, and recognized the subject of an illiberal polity, she lacks the Rousseauian dignity of being self-governing.

Although it is an empirical question amenable to new evidence, we would be quite surprised to find that we could live happier, more dignified, more egalitarian, and overall more satisfied lives in an undemocratic, illiberal regime than in a liberal democracy. We cannot rule out such a surprise, but in the absence of a preponderance of evidence to the contrary, the theoretical case that, over the long term, liberal democracy will most likely land upon and enshrine the correct political principles should win our endorsement. That it is an endorsement open to revision in light of new evidence does not make it a tepid endorsement. It is a mistake, unfortunately common, to confuse nondogmatic beliefs with a weak will to defend and enact them. One does not have to be certain that liberal democracy is the best form of government to act confidently and decisively in its defense. Nonetheless, those who construe all pragmatisms as forms of relativism, and all admissions of fallibility as disabling doubt, will judge RP a poor foundation for a confident liberalism. As it is, many already think liberalism, and "wishy-washy" liberals, ill-suited for staunch defense of any social values. Grounding liberalism in an explicitly pragmatic, fallibilist epistemology might serve to heighten those concerns.

It shouldn't. RP's conceives of knowledge as relative only to a social system; with regard to anyone, we will ever know the truth is absolute. RP applies a single standard to anyone with whom we dispute social policies. It provides no theoretical bases for waffling equivocation. When we have a genuine political disagreement, someone is right and someone is wrong. Our argument is not about whether there is political truth, only about what is true in the matter at hand. RP can argue for the truth of liberalism as confidently as clerics can for theocracy, and with better reasons.

Belief that there is political truth is a prerequisite for seeking it. Belief that you can never be certain you've found it, RP's fallibilism, does not preclude forceful commitment to what you have found. Although we can never be certain who, if any, among disputants is right, uncertainty need not be paralyzing or enervating. Doubtful outcomes do not deprive athletes of competitive drive or soldiers of fighting morale. Most struggles are uncertain of victory without loss of vigor. When uncertainty is lodged in the rightness rather than the likelihood of the outcome, belief in probable rightness remains as motivating as belief in possible achievement. If we feel it is important that we win, so long as our prospects are not hopeless, not an absurd longshot—in love, war, or sport—the *possibility* of defeat does not weaken our efforts. If we feel it is important that the right prevail, so long as we think we are likely right—the *possibility* we are wrong should not weaken our commitment.

Consciousness of the possibility of error might cause hesitation where dogmatic belief would spur headlong engagement. He who hesitates is, indeed, *sometimes* lost. But far more often, a reflective pause prior to commitment, a pause motivated by the possibility that we might be wrong, is beneficial. This is especially so in social policy, where complexity of effects and difficulty evaluating results make second and third thoughts apt. Existential dread that you might be wrong should accompany any action that will have large-scale, long-term consequences. Ongoing willingness to question an ongoing commitment, again sometimes, might weaken efforts, but more often openness to midcourse corrections is a benefit. Knowing she might be wrong does not divest the RP liberal of political commitment or energy. It might slow her down, but that is generally to the good. Critical forethought is compatible with enthusiastic engagement.

A very different group of critics might object to RP's as a theoretical justification for liberalism because they view it as incompatible with the central liberal ideal of tolerance. These critics think relativism the natural ally of tolerance, and any belief in singular political or moral truth the high road to suppression of dissent. But this discounts RPs fallibilism and confuses RP's doctrine that there is a truth, with the belief that we certainly possess it, and possess it whole. RP holds that no set of current beliefs are the full truth and accepts that anyone's beliefs, including one's own, might be further from the truth than an opposing set of beliefs.[7]

It is relativism which leaves vulnerable the ideal of tolerance. If there is no political truth, or if one "truth'" is as good as another, all that remains is to work for the triumph of one's own preferences. Nothing is lost by suppressing others' opinions or values, for there is nothing there to lose. If we cannot be wrong we cannot do wrong by shutting down others. RP's twin securing of tolerance, as a way of hearing the truth, and a way of realizing the truth that self-expression is a universal goal, is unavailable to the relativists who have drained truth of its power to support rational judgment.

3. SOCIALIST VALUES

If morality is the realm of practical reason that prescribes how we ought to treat each other, politics is the realm of practical reason that constructs the institutional setting for that treatment. The dichotomy, of course, is not that sharp. How we treat each other creates social institutions—explicitly in drafting constitutions, legislation, and law enforcement, implicitly in the daily creation and recreation of political culture. Hence, morality is political.

And politics is morally fraught; in the creation of institutions, we employ and endorse interpersonal principles. Still, the differences between the direct interpersonal application of practical reason—morality, and its application to social structure formation—politics, calls for distinct principles.

In chapter 6, I argued that "no double standards," is the fundamental norm of practical reason because it best expresses the egalitarianism at the heart of RP; rudimentary egalitarianism initiates objectivity, and objectivity reveals the truth of egalitarianism. The belief that others are of my kind, equally capable of responding to reasons, generated the moral principles of chapters 6 and 7.

Egalitarianism is no less central to RP's political implications, for true political principles must also meet the standard of objectivity. Socialism, the historical ideology that most consistently champions egalitarianism,[8] prominently features the values that should guide RP inspired politics. No metaethics, including RP, will have clear policy implications, and, even if it did, the term "socialism" in both theory and practice has been used to designate such an extremely broad set of policies, it would be absurd to say that RP supports "socialism." However, the commitment to actual human equality and material equality's role in realizing it I think is fairly called a (perhaps the) socialist *value*, and RP does help ground that value. Yet RP support for the value is not necessarily support for traditional socialist strategies for realizing it. Indeed, there are reasons to believe that some cherished socialist nostrums are undermined by the moral principles RP would seem most to support.

Socialism recognizes that equality of personhood, a liberal ideal, is not separable from material equality. Marxist materialism, socialism's canonical metaphysics, does not deny spirit, but it rejects the idea that spirit floats free from practical relations of material production and distribution. Formal political and legal equality falls short of respecting equality of personhood, because personhood is about more than an abstract, impersonal official status. A person has specific, concrete, *personal* goals, and if social arrangements are biased to favor the achievement of some persons' goals, thereby disadvantaging others', equality of persons is diminished. The socialist value of meaningful, practical equality promoted through social arrangements politicizes rationalist pragmatism's fundamental recognition that others are like me and consistency demands they be treated as such. It follows that securing material equality should be the default principle of governance. At a minimum, social arrangements must provide the food, housing and health care that sustains life. Respect for personhood must begin by ensuring its embodiment. Moreover, if that assurance forces some, but only some, to struggle for the basics, consuming all their time and energy, crowding out the pursuit of any goals beyond biological survival, their personhood has been discounted. If it is true that all people's goals count equally, then Reason requires that all be fed, housed, and healed, and none be confined to that minimal state while others transcend it.[9]

Besides sustaining life and freeing-up energy for goals beyond survival, material resources enable effective pursuit of projects with a material element. Not all projects do, and perhaps some of the most important don't. But many endeavors require goods and services, or are helped by them. Often, the more material resources, the merrier. The universal utility of wealth is a truth universally acknowledged. East European dairymen and English gentlewomen all want to be or marry a rich man. Nearly every departure from material equality favors some individuals' goals and demotes others in comparison. The RP ethic of treating people consistently would have us value material equality and promote it through policy.

However, lack of material resources is not the sole impediment to goal achievement, and it may be that at some times and in some ways, maintaining or striving for *strict* material equality will damage other dimensions of equality. The extent to which generating extensive social wealth requires differential material distributions is an empirical question, but it does appear, contra socialist hopes, that intense, reliable labor and efficient investment, at least over time and distance, must appeal to narrow material self-interest. Apparently, ideological commitment and moral education cannot sustain high levels of production.[10] It may not be an iron law of human nature or economics, but hard work and well-calibrated risk taking seem to be both needed to create wealth and most reliably elicited by compensating individuals who work hard and calibrate their risks well. You get what you pay for. Distribution divorced from productive roles might lead to fewer material resources for all.[11]

An enforced universal egalitarian poverty is not simply overvaluing equality at the expense of other values (e.g., happiness)[12] it also turns equality into an empty abstraction removed from concrete, practical equal respect of persons. There is a formal equality when all are equally *un*able to fulfill their goals, but concretely that is an equal disrespect for persons—hardly the sort of equality that RP or socialism values. *Nobody can do what they want* is not a realization of equal respect for persons. Complete socialization of economic activity is not a morally enjoined policy if its consequences were that personal goals were, in general, harder to realize.

Even if it were empirically possible to produce great wealth with a strictly equal distribution of that wealth, so long as that abundance fell short of meeting all material desires, equality would require differential distributions. As long as not everyone can have everything, giving everyone the same amount of money is not treating them equally. Not all goals are equally dependent on material resources: the contemplative needs solitude, the scholar time, the performer attention. Social arrangements that afforded all equal and great purchasing power, but none solitude, would respect the house-proud person more than it would the aspiring hermit. Equal income for all under a regime of compulsory 80 hour work weeks, even if it made us all rich, would leave many a leisure lover treated as a lesser person. And equal compensation, however adequate for typical human ambitions, would leave those whose goals were heavily dependent on wealth, with less wealth than they wanted. Such material girls (and material boys, women and men) would be disadvantaged relative to those whose goals were more ethereal. Enforced income equality would rob those of a consumerist bent of the power to direct their talent and energy to the achievement of their goals. Distribution policies should be structured so that individuals can tailor their efforts to acquire the material resources that best match their priorities.[13]

The limits of material equality to realize full equality is obscured by the thoroughness of contemporary capitalism's ability to commodify all value. Solitude, time, attention, and almost any other object of desire are purchasable. When all objects of value enter the market, material equality seems a very close stand in for equality of persons. But material equality's imagined ability to mimic true equality by empowering all to purchase all they yearn for in a world where everything is for sale is an illusion of equality. All-pervasive markets are incompatible with material equality, and real equality incompatible with pervasive markets.[14] Everything simply wouldn't be for sale or affordable in a world without disparities of wealth; who would be the servant and who the master, who the mogul and who the trophy spouse? Not *all* goals could be bought if all buyers and sellers were equally wealthy. And when all things can be bought, true equality is impossible because those who seek goods which are destroyed by commodification would find those goods impossible to realize. There could be no just deserts if all deserts were for sale and one's conception of justice was something other than "fully paid for." Some things are essentially transformed when bought and sold, and so all-pervasive markets would deprive individuals who sought the untransformed originals. Respecting all persons' goals equally requires both more and less than material equality: more in that material equality alone does not guarantee equal consideration of all, less in that material equality can undermine deeper equalities.

What socialism gets right is that departures from material equality are in need of a broader justification, a justification whose plausibility wanes as the material inequality waxes. Material equality is too germane to true equality to allow significant wealth disparities without demonstrable gains of respect for all persons. There are probably empirical reasons, and certainly moral reasons to believe such gains flow from permitting *some* material inequality, refuting the rightness of the traditional socialist political agenda. However, socialism is right to see constraints on material inequality as necessary in the struggle

for genuine equality, and right to see the pursuit of genuine equality as the
basic principle of rational politics.

4. COSMOPOLITANISM

Are disparate treatment based on social identity ever endorsed by rationalist pragmatism? No detailed derivation is needed to understand that RP
grounded politics prohibits policies that systematically disadvantage any
subset of persons. However, the protections afforded "protected categories"
of American legal parlance are justified. Mere formal status equality is insufficient to fulfill RP's political ideals. Policies that effectively equalize the
goal achievement of individuals' in these groups with those of others' are
clearly justifiable when, as RP requires, their experiences are included in our
standard of political truth. It is not enough to make public bigotry illegal;
public life must be structured to value the well-being of all on equal terms.
What that structuring looks like depends on circumstances and actual effects
of particular policies. So, for example, while we cannot rule out a regime of
total "color blind" policies, some color-conscious policies are justified so
long as racial identification tends to socially discount the value of some persons' goals. The elevation of all into "people who count" is no more than the
traditional utilitarian injunction that all count for one, modified so that what
is being counted is not their happiness, but their viewpoint. It is a practically
consequential modification, for it is easy to misjudge the value of others
happiness unless we hear them evaluate it, and they get to pronounce on the
significance of their testimony.

Because many cherished (some have argued all)[15] goals are embedded
in specific cultural traditions, policies that are attentive to maintaining and
nourishing particular cultures are important parts of egalitarian politics. If the
culture of the Basque loses vitality, persons whose goals are inseparable from
Basque culture are disadvantaged relative to persons whose goals are housed
in Spanish or French traditions and words. The correct policies for respecting
cultures may be nothing more than permitting private cultural initiatives, or,
toward the other end of the spectrum, may require extending public educational and financial support to endangered cultural groups. At the farthest end
of the spectrum, complete cultural autonomy—the "nation state"—may be in
order. However, for rationalist pragmatism, nation states present dilemmas as
means of achieving "cultural equality" of persons.

Historical circumstances may make political autonomy of a cultural group
the only way of ensuring personal equality, and so a "right to national self-
determination" may be earned by a history of group oppression or circumstances of cultural vulnerability. However, unlike policies aimed at realizing

the equality of other groups, such as sanctioning same sex marriage, which only undoes baseless inequality, or affirmative action and access-for-disabled regulations, which only attempt to compensate for ongoing inequalities, all without creating further inequalities, political sovereignty to ensure cultural viability raises some serious egalitarian concerns in the course of addressing others.

The problem is not that political sovereignty is instituted to protect a culture, it is that it is instituted at all. While there are moral difficulties peculiar to the nation-state, any state which doesn't count all persons anywhere in the world as its citizens is seriously morally flawed. Noncitizens, whether resident in the state territory or not, are explicitly left unrepresented in that state's policy formation. Even if their views are considered, their disempowerment inevitably degrades the quality of that consideration. The distinction between citizen and noncitizen enshrines in law differential treatment of persons. While personal biases favoring family and friends within a legal structure that defines the scope of such personal favoritism is justifiable,[16] and even local government and civic associations may privilege residents and members, the sovereign authority, whose job is to ensure equal respect of persons, must be absolutely unbiased. Any multiplicity of sovereignties produces ultimate authorities prejudiced against some people. Even the most enlightened and cosmopolitan of states, if it has a substantial notion of citizenship, excludes persons.

Nor does the possibility, or the fact, of the excluded persons' citizenship in other sovereignties remedy the inequality. At best it adds a reciprocal inequality. Disregarding some is not made rational by their being regarded by others, nor by those doing the disregarding themselves being the objects of others' disregard. Mutual disregard does not cancel-out the inequality inherent in disregard. Citizen and noncitizen remain unequal, even if the inequality gets reversed with spatial location. Although a world without stateless persons, along with a world of only liberal, democratic states, would go a long way to mitigate the inequality, as would humane, protective policies to foreigners, a multiplicity of states is in principle politically unjust.

Ultimately, because the people of the world are part of the same social system, only world government can implement full equality. Such government might only consist of a small list of rights, a world court to judge of alleged violations, and universal agreement from local government to enforce the court's judgments. It need not have the panoply of functions and functionaries we associate with a sovereign state. It could, and probably should, leave enormous swaths of policy to the discretion of inferior governments. But it must have the authority and power to protect the equal personhood of all. World government is usually urged as the only path to world peace. War of course is always a plague of disrespect for persons, but a more general disrespect for persons is also defeated by world government. A perfected union of we the people must include all people.

There is nothing inevitable or natural about liberal democracy, much less liberal democratic world government. Whether long-term developments incline that way is for political scientists to judge. However, there is a sense in which liberal democracy and world government is the political *telos*: it is the ultimate political aspiration of the genuinely rational. Like other ultimate aspirations, it is irrational to seek it prematurely, to attempt it under conditions in which other political forms will better approximate equality. This is an end which may never, and perhaps should never, arrive, as circumstances for its correct actualization may never ripen. It can certainly not be forced. However, the concept of a liberal, democratic world order can help orient us in a quest for sound political principles.[17]

5. CONCLUSION AND METAPHYSICAL CODA

Persons—selves—have goals, and necessarily conceive of themselves as situated with others of their kind in a common world. The world is where selves meet and speak in cooperative pursuit of their goals. In service to the coordinated common working of the world, selves come to value truth, and create the standard for judging the truth of beliefs, including moral beliefs. That standard evaluates beliefs by their ability to effectively realize goals. Beliefs' effectiveness, and hence our knowledge of their truth, can only be discovered by attending to the experience and judgments of all selves—all the possessors of goals in our world who can affirm and deny. Anything less falls short of the objectivity that is the essence of justification. Falling short of justification diminishes our rationality. Reason therefore requires treating all persons equally, especially as beings who know, suffer, fail, and succeed—as beings that can verify and report on the status of their goals. Such is pragmatism's account of our morality.

Beyond the conviction that there are selves with goals, pragmatism is an epistemological stance that eschews metaphysics, but its epistemic views can favor particular metaphysical attitudes. If pragmatism has us recognize true beliefs because they "work best," then, for now, pragmatism is a friend of materialism. Our most serviceable theories, those we honor with the term "science," promote beliefs that treat the fundamental constituents of the universe as unthinking, unperceiving, goalless entities. Fermions have no feelings, bosons no beliefs. The raw ingredients of Being neither judge nor want. The strong force, weak force, electromagnetism, and gravity do not intend, understand, appreciate, or fear. Our current candidates for best beliefs make all things emerge from these mindless bits. They are materialist beliefs.

Idealisms, whether theistic or more abstractly philosophical, are, if not out-right inconsistent with our best science, an awkward fit. In the beginning was neither the Word, nor the Idea, nor acts of love or will. There was no eternal, uncreated spirit doing the creating. What appears to be true, what appears to comport with values, discoveries, and ambitions of science, what appears to be the most powerful beliefs for reaching our goals is that we are made from things that go bump in the night. This darkling plain of ignorant, clashing, hordes of particles is how we, as a kind, began and where we, as individual organisms, begin. Acceptance and understanding of these beginnings is the beginning of materialist wisdom. It is not, however, the end.

Idealists too often treat materialists as deniers of the spiritual. It is a charge which may stick to the crudest of materialists, but misunderstands the deepest materialist program, which is to explain spirit in order to better support it. Materialism does not hold spirit an illusion, it only holds illusory spirit's ontological separateness from matter. Contemporary pragmatism comes to its materialism through highly spiritual categories: goodness and truth. Pragmatism recognizes true belief by the good it does, and both truth and goodness are spiritual beings. These spiritual tools report that our best beliefs—the theses of contemporary physics, biology, and psychology—treat spirit as organized matter. Our spiritual nature, our commitment to truth, has led us to conclude our origins and components are material, and that our spiritual nature ignores this fact at its peril.

Nietzsche, the most spiritual and profoundest of materialists, says spirit is something about the body.[18] Spirit is better thought of as many things about the body, and the most valued forms of spirit materialize when the body forgets itself. This forgetting is a luxury that bodies can only fully indulge when they are running smoothly. The sweetest spiritual fruit, such as freedom and beauty, arise when their earth-bound roots are well nourished and their fleshy vines bathed in light. The struggling body enlists its spiritual creations in its struggles; our senses, perceptions, emotions, and intelligence are directed to bodily survival and alleviation of bodily stress. Indeed, evolution teaches that these spiritual forms come into being just because they do serve the body. Impressed to that service, spirit neglects its interests. "There was never yet philosopher who could endure the toothache patiently," may be hyperbole, but, although the "starving," artist is not all myth, the distressed, pained body (as opposed to the memory of the pained, distressed body) is rarely the source of music, poetry, humor, insight, or love. When it is, we recognize the accomplishment as heroic. The body at ease can release spirit to attend to spirit's own ends. Once satisfied the body puts spirit on holiday, where it plays and chooses its own destinations.

Truth is a product of the social body, and like other forms of spirit, is best bred in times of health. Social harmony—not to be confused with a repressive stability—allows us to work together toward more adequate beliefs. While great progress in knowledge has been born in revolutions, it is not social conflict that brings us nearer to the truth, but rather the attempt to overcome the source of social conflict, the falsehoods enacted by privilege and domination. All kinds of social deficiencies will suppress truth, but their common feature will be inequality among persons. Striving for equality is striving for truth—not just the truth that we are equal, but all of the objective truths that become manifest through social equality.

We cannot ever expect to be in full possession of final truth because although we can forever get increasingly close, complete, enduring, social equality will be as elusive as complete, enduring individual health. Even the healthiest person remains dimly aware of gravity and mortality. The body never can fully forget itself. No social order will be without status markers that tarnish the equal respect that all are always due. Disease-free immortality is an attribute of the gods, and domination-free social arrangements an attribute of heaven. But mythical status does not render the gods or heaven unworthy of emulation. That we will never have the bodies of Zeus or Aphrodite is no cause to abandon the quest for better health, strength, and beauty, and that we will never have an egalitarian Eden is no cause to abandon the quest for a society of full equality for all persons.

NOTES

1. If history testified against liberal democracy no theoretical arguments in its favor should persuade us of its rightness. There is however, no compelling empirical refutation of the practical superiority of liberal democracy. Historical teaching, as ever, appears equivocal; there is no decisive empirical case for the correctness of liberal democracy, but neither is there one against it. While this might change, in the absence of an empirical refutation, the theoretical case for the objective correctness of liberal democracy carries conviction. It may, however, seem that there is, at least prima facie, an empirical case that nondemocracies do better or as well as liberal democracies at meeting the goals of all who are under their rule. Pre-modern nondemocratic regimes in Samaria, Egypt, China, Rome, and Peru for example, were enduring, orderly and even peaceful for long periods (discounting state violence against its own subjects). Countless other monarchies and traditional authoritarian regimes appear to have been effective government that "delivered the goods." However, if we hear few complaints from the subjects of many of history's nondemocracies, largely slaves or peasants of one sort or another, it is implausibly attributed to the high general level of goal fulfillment. We must imagine the mute, illiterate denizens of history's ancient regimes as wretched even when politically docile. However, well served the thinly populated nobility and their immediate servants, officials, and ideologists may have been in their authoritarian states, if we count as persons the vast majority doing the heavy lifting, pervasive discontent surely prevailed. Of course, material

scarcity in undeveloped pre-modern societies, rather than their political institutions, may be responsible for their discontents. Poverty frustrates regardless of politics. And while poverty, especially relative poverty, is not independent of politics, the empirical case for liberal democracy must rest on either grounds separate from prosperity, or liberal democracy must be shown to be a prerequisite for prosperity. The case that it is a prerequisite looks shaky. Recent history has demonstrated that social wealth, and especially the exponential increase of productivity which creates it, does not depend on democracy, liberal, or otherwise. Singapore has achieved widespread prosperity; China and Vietnam have made great strides in wealth. Raising masses of people up from oppressive poverty, many into comfortable middle-class circumstances, apparently is possible with neither democracy nor liberalism. We can, of course, doubt the long-term sustainability of growth under authoritarian rule, and also doubt the stability of authoritarian rule in a middle-class society. In addition, we can note that by and large stable, enduring democracies rarely appear on the list of the poorest nations— but historical evidence by itself makes only the most tentative case for liberal democracy's economic utility. Is the evidence more robust for liberal democracies general utility? Do such societies in fact do better than competitors at realizing its members' goals? I don't know, and am doubtful anyone does. The relevant evidence is not easily identified, collected, or evaluated. It is difficult to measure "goal achievement" with precision (see the appendix). Surveys of self-reported happiness, satisfaction or contentment levels may be measuring something vaguely similar, but there is little reason to believe them valid tools for comparing inter-social goal satisfaction levels. And even if we could accurately now measure a society's relative goal achievement level, there are so many variables that affect goal-satisfaction, that it would be difficult to assess political structures' contribution to the total. When we throw in the small sample size, our inability to run controlled trials, and the fact that many plausible causal factors tend to correlate with political forms, it is clear we are confronting an especially devilish social science problem. Not a theoretically insoluble one, so we cannot be closed to possible evidence counting in favor of nondemocratic government. Certainly, the sometimes shockingly poor results of relatively liberal democracies (I write in 2019 United States) must count against dogmatic confidence in democracy's general utility.

2. Instrumental concern for constituent s' goals may transform into intrinsic concerns, just as the violoinist may eventually attach value to the violin's particularity apart from the music it can make, and the old soldier to the no longer functional rifle. Politicians may only care about wage levels because their voters do, but that is still caring, and caring about wage levels intensely and long enough to please wage earners, a politician may find herself with an intrinsic care for wage levels.

3. John Stuart Mill (1861c, chapter 3) makes similar arguments pointing out the epistemic advantages of representative democracy, but he does not focus on the way democracy also incentivizes representative governors to acquire and employ that knowledge.

4. The classic brief for the epistemic virtues of a liberal society is made in J. S. Mill's *On Liberty* (1861b), a version of which the argument in the text recapitulates in an RP context.

5. The tone of certainty in the paragraph should not be taken as a retreat from fallibilism. Of course, like any belief, the contemporary ones I cite as commonplace "truths" that I share with my likely readers may be false. The point here is that we think they are true and have discovered them because of liberalism. It will be the application of liberal principles that will prove them false if they are false.

6. For example, same-sex marriage (although, I grant, some still reject it).

7. Mill (1861b) is excellent on this and closely related points.

8. As ideology, not as implemented by communist states. Other than widespread poverty, very little is egalitarian about North Korea.

9. Much of my discussion of the rationale for material equality, and reasons I will give for departing from strict material equality arises from the same considerations that motivate Rawls' contractors in the Original Position (1971). Here I am concurring with Rawls' "thin theory of the good"—the notion that everyone finds possession of material resources valuable.

10. I take the best evidence of this not to come from communist societies whose tyrannies distorted all phases of life, but from communes situated in relatively democratic settings (e.g., kibbutzim) where resentments over the lack of correlation between consumption and productive contribution accumulated over the decades.

11. Their belief (and Rawls') that this may be the case leads Rawls' (1971) contractors to modify strict equality with the "difference principle," which permits inequalities precisely to the extent they raise the material floor.

12. This is Isaiah Berlin's reason for limiting the scope of egalitarian principles in politics (1998), and I agree with Berlin's value pluralism, that is, equality is not the only good thing, and agree that politics must allow for the emergence of those other good things (my point above). However, if I understand Berlin correctly, I disagree with him that these propositions entail that politics should sometimes abandon egalitarian principles. I think they only entail, as I will argue above, that politics should sometimes abandon strict *material* equality as an end of rational politics.

13. Rawls (1971) acknowledges this point by making equal liberty the first principle of justice. But this too much makes it appear that freedom is being counterpoised to equality. I think it more accurate to say that true equality—equal respect for all persons—entails promoting the highest degree of effective autonomous agency, which in turn permits, if not requires, limited material inequality.

14. For a good discussion of markets' relation to egalitarianism see Satz (2010).

15. MacIntyre (1984), Taylor (1989).

16. See the discussion of saints, chapter 7, section 2.

17. This concise defense of political cosmopolitanism elides many distinctions, objections and analyses of cosmopolitanism and closely related issues. For such discussions look at Singer (2002), Appiah (2006), Kymlicka (2001), and many of the essays collected in Brown (2010), and McKim (1997).

18. Nietzsche (1882).

Appendix

On Weighing Goals

A theory that rests morality on the justification of belief, and belief justification on goal satisfaction, ought to describe how goal satisfaction could be, however roughly, measured.

In chapter 4, I introduced a technical concept constructed to elucidate the idea of justification: "a social system." A social system consists of a group of socially (as opposed to merely causally) interacting individuals who have beliefs and are agents. This is a broader concept than that which is typically denoted by terms like "society," "community,"[1] or "culture," for any social interaction, by which I mean interaction in their capacity as believers and agents, however mediated, sporadic, or slight in effect, places individuals in the same social system. We are in the same social system as Montezuma because he had beliefs and took actions that we can respond to *as beliefs* and *actions*. Should we ever exchange beliefs with extraterrestrials, they will be part of our social system. Any individual who can challenge or accept each other's assertions belong to the same social system.[2] The relation is transitive. That is why you and I are in the same social system as Montezuma and any putative Vulcans that communicate with our descendants. The degrees of separation may be many, but if they are finite, the social system is one. There may be other elements of a social system which are not reducible to individuals, but individuals with beliefs and the capacity to act are, at a minimum, its necessary elements.[3]

A social system of beliefs (SSB) is the collection of all beliefs of every contemporaneous individual in a social system. Strictly speaking (which, of course, is not how we do or should speak when not philosophizing), only SSBs (and their expressions) are true or false. An SSB is justified if it serves the individuals of its social system as well as any alternative SSB.[4]

How might we determine, even in theory, that a SSB is serving the individuals of a social system better than an alternative SSB, and is therefore the (or at least a) true (i.e., fully justified) social system of belief (TSSB)?[5] Although we will never arrive at a TSSB, its explanatory function in RP is undermined if we cannot attach any meaning to an SSB serving the totality of goals in a social system better than an alternative SSB. We need to be able to compare one state of affairs to another, and say in terms of goal achievement which is the better.

Our fundamental strategy for determining how well beliefs serve a social system attributes comparative value through idealized hypothetical choices. Through a series of such choices, we can give meaning to the idea that a social system is better served by one SSB than it is by another. A TSSB provides optimal value (goal achievement) to a social system, and the degree of value is known by choices that would be made in idealized circumstances.

The idea of choice presupposes minds, acts, and options. Choosing occurs only where a mind conceives of alternatives states of affairs and acts to realize some and leave others unrealized. Choices can aim at maintaining or changing a status quo, and the act of choosing may fail to realize its aim. The aims of choices are goals, but not all goals are chosen. States of affair can be sought even if they must be sought. One can be compelled, by nature, irresistible desire, or failure to imagine alternatives to aim at a state of affairs. It is then an unchosen goal.

That something is a goal, a state of affairs sought by sentient beings, is a fact forged by natural or historically fashioned desires and beliefs. Desires typically nominate goals, and goals are the raw material of value. Choosing—selecting one goal and rejecting another—indicates the goal's degree of value—its "weight." Weight is a comparative concept. It is only in the presence of other goals that a scale is needed to measure the value of competing pursuits. A goal's weight is its ranking among other goals, and is best specified by the philosophical imagination. The core idea is provided by John Stuart Mill. The more valuable of two items is the one that would be chosen by a *competent* chooser. Competency requires full appreciation of the features of each item, in particular, acquaintance with the experiences a state of affairs would engender. Whatever would be chosen by such a chooser(s) is the more valuable. We may call any hypothetical procedure that determines degree of value by what would be chosen in specified circumstances an "ideal measure of value procedure" (IMVP). Mill has sketched one IMVP.[6]

It should be kept in mind that choices made in an IMVP do not reveal, let alone create, value. Mostly desire does. Desire for a state of affairs, or desire for its absence provides us with most, if not all, goals.[7] Goals (more precisely their achievement) are the items on our value continuum. An IMVP is meant to tell us where on the continuum a goal falls, not what qualifies to be on the value continuum. To say that all goals are on the value continuum does not imply every goal has positive value. An IMVP may reveal that the goal of not- X places the goal of X in the negative region of the continuum. Goals tell us what things are good or bad.[8] An IMVP tells us how good or bad they are.

An IMVP must create an ideal chooser(s) and choosing procedure that produces comparative weights without building biasing desires into the creation. This requirement is tricky. Initial goals, likely deriving from given desires, are necessary features of a chooser for her to produce any choice at all. She has to start off seeking some things before her choice can reveal which things she seeks more. However, the initial set of desires assigned the chooser can create biases by limiting the alternatives or rigging the scales. Roughly speaking, the biases can be of two varieties: the selected initial desires can privilege goals of particular origins, or the initial desires can tend to particular preferences. An example of the first is a chooser that starts off caring more about me than you, so her choice of my well-being over yours is not an impartial measure of our well-beings' comparative values. An example of the second type of bias is a chooser who begins with a sweet tooth. Her choice of a perfect dessert over a perfect savory, even granting she appreciates all of the features of each that makes it perfect of its type, is biased by her sweet tooth. It is unclear that any set of initial desires can escape this sort of bias. Yet an IMVP ought to provide a chooser with nonbiasing initial desires.

Subjective value is the value of a goal to a particular person.[9] In this sense, it is a candidly biased kind of value—it is the value of a state of affairs to a specified subject. The area of practical reasoning concerned solely with subjective value we may term "proto-rationality." Acting so as to achieve what one most values is acting proto-rationally. But prior to proto-rationality, there is impulse, the immediate satisfaction of the currently prevailing desire.[10] Proto-rationality is the efficient management of impulse in service to maximizing subjective value.

As noted earlier, desire is the kernel out of which most goals and therefore most value is constructed. However, the value generated by isolated desires is not yet subjective value because there is no subject. We get the beginnings of a subject for whom there is value, when multiple desires are attributed to a common desirer. Ultimately, we are interested in objective value, because it alone makes an SSB a TSSB. However, as a step toward it, before deploying an Ideal Measure of Value Procedure to measure objective value, we will construct an IMVP that measures subjective value.

Suppose the simplest situation: mutually exclusive states of affairs, X and Y. If a person, P, chooses to pursue X, knowing all the consequences of both X and Y, then according to a basic, but incomplete, IMVP which requires only full information for its chooser, X is more valuable than Y to P. But, if

P is indeed to be a person, then P must persist through time, and even with an unchanged understanding of the full consequences of each choice, P might change her mind and at a later time choose Y over X. So which is more subjectively valuable, that is, valuable to the person P, who made different choices at different times, X or Y?

Choice depends on belief. In the spirit of Mill, IMVPs usually posit a fully informed chooser. The true weights of values are given by the choices of all-knowing choosers. However, what would be chosen clearly can be affected by the chooser's desires as well as her beliefs. Choosers, however omniscient, will differ in desires and often make different choices. Proto-rationality varies across persons. Even within a single life, a chooser's desires change. Omniscient Patty at eighteen might not choose as would omniscient Patty at eighty, because, although cognitively identical, Patty at eighteen has different desires than Patty at eighty. If the IMVP is to provide anything beyond an evanescent, momentary notion of value, we must specify the chooser's desires. When P is considered as a self, the value of X to P should be measured by its value to P in the context of her entire life, but as a chooser, P will not be the same throughout that life, and yet the IMVP requires a *specifiable* chooser, with enough specific desires to determine a choice. Who chooses for P? What sort of chooser evaluates X for P?

Before describing the chooser, more needs to be said about the choice. Being fully informed, and choosing as a temporally extended self, P's choice of X is a choice of a life wherein X is chosen. The apt IMVP here should interpret every choice of P as a choice of a life. A stage of P can choose X over Y, and even though fully informed, the choice only gives us the value of X for that stage of P, and that stage of P is not P herself, for P consists of many P stages. When we seek to assess the value of X for P, we presume what P ultimately values is a good life. When the chooser for P picks X over Y, it indicates that P's life with X is better, in P's assessment, than her life with Y. The claim that Patty's choice to attend law school would lead to more subjective value than a choice to attend business school is the claim that Patty would have chosen the life the law school choice led to over the life the business school choice would have led to.[11] But which stage of Patty gets to make that judgment?

The most plausible chooser of a good life for P is P, but, our chooser chooses at a time, and so can only be a stage of P, whether actual or hypothetical. The designation of life stage matters. One possibility is to imagine a new stage of P that has all of the desires P ever had in the same intensity that P had them when they were had. However, this creation, besides being very unlike any stage of P, does not seem to be a good representative of P herself. P is a stretch of history, not a museum. The hypothetical stage that includes all previous stages makes a melody into a chord, and probably a discordant one at that. The collected desires of P's every stage would not yield plausible preferences of P, but rather the preferences of some nightmarish monster made from P parts. A "Patty" simultaneously besieged by her infantile, adolescent, mature, and senescent desires would yield no choices plausibly representing subjective value for the actual Patty.

The desires of an actual life stage of P, combined with hypothetical full knowledge, are a more plausible determiner of subjective value than a hypothetical stage of P that concurrently had all of the desires P ever had. However, the life that fully informed eighteen-year-old P would choose is not the life fully informed eighty years old P would choose. Although in reality, the different values of an eighteen and eighty years old is substantially due to relative knowledge (at eighty one knows more about the life choosing X leads to than one does at eighteen), even stipulating that each age of P is fully informed does not erase the possibility of different choices. Unless the strong Platonic line is correct, and all fully informed choosers would make the same choice, a chooser often chooses with more than mere knowledge—she chooses with desire, and so the IMVP determination of subjective value must specify more than just the knowledge state of the chooser. The chooser will have desires and goals that partially determine her choice. And different stages of P would have different desires and goals informing her choice of the best life for P.

P's oldest stage (assuming fully informed includes vividly remembering the attitudes, satisfactions, and preferences of all earlier stages) should be the hypothetical chooser. This is not because she knows more—*ex hypothesi* she does not—but because there is at least one plausible crucial element that adds value to a life which can only be authoritatively judged from the latest stage: an ever-improving life.[12] If one would choose a life that tended to get better over time—and that seems like a plausible factor that should figure in determining choice, then the oldest stage of life is the best chooser, for only the oldest stage of life can declare life improved. The property of "improvement" has a temporal component. Just as the "best life according to a 5 year old" must take the five-year-old's opinion as authoritative, an "ever-improving" life must take the final life stage's opinion as authoritative. An eighteen-year-old Patty that clairvoyantly saw and appreciated all that Patty experienced in her eighty years may think her life would be increasingly better over time were she to choose X, but if at eighty Patty would have a different judgment, then it cannot in fact be judged as ever-improving. Improvement is necessarily judged in retrospect.

This is not to argue that an improving life is the most important subjective good let alone the sole subjective good. It is merely to claim that it is a significant part of subjective value. If all other subjective values, unlike the value of an improving life, are equally accessible to every life stage, the value of an improving life can serve as a tie-breaker, a nonarbitrary way of selecting a particular life stage of Patty to choose for Patty.

The upshot is that X is more subjectively valuable than Y, if an idealized final stage of P, that is, as mentally acute as she has ever been and in full vivid recall of all of P's past inclinations, would want X to be chosen, in light of the life X would help create. Thinking of P as a self that endures over time, we suppose her idealized choices definitively indicate her subjectively best life, and we take leading her best life to be her goal. Although final stage P is using her final stage values to choose, she is choosing what she takes to be best for P, not best for final stage P. Eighty-year-old Patty is conceived of as (atemporally) proto-rational; she cares about her entire life.

Objective value requires an IMVP that confronts difficulties of specifying the chooser that are analogous to those of subjective value, but are not amenable to the same solution.[13] The difficulty common to knowing subjective and objective value through an IMVP is finding a chooser or choosing procedure that designates a preferred goal without unjustifiably biasing the choice against either a person-stage (in the subjective case) or a particular person (the objective case).[14] Just as there are many stages of a person that might make different choices even if each stage were fully informed, there are many people in a social system that would make different choices although all of them were fully, and therefore equally, informed.

In the subjective case, our solution was enabled by focusing on a good that was not a good for any stage of the person, but rather was a good—the good life—that was a property of a person, a self. While composed of life stages, the self is more than a stage, and most importantly, it has a good of its own, a good, that superseded the goods of life stages, a good to which the goods of life stages were mere means.

Social systems are different from selves. They have no good that is not reducible to the good lives of their members. The goods of stages of a life can be treated as instrumental values and assessed for their contribution to a good life, but individual lives cannot be aggregated as proximate goals serving a larger ultimate goal, the way stages of life can be aggregated into a single life.[15] Our task is to describe a choosing mechanism, an IMVP with a chooser, whose choices can be viewed as evaluating alternative collections of life courses, without the collection itself having any independent good.

If the social system contains no higher good than its individual members' good, we must devise an IMVP that represents each individual's good as an end in itself, not solely as a contributor to the nonexistent good of the social system. It is not enough that every person "counts"; they all must be well served.[16] However, just as in the subjective case, an IMVP determining comparative objective value must specify a chooser or choosers. This presents problems: If a single chooser is designated, how do we give her the specific desires with which to choose without biasing the scales against individuals inclined to make different choices. If we conjure a collection of choosers, which seems more suited for choosing a collection of individuals' good, why believe there would be anything approaching agreed choices?

Ideal Observer Theory, in its many varieties, attempts to construct a single unbiased chooser to reveal the good. Like most IMVPs, ideal observers are made fully informed. One approach to achieving impartiality has been to have the ideal observer live each individual life. The idea is to make the ideal observer's relation to individual lives the same as the relationship a stage of life has to a person's entire life. But that approach will not work for two reasons. First, it would allow the ideal observer to sacrifice one life for the good of another because the ideal observer had both, just as P is constituted by the various stages of P. In other words, it would create a social system good that isn't reducible to the goods of the individuals in the system—and there is no such irreducible social system good.

Second, depending on how it is thought of, the ideal observer who is living every life herself, is either just another unique individual with an enormous array of desires which in turn create unique, but not privileged, second-order desires (desires about or derived from her segmented lives) or the all-lives-lived ideal observer is not actually constructed to make ideal choices.

Consider how each conception only leads to an unrepresentative new individual: if in living the lives of each individual, the ideal observer is subjectively aware of her past lives, that is, remembers them, she is no longer a collection of lives but rather a new complex life, who has not actually lived our lives, which are very much structured by the finitude of their subjectivity, but a different life, that although it contains episodes similar to our lives as subsets, is itself another life. To truly live each life as it is lived is to never experience other lives. Our all-lives-lived ideal observer would have desires generated by her memory of past lives and anticipation of future lives. Now consider the alternative conception: if the ideal observer forgets the past lives, there is no longer any sense in which we have retained an ideal observer. At every choice point, she would choose with the desire set of the particular life she inhabited and her choices would be biased by the values and concerns of that life. No individual, however, conceived, by mere dint of her construction, can be assigned self-interested desires that impartially represent each of our well-being.

Instead of making the ideal observer the liver-of-all-lives, we can achieve impartiality by simply making her care equally about all lives (which, of course, is in line with this book's thesis that rationality calls for objectivity with regard to others' goals). An "equal care" stipulation directly addresses a bias in favor of particular persons. Indeed, God (the folk ideal observer) is traditionally conceived of as caring for all; we are his children and he is a loving father. However, making the ideal observer care equally for all still leaves her with a crucial deficiency: even if she cares equally about all members of the social system, what does our ideal observer care about in its caring? We need to specify not only the subjects of her concern; we need to specify what she wants for them.

Does the ideal observer have any initial desires? Presumably, she wants that each individual have the subjectively best possible life. The good of the ideal observer is simply the subjectively good lives of all lives she observes. What the ideal observer cares about, what she desires, is that each person live the best possible subjective life. The ideal observer, knowing for every P what choices final stage, fully informed P would make, knows what each P's subjectively best life is. We can call the ideal observer's goal the perfect collection of lives, the collection of lives in which each leads her best subjectively valuable life.

However, there is no reason to believe that the realization of the subjectively best life for each and every individual in a social system is possible. If, in my best life, I am married to you, and in your best life, you are not married to me, what would the ideal observer, although loving us both completely and equally, choose? The problem for the ideal observer is that in picking a collection of lives, if there is no collection in which everyone in the social system leads her subjectively best life, (and there is no reason to believe there is such a collection), then the ideal observer must choose among collections in which some individuals fall short of their best lives. Which of these nonperfect collections would an ideal observer pick? It will not do to invoke some formal measure that evaluates how "close" a collection of lives is to the perfect collection. No matter which formal measure we choose to evaluate relative proximity to an ideal collection of lives, there will be circumstances in which the formal measure will endorse a few miserable lives because those circumstances minimize the formal distance to the ideal. No measure of a central tendency, or measure of variability, eliminates that possibility. A quantitative approach can always justify a single, outlying miserable life.[17] But such sacrifices belie the concept of caring equally for each life. No loving parent of a billion children would consent to having one child lead an agonizing life so that his billions of sibling could lead near perfect lives if there was an alternative in which they all could live reasonably contented lives, albeit none came close to perfection.

However, caring for the goodness of each life equally would not lead an ideal observer to strive for proximity to strict equality of life outcomes (presuming that was determinable) either. Strict equality would not trump all other considerations for an ideal observer who cares equally for all. Again, resorting to the metaphorical loving parent of billions, varying levels of good lives for their multitudinous offspring would be chosen in preference to choosing equally middling lives for each. Neither strict equality of outcome nor a quantitative measure of proximity to perfection is a plausible principle of choice for the lover of all. We must resort to vaguer principles.

As the history of American constitutional interpretation vividly demonstrates, the application of vague principles is ineluctably subjective. The application must be made from a particular perspective that is partially defined by values. Although, knowing just what a collection of perfect subjective lives would be, and motivated to come "as close as possible" to that collection, our ideal observer's judgment of "closeness" would have to introduce values to realize a conception of proximity. There is no value neutral measuring rod of "closeness to the collection of perfect subjective lives."

So we are forced to imagine an ideal observer, a chooser who not only loves/cares for each life in the social system, but in addition has values. But which values to assign the ideal observer? It will make a difference. Two parents, each equally loving common children, each unmoved by any self-interest, each only wanting the children to have their subjectively best possible lives, confronted with the impossibility of both children leading perfect subjectively valuable lives might yet choose different "second-best" collections of lives for those children. Suppose Merle and Bret Johnson, the parents of Jack and Jill knew that Jill's most subjectively valuable life had her doing carpentry and Jack's would be as a nurse, but, in the Johnsons' world, these lives are inconsistent. Merle might judge that Jill being a carpenter and Jack being a teacher was closer to the ideal world, and Bret judge Jack being a nurse and Jill being an accountant closer to their children's collective ideal. These differing judgments would be informed by differing, biasing values.[18] However, an ideal observer without values cannot choose, and so could not function as a ranker of values.

In sum, we cannot devise an ideal observer that is above the fray of weighing values, which means the ideal observer cannot serve as the neutral source of objective evaluation. Knowledge of objective *perfection* can be given the ideal observer because it can be constructed entirely from subjective value, but knowledge of comparative value short of perfection requires an ideal observer with values of her own. However, an assignment of any particular initial values biases the ideal observer, and the assignment of all actually held subjective values into some leviathan chooser would create new particular desires just as biased.

An alternative approach creates an IMVP that is an assemblage of choosers, representing all actual lives, each with its own subjective values. We also imagine each chooser as, after the fashion of ideal observers, fully informed, including knowledge of her own and all others' subjective values. Finally, the choosers assembled care about every member of the assembly (themselves included) equally: a congregation of mutual, equal, and universal love. Each uses subjective values to choose, but the goal of each is not her best life, or at least not any more than it is the best life of any member of the social system. We shall call this assembly the ultimate position.

The nature of this IMVP is usefully compared to its inspiration, John Rawls' original position, which is also an assembly of choosers. The original position is an idealized choosing situation designed to reveal principles of justice rather than relative value, but it confronts the same issue of motivating choice in circumstances meant to ensure impartiality. Rawls motivates the choice by assigning each chooser identical initial motives—undefined self-interest, with freedom and the "thin theory of the good" as universally desired instrumental values for its pursuit.[19] Impartiality is achieved through the veil of ignorance—each chooser does not know who she is, or what her idea of a good life (our "subjective value") is—although she does know the range and variety of subjective values. The veil of ignorance disables both biases discussed above. A chooser in the original position has no reason by virtue of her identity (because she doesn't know it) to care more about one person than another, and the chooser in the original position is not employing any values not shared by every chooser. Neither one's identity nor tastes come into play in the original position.

Our assumption of universal, equal care for all, contrasts with the self-interested motives of choosers in the original position. The assumption of equal care for all effectively removes the first bias, the bias toward particular persons' well-being. The original position disables a bias toward particular persons through the veil of ignorance. Rawls requires the veil of ignorance because the only form of rationality he imbues his choosers with is prudence (proto-rationality), the quest to realize self-interest. We however, by presuming the rationality of objectivity (a presumption I hope the arguments of this book have entitled us to), of universal, equal care for all, defuse the danger that knowledge of their own identities in the ultimate position will bias choosers to particular persons.[20]

What about the bias that arises because a chooser must choose with a set of specific given values? Rawls seeks to avoid this bias by restricting his choosers to the universally useful instrumental values of freedom and material resources. But, if a chooser cannot ensure complete freedom and an abundance of material resources to pursue self-interest, these instrumental values by themselves determine no choice. Without additional personal preferences regarding risk and the evaluation of payoffs, all equally possible preferences, a chooser in the original position cannot determine what counts as maximization of these instrumental values. Indeed, Rawls' maximin strategy (in which the chooser seeks to maximize her worse case outcome) imports the substantive value of complete risk avoidance, that is, the highest possible floor is judged closer to perfection than the most likely particular outcome (the highest mode), or maximizing the likely outcome-region (highest median or mean) or indeed the highest possible ceiling (a maximax strategy). Rawls has the choosers choose with a particular and therefore biased value for ranking outcomes.

The choosers in the ultimate position, in contrast to Rawls, choose with their own subjective values. However, although the choosers in the ultimate position are biased by their personal desires, their collective choice is not necessarily biased. The ultimate position can harness particular inclinations to generate interpersonal, objective, valuations.

Whereas the original position suggests a negotiation among self-interested parties that is fair, the ultimate position posits a conversation among mutually caring members of a social system. Fairness is replaced by love. The parties in the ultimate position have different views of what is best for themselves and each other, but aspire to fully understand each other to reach a common view of what is objectively best for all. It is analogous to a perfect family dynamic. Fair negotiation is apt for rendering justice, loving deliberations for goodness.[21]

What choices are made in the ultimate position? We need not here employ the ultimate position to catalog and rank objective values. We need only show that it can, and how it can, assign goals relative weight. Our image of the dynamics of a perfectly loving family is the right intuition pump. It allows us to make doubtful some candidates as guiding principles in the ultimate position. A loving family, for example, does not try to maximize total happiness without regard to distribution. No matter how close to a perfect life being king would be for Dad, the perfectly loving family, each member of which is omniscient and supposed to have the typical mix of subjective values, would not consign Mom to a miserable life to crown Dad. Nor would it be guided by a maximin strategy, wherein the family would ensure that the least subjectively good life in the family were as good as possible regardless of how it hampered other family members' lives. Suppose sister's life as an architect would create a significantly better subjective life for her than her life as a cardiologist, and brothers' life as a chemical engineer a marginally better life than the one as a mechanical engineer. Even if sister's life as a cardiologist would still be quite good, and in fact slightly better than brother's life as a chemical engineer, and so a maximin principle would require careers of sister cardiologist and brother chemical engineer, the loving family would unanimously (loving brother and equally loving sister too) choose to enable her architectural life although it required brother to be a mechanical rather than a chemical engineer. However, if she'd be happy enough as a cardiologist, and the only way to make her an architect would be to force brother to become a lawyer, which would make him fairly unhappy, the loving family would opt for the cardiologist/chemical engineer state of affairs. Or at least that is my prediction of the upshot of a perfectly loving family's conversation.

In general, I think a loving family wants as high a floor for the goodness of the life of each of its members but also would choose to sacrifice small gains for one life to achieve significant gains for another. This is not a precise enough formula to determine all ultimate position choices, depending as it does on vague terms such as "small," "significant," "marginal" and so forth. Indeed, an ultimate position is not an effective decision-making procedure guaranteed to produce a result in a finite number of steps. Rather it describes the motives (universal caring—a desire to make every life as good as possible) and values (the subjective values that would emerge from the actual values of each member at the last stage of life) with which our fully informed choosers in the ultimate position deliberate. We, of course, can only imagine the results of such a deliberation, or rather the course of such a deliberation, for it is bound to be nonending. Objective weights might never be decisively determined, even in an actual ultimate position, and certainly not in our imagined approximations. Nevertheless, the ultimate position is an IMVP that gives us a tool to think about the weights of goals and a *rough* standard to measure them by.

NOTES

1. Although "community"'s connotation of common communication captures the essential element of social system. For more discussion of my concept of a social system see chapter 4.

2. As I pointed out in note 17 in chapter 7, section 4, because there is an asymmetry in our communicative relations to past persons—we can respond to them but not them to us—their status in the social system is problematic. They had goals, some of which we are aware of, and there seems no reason to discount their goals for judging a belief's utility. However, they can no longer participate in the ongoing activity of justifying beliefs. Yet unlike animals, who are of moral concern because our principles apply to their condition even though they do not verify the principles, past persons had been verifiers, and so not only should their goals be used to recognize truth, it strikes me that their judgments should be attended to (not of course necessarily agreed with) in spite of their inability to continue to defend or revise them. I conclude that they are in the social system, but SSBs are restricted to the belief sets of synchronous slices of the social system.

3. It is unclear whether there exists other social systems than the one we belong to, and unclear how we could come to know of their existence if there were any. How could we know there were others with beliefs if we could not accept or reject their beliefs? How could we know there were other agents if we could not recognize any of their purposes? Still, although we could not know of them without a merging of our social systems, nothing in principle rules out a multiplicity of social systems. Not

everyone in a social system need be able to communicate with everyone else in that system without a translator—whether cultural, technical, or linguistic. Brian Epstein (2015) argues that the ontology of social science requires more than individuals, and even a stipulated social concept, such as a "social system" might require primitive elements beyond individuals to be fully coherent.

4. For a given social system, it is theoretically possible for there to be multiple justified social systems of beliefs (TSSB), because alternative SSBs might serve its members equally well. This is unlikely, but in any event, for any social system there will be vastly more false (unjustified) SSBs than TSSBs.

5. Note that this is an important theoretical problem, but not at all a practical issue because we never assess our SSB, only much smaller subsets of it. How we do that I discussed in chapter 4 Section 7.

6. Mill (1861a). An IMVP is just the sort of entity that its critics find most objectionable in "ideal" moral theory (see the introduction). It imagines and then draws conclusions from impossible scenarios, whose impossibility they argue, deprives them of any relevance to our world. But the criticism misunderstands the function of such thought experiments. They are tools for clarifying intuitions and logical relations, and the only impossibilities they must avoid are logical. Like riding on a light beam or being in an absolute vacuum unaffected by the gravity of other bodies, many thought experiments cannot be realized. Trying to use them as engineering blueprints rather than for insight is madness, but refusing their illumination is positivistic myopia. Of course, in the application of whatever insight they afford the differences between reality and the thought experiments requires attention, and sometimes those differences will render the thought experiment as irrelevant to reality as the critics of ideal theory claim they all always are. But sometimes they help uncover the conceptual heart of an issue, or suggest a creative approach to a problem. Each thought experiment must be judged on its own merits.

7. This is consistent with my claim that an original desire on the part of an agent is not required for *that agent's* motivation. (See chapter 5 "Morality's Motivational Powers.") Somebody at some time usually has to want something for a goal to be formed, but a person doesn't have to want some state of affairs prior to its becoming a goal. I can value something because I *believe* someone else desires it, and because I believe it valuable it can become a goal of mine. The claim that if there were no wants there would be few goals and values (which I make in this appendix) is distinct from the claim that all motives contain a nontrivial desire attributable to the motivated agent. I do not rule out the possibility of value without desire, only because it is an empirical question whether someone can formulate a goal without her or anyone she knows or conceives of having an emotional attitude toward it achievement. I am doubtful.

8. Things are good insofar as they are a goal, bad insofar as their negation is a goal. And what is a goal? A goal is a state of affairs X such that 1. Person P believes he can act so as to increase the likelihood of X and 2. P believes he will so act just *because* he believes his actions will so increase the likelihood of X. Note that P does not need to have any emotional attitude toward X, although typically *someone* will desire that X (not necessarily P) if X is a goal of P. Their own best life, the maximal

achievement of their various goals, is presumably everyone's goal. In part, this appendix tries to clarify how other goals contribute or relate to that goal. There is a distinction to be made between goals and stages to a goal, or, if you will, instrumental goals and intrinsic ones. For example, in tennis winning a point is usually just a stage toward the goal of winning a game, and so with games to sets, sets to matches. Instrumentality versus intrinsicality, stage to goal, is relative: winning a tennis match is intrinsic compared to points, games, and sets, but could be instrumental relative to achieving fame and fortune. Abstractly, a goal's achievement has some intrinsic value, whereas stages to goals, or purely instrumental goals, are valueless in themselves.

9. It is not the value she thinks it has to her; it is the value it actually has to her.

10. Cf. Sidgwick (1901, 124).

11. As Dewey (1932, 197) puts it "a satisfaction that is seen by reflection, based on large experience, to unify in a harmonious way [a] whole system of desires . . . is [appropriately} denoted by the term 'happiness.'"

12. See Kazez (2007).

13. The distinguishing difficulty is not that a stage of life can be presumed to care about the entire life, whereas one person's life cannot be presumed to care about another's. To presume that eighteen-year-old P cares about eighty-year-old P is simply to presume she is proto-rational. The eighteen-year-old P who had no concern with the eighty-year-old P makes no logical mistake or observational error; we simply include such a concern in proto- rationality and hold that a stage of P indifferent to "her" future would be proto-*ir*rational. Similarly, the concern for others is baked into our notion of objectivity, which in turn is constitutive of full rationality. *Here* we presume an aspiration to objectivity; we are not trying to justify objectivity (I am hopeful that readers will agree "been there done that" earlier in the book), instead, we are trying to understand what objectivity involves. Our chooser is constructed to provide objectivity. The difficulty is describing such a chooser, not justifying the motives for the construction.

14. The structural similarities between prudence (comparable to proto-rationality) and morality is extensively discussed in Nagel (1970).

15. This insight has been a major objection to utilitarianism.

16. Classical Utilitarianism holds that including the positive and negative experiences of everyone in its hedonistic calculus discharges the obligation to objectivity. But a person's well-being is more (or less) than the sum of her experiences, and so the experiences of a group of persons is not fungible, not detachable from their personal context. This defeats utilitarian summing. Rawl's (1971) solution to "the separateness of individuals" problem is to keep choosers' individuality in his IMVP by making them self-interested, but achieving consensus by making them identical individuals; he gives the choosers a common set of proclivities (the thin theory of the good) and common appreciation of the instrumental value of freedom and no individual preferences beyond that—which may get to fairness but hardly to a measure of value.

17. Sidgwick (1901, 124) makes an analogous point.

18. Another way to put the point being made is that any maximization scheme requires a single unit of value. In the subjective case, that unit was the preference

satisfaction of the last stage of the person. Whose preferences set the common unit values for Brett and Merle?

19. Rawls (1971, 94) calls these instrumental values "primary goods."

20. Rawls considers this approach (1971, 148–149) but prefers the veil of ignorance to "benevolence" because it is simpler, requires a weaker assumption regarding motives, and more easily leads to definitive results. The assumption that the choosers are self-interested, however, is weaker than the assumption that they are benevolent, only because we tend to believe that self-interest is subjectively a more reliable motive than benevolence. But this book's arguments that altruism is inherent in objectivity has already done (or at least claims to have done) the heavy lifting that makes "benevolence" a feature of the ultimate position, which is meant to figure out the weight of objective values, not derive the existence or prove the reliability of objective values. And because we are interested in the deliverances of ideal objectivity, our assumption is also simple: the benevolence is complete, the choosers are just as interested in each member of society's well-being in the ultimate position as a chooser is interested in his own well-being in the original position. There is no complexity about the strength of benevolent interest. Rawls is correct that the ultimate position assumption of benevolence yields no definite result, but it is questionable whether the original position does either (as I argue in the text). But even if the original position does give a definite result, it yields only principles of justice, not answers about the objective moral value resulting from every possible choice. Justice is morally valuable, but it is not the sole moral value.

21. An important structural difference, between Rawls' Original Position and the Ultimate Position, reflecting the different roles they are playing in their home theories, is that Rawls is using fairness to get to justice, whereas love (i.e., the caring about others entailed by objectivity), already established as a *consequence* of justice, is being employed to measure its degree.

Works Cited

Aikin, Scott. 2017. "Modest, But Not Self-Effacing, Transcendental Arguments." *The Philosophical Forum* 48 (Fall): 287–306.

Alston, William. 1993. *The Reliability of Sense Perception*. Ithaca, NY: Cornell University Press.

Anderson, Elizabeth. 2010. *The Imperative of Integration*. Princeton, NJ: Princeton University Press.

———. 2015. "Moral Biases and Corrective Practices: A Pragmatist Perspective." *Proceedings & Addresses of APA* 89 (November): 21–47.

Antony, Louise. 1993. "Quine as Feminist: The Radical Import of Naturalized Epistemology." In *A Mind of One's Own*. Edited by Louise Antony and Charlotte Witt. Boulder, CO: Westview Press.

———. 2016. "Things Oughta Make Sense." *Proceedings and Addresses of the American Philosophical Association* 90 (November): 21–39.

Apel, Karl-Otto. 1998. *From a Transcendental-Semiotic Point of View*. Edited by Mariana Papastephanou. Manchester: Manchester University Press.

Appiah, Kwame Anthony. 2017. *As If*. Cambridge, MA: Harvard University Press.

Aristotle. c. 340 BCE. *Nicomachean Ethics*. Translated by Richard McKeon. 1941. New York: Random House.

Austin, J. L. 1962. *How to Do Things with Words: The William James Lectures Delivered at Harvard University in 1955*. Edited by J. O. Urmson and Marina Sbisà. Oxford: Clarendon Press.

Ayer, A. J. 1936. *Language, Truth, and Logic*, 2nd Edition. London: Gollancz, 1946.

Bagnoli, Carol. 2013. "Constructivism in Metaethics." *Stanford Encyclopedia of Philosophy*. https://plato.stanford.edu/archives/win2017/entries/constructivism-metaethics/.

Bentham, Jeremy. 1789. *The Principles of Morals and Legislation*. Republished 1973. Garden City, NY: Anchor Books.

Berlin, Isaiah. 1998. *The Proper Study of Mankind: An Anthology of Essays*. Edited by Henry Hardy and Roger Hausheer. New York: Farrar, Straus & Giroux.

Brandom, Robert. 1994. *Making It Explicit*. Cambridge, MA: Harvard University Press.

———. 2010. "Reply to Dennett." In *Reading Brandom on Making It Explicit*. Edited by Jeremy Wanderer and Bernhard Weiss. New York: Routledge.

———. 2011. *Perspectives on Pragmatism*. Cambridge, MA: Harvard University Press.

Brown, Garret, and David Held (eds.). 2010. *The Cosmopolitan Reader*. Cambridge: Polity Press.

Buber, Martin. 1923. *I and Thou*. Translated by Ronald Smith. 1958. New York: Charles Scribner and Sons.

Buckwalter, W., and S. Stich. 2014. "Gender and Philosophical Intuition." In *Experimental Philosophy, Vol. 2*. Edited by J. Knobe and S. Nichols. Oxford: Oxford University Press.

Chrisman, Mattthew. 2016. *The Meaning of Ought*. Oxford: Oxford University Press.

———. 2018. "Two Nondescriptivist Views of Normative and Evaluative Statements." *Canadian Journal of Philosophy* 48, nos. 3–4: 405–424.

Copp, David. 2015. "Explaining Normativity." *Proceedings & Addresses of APA* 89 (November): 48–73.

Danto, Arthur. 1987. *Mysticism and Morality*. New York: Columbia University Press.

Darwall, Stephen. 2006. *The Second Person Standpoint*. Cambridge, MA: Harvard University Press.

Davidson, Donald. 1967. "Truth and Meaning." In *The Philosophy of Language*. Edited by A. P. Martinich. 2008. Oxford: Oxford University Press.

———. 1973. "Radical Interpretation." In *Inquiries into Truth and Interpretation*, Edited by Donald Davidson, 2nd edition. 2001. Oxford: Clarendon Press.

Dennett, Daniel. 1984. *Elbow Room*. Cambridge, MA: MIT Press.

———. 1987. *The Intentional Stance*. Cambridge, MA: MIT Press.

———. 1995. *Darwin's Dangerous Idea*. New York: Simon & Schuster.

———. 2003. *Freedom Evolves*. London: Penguin.

———. 2010. "The Evolution of 'Why'." In *Reading Brandom on Making It Explicit*. Edited by Jeremy Wanderer and Bernhard Weiss. 2010. New York: Routledge.

Descartes, Rene. 1641. *Meditations on First Philosophy*. Translated by Donald Cress. 1979. Indianapolis, IN: Hackett Publishing Co.

Dewey, John. 1932. "Ethics." In *The Later Works of John Dewey*. Edited by Jo Ann Boydston. 1985. Carbondale: Southern Illinois University Press.

Emerson, Ralph Waldo. 1841. "Self Reliance." In *Selected Essays*. Edited by Larzer Ziff. 1982. London: Penguin.

Epstein, Brian. 2015. *The Ant Trap*. Oxford: Oxford University Press.

Fesmire, Steven. 2003. *John Dewey and Moral Imagination*. Bloomington: Indiana University Press.

Feuerbach, Ludwig. 1841. *The Essence of Christianity*. Translated by G. Elliot. 1957. New York: Harper Torchbooks.

Fotion, Nick. 2014. *Theory vs. Anti-Theory in Ethics*. Oxford: Oxford University Press.

Franklin, Benjamin. 1787. *The Autobiography of Benjamin Franklin*. Philadelphia: Independence Hall Association, 1999.

Fricker, Miranda. 2007. *Epistemic Injustice*. Oxford: Oxford University Press.

Fukuyama, Francis. 2011. *The Origins of Political Order*. New York: Farrar, Straus, & Giroux.

Garfield, Jay. 2015. *Engaging Buddhism*. New York: Oxford University Press.

Garner, Richard. 1994. *Beyond Morality*. Philadelphia: Temple University Press.

Gilligan, Carol. 1982. *In a Different Voice*. Cambridge: Cambridge University Press.

Goodman, Nelson. 1955. *Fact, Fiction, and Forecast*. Cambridge, MA: Harvard University Press.

Gould, Stephen Jay, and Richard Lewontin. 1979. "The Spandrels of San Marco and the Panglossian Paradigm: A Critique of the Adaptationist Programme." *Proceedings of the Royal Society B: Biological Sciences* 205: 581–598.

Grice, H. P. 1957. "Meaning." In *The Philosophy of Language*. Edited by A. P. Martinich. 2008. Oxford: Oxford University Press.

———. 1961. "The Causal Theory of Perception." *Proceedings of the Aristotelian Society* 35 (Suppl.): 121–152.

Haack, Susan. 1993. *Evidence and Inquiry*. London: Basil Blackwell.

Habermas, Jurgen. 1971. "Reflections on the Linguistic Foundations of Sociology." In *On the Pragmatics of Social Interaction*. Translated by B. Fultner. Cambridge, MA: MIT Press.

———. 1981. *The Theory of Communicative Action*. Translated by Thomas McCarthy Vol. I. 1984. Volume II. 1987. Boston: Beacon.

———. 1983. *Moral Consciousness and Communicative Action*. Translated by C. Lenhardt and S. W. Nicholsen. 1990. Cambridge, MA: MIT Press.

———. 1996. "Inclusion of the Other." In *Studies in Political Theory*. Edited by C. Cronin and P. DeGreiff. 1998. Cambridge, MA: MIT Press.

———. 1998. *Inclusion of the Other: Studies in Political Theory*. Translated by C. Cronon. Edited by C. Cronin and P. Degreiff. Cambridge, MA: MIT Press.

Haidt, Jonathan. 2001. "The Emotional Dog and its Rational Tail." *The Psychological Review* 108, no. 4: 814–834.

———. 2012. *The Righteous Mind: Why Good People are Divided by Politics and Religion*. New York: Pantheon.

Hegel, G. W. F. 1807. *Phenomenology of Spirit*. Translated by A. V. Miller. Oxford: Oxford University Press.

Held, Virginia. 1990. "Feminist Transformations of Moral Theory." In *Ethics*. Edited by Steven M. Cahn. 2012. Oxford: Oxford University Press.

Hempel, Carl. 1962. "Deductive-Nomological vs. Statistical Explanation." In *Scientific Explanation, Space & Time* (Minnesota Studies in the Philosophy of Science, vol. III). Edited by Herbert Feigl and Gordon Maxwell. Minneapolis: University of Minnesota Press, 98–169.

Heney, Diana. 2016. *Toward a Pragmatist Metaethics*. New York: Routledge.

Herrick, Paul. 1994. *The Many Worlds of Logic*. Fort Worth, TX: Harcourt Brace College Publishers.

Hobbes, Thomas. 1651. *Leviathan*, Fourth Edition. London: Penguin Classics, 1982.

Hume, David. 1739. *A Treatise of Human Nature*. Edited by L. A. Selby-Bigge. 1888. London: Oxford University Press.

———. 1748. *Enquiry Concerning Human Understanding*. Edited by Tom L. Beauchamp. Oxford/New York: Oxford University Press, 1999.

Hutcheson, Francis. 1723. *Inquiry Concerning Moral Good and Evil*. London: Midwinter&Bettesworth.

James, William. 1891. "The Moral Philosopher and the Moral Life." *The International Journal of Ethics*. April. Reprinted 1979. New York: Bobbs-Merrill.

———. 1896. "The Will to Believe." In *Pragmatism The Classic Writings*. Edited by H. Standish Thayer. 1970. New York: New American Library.

———. 1905. "What is Pragmatism." In *Pragmatism: The Classic Writings*. Edited by H. Standish Thayer. 1970. New York: New American Library.

Joyce, Richard. 2001. *The Myth of Morality*. Cambridge: Cambridge University Press.

Kahneman, D. 2011. *Thinking, Fast and Slow*. New York: Farrar, Straus, & Giroux.

Kant, Immanuel. 1785. *Groundwork of the Metaphysics of Morals*. Translated by H. J. Paton. 1964. New York: Harper & Row.

Kazez, Jean. 2007. "Necessities." In *The Ethical Life: Fundamental Readings*, 1st edition. Edited by Russ Shafer-Landau. 2010. Oxford: Oxford University Press.

Kirkham, Richard. 1992. *Theories of Truth*. Cambridge, MA: MIT Press.

Korsgaard, Christine. 1996. *The Sources of Normativity*. Cambridge: Cambridge University Press.

Kripke, Saul. 1975. "Outline of a Theory of Truth." *The Journal of Philosophy* 72: 690–716.

Kuhn, Thomas. 1962. *The Structure of Scientific Revolutions*. Chicago: University of Chicago Press.

Kupperman, Joel. 2006. *Six Myths about the Good Life*. Indianapolis: Hackett Publishing Co.

Kymlicka, Will. 2001. *Politics in the Vernacular*. Oxford: Oxford University Press.

Lackoff, George, and Mark Johnson. 1980. *Metaphors We Live By*. Chicago: University of Chicago Press.

Levine, Steven. 2010. "Rehabilitating Objectivity: Rorty, Brandom, and the New Pragmatism." *Canadian Journal of Philosophy* 40, no. 4 (December): 567–590.

———. 2019. *Pragmatism, Objectivity, and Experience*. Cambridge: Cambridge University Press.

Levinas, Emmanuel. 1999. *Alterity and Transcendence*. Translated by Michael B. Smith. New York: Columbia University Press.

Lewis, David. 1986. *On the Plurality of Worlds*. Oxford: Blackwell Publishers.

Lillehammer, Hallvard. 2007. *Companions in Guilt*. London: Macmillan & Co.

Lloyd, Genevieve. 1984. *The Man of Reason*, 2nd edition. 1993. London: Routledge.

Locke, John. 1690. *The Second Treatise On Government*. Indianapolis, IN: Bobbs-Merrill Inc, 1952.

Machery, E., R. Mallon, S. Nichols, and S. Stich. 2004. "Semantics, Cross-Cultural Style." *Cognition* 92, no. 3: B1–B12.

MacIntyre, Alasdair. 1984. *After Virtue*, 2nd edition. South Bend, IN: Notre Dame University Press.

Mackie, John. 1977. *Ethics: Inventing Right and Wrong*. London: Penguin.

Marks, Joel. 2013a. *Ethics without Morals*. New York: Routledge.

———. 2013b. *It's Just a Feeling*. Seattle: Createspace.

———. 2016. *Hard Atheism and the Ethics of Desire*. New York: Palgrave.

Marx, Karl. 1844. *The Economic and Philosophic Manuscripts*. Translated by Martin Milligan. 1988. New York: Prometheus Books.

———. 1859. *Contribution to a Critique of Political Economy*. New York: International Publishers, 1979.

McKim, Robert, and Jeff McMahan (eds.). 1997. *The Morality of Nationalism*. Oxford: Oxford University Press.

Mead, George Herbert. 1913. "The Social Self." In *Pragmatism: The Classic Writings*. Edited by H. Standish Thayer. 1970. New York: New American Library.

Mill, J. S. 1861a. *Utilitarianism*. Edited by George Sher. 1979. Indianapolis, IN: Hackett Publishing Co.

———. 1861b. *On Liberty*. Indianopolis, IN: Hackett Publishing Co.

———. 1861c. *Considerations on Representative Government*. Project Gutenberg Ebook. 2004. www.gutenberg.org.

Millikan, Ruth. 1990. "Truth Rules, Hoverflies, and the Kripke-Wittgenstein Paradox." In *The Philosophy of Language*. Edited by A. P. Martinich. 2008. Oxford: Oxford University Press.

———. 2013. "Reply to Shea." In *Millikan and Her Critics*. Edited by Dan Ryder, Justine Kingsbury, and Kenneth Williford. Chichester: Wiley-Blackwell.

Mills, Charles. 2005. "'Ideal Theory' as Ideology." *Hypatia* 20, no. 3: 165–184.

Misak, Cheryl. 2000. *Truth, Politics, Morality: Pragmatism, and Deliberation*. New York: Routledge.

———. 2004. *Truth and the Ends of Inquiry*. 2nd edition. Oxford: Oxford University Press.

———. 2011. "American Pragmatism and Indispensability Arguments." *Presidential Address, Transactions of the C. S. Peirce Society* 27, no. 3: 261–273.

———. 2018. "There Can Be No Difference Anywhere that Doesn't Make a Difference Somewhere." *Transactions of the C. S. Peirce Society* 54, no. 3: 417–429.

Moyn, Samuel. 2005. *Origins of the Other*. Ithaca, NY: Cornell University Press.

Nagel, Thomas. 1970. *The Possibility of Altruism*. Oxford: Oxford University Press.

———. 1978. "Ruthlessness in Public Life." In *Public and Private Morality*. Edited by Stuart Hampshire. 1978. Cambridge: Cambridge University Press.

———. 1986. *The View From Nowhere*. Oxford: Oxford University Press.

———. 1991. *Equality and Partiality*. Oxford: Oxford University Press.

Nietzsche, Friedrich. 1882. *The Gay Science*. Translated by Walter Kaufmann. 1974. New York: Random House.

———. 1887. *On the Genealogy of Morals*. Translated by Walter Kaufmann. 1967. New York: Random House.

Noddings, Nel. 1984. *Caring: A Feminine Approach to Ethics and Moral Education*. Berkeley: University of California Press.

Nozick, Robert. 1993. *The Nature of Rationality*. Princeton, NJ: Princeton University Press.

Parfit, Derek. 1984. *Reasons and Persons*. Oxford: Oxford University Press.

———. 2011. *On What Matters: Volumes I and II.* Oxford: Oxford University Press.

Perry, John. 1979. "The Problem of the Essential Indexical." In *The Philosophy of Language.* Edited by A. P. Martinich. Oxford: Oxford University Press.

Pierce, C. S. 1877. "The Fixation of Belief." In *Pragmatism The Classic Writings.* Edited by H. Standish Thayer. 1970. New York: New American Library.

———. 1878. "How to Make Our Ideas Clear." In *Pragmatism The Classic Writings.* Edited by H. Standish Thayer. 1970. New York: New American Library.

Pölzler, Thomas. 2018. *Moral Reality and the Empirical Sciences.* New York: Routledge.

Popper, Karl. 1945. *The Open Society and its Enemies.* Princeton, NJ: Princeton University Press.

Prinz, Jesse. 2007. *The Emotional Construction of Morals.* Oxford: Oxford University Press.

Putnam, Hilary. 2004. *Ethics Without Ontology.* Cambridge, MA: Harvard University Press.

Quine, W. V. O. 1951. "Two Dogma's of Empiricism." In *The Philosophy of Language.* Edited by A. P. Martinich. Oxford: Oxford University Press.

———. 1960. *Word and Object.* Cambridge, MA: MIT Press.

Rawls, John. 1971. *A Theory of Justice.* Cambridge, MA: Harvard University Press.

———. 1980. "Kantian Constructivism in Moral Theory." *Journal of Philosophy* 7, no. 9: 515–572.

Richard, Mark. 2008. *When Truth Gives Out.* Oxford: Oxford University Press.

Rorty, Richard. 1979. *Philosophy and the Mirror of Nature.* Princeton, NJ: Princeton University Press.

———. 1989. *Contingency, Irony, and Solidarity.* Cambridge: Cambridge University Press.

Ross, W. D. 1930. *The Right and the Good.* Oxford: Oxford University Press.

Rousseau, Jean Jacques. 1762. *The Social Contract.* Translated by Maurice Cranston. 1968. London: Penguin.

Russell, Bertrand. 1903. "Appendix B: The Doctrine of Types." In *The Principles of Mathematics.* Cambridge: Cambridge University Press.

———. 1940. *An Inquiry Into Meaning and Truth.* London: George Allen and Unwin.

Satz, Debra. 2010. *Why Some Things Should Not Be For Sale.* Oxford: Oxford University Press.

Schwitzgebel, Eric, and Fiery Cushman. 2015. "Philosophers' Biased Judgments Persist Despite Training." In *Cognition:* journal homepage: www.elsevier.com/locate/COGNIT.

Sellars, Wilfrid. 1966. "'Ought' of Moral Principles." Unpublished. diText.com/sellars/omp.html.

Sepielle, Andrew. 2017. "Pragmatism and Metaethics." In *The Routledge Handbook of Metaethics.* Edited by Tristram McPherson and David Plunkett. New York: Routledge.

Sidgwick, Henry. 1901. *The Methods of Ethics.* London: Macmillan & Co.

Silver, Mitchell. 1980. *Self-Concept and Self-Interest: A Study of Thomas Nagel's The Possibility of Altruism.* Unpublished doctoral dissertation. Storrs: University of Connecticut.

———. 2002. "Reflections on Determining Competencies." *Bioethic*s 16, no. 5 (September). Oxford: Blackwell.

———. 2006. *A Plausible God.* New York: Fordham University Press.

Singer, Peter. 1979. *Practical Ethics.* Cambridge: Cambridge University Press.

———. 2002. *One World.* New Haven, CT: Yale University Press.

Smart, R. N. 1958. "Negative Utilitarianism." *Mind* 67: 542–543.

Stawson, P. F. 1959. *Individuals.* Abingdon: Routledge.

Stevenson, C. L. 1944. *Ethics and Language.* New Haven, CT: Yale University Press.

Stich, Stephen. 1983. *From Folk Psychology to Cognitive Science.* Cambridge, MA: MIT University Press.

Tarski, Alfred. 1933. "The Concept of Truth in Formalized Languages." Translated by J. H. Woodger. 1935. In *Logic, Semantics, Metamathematics*, second edition. Edited by J. Corcoran. 1983. Indianapolis: Hacket.

Taylor, Charles. 1989. *Sources of the Self.* Cambridge, MA: Harvard University Press.

Wanderer, Jeremy. 2008. *Robert Brandom.* Montreal: McGill-Queen's University Press.

Wanderer, Jeremy, and Bernhard Weiss. 2010. *Reading Brandom on Making It Explicit.* New York: Routledge.

Williams, Bernard. 1981. *Moral Luck.* Cambridge: Cambridge University Press.

———. 1985. *Ethics and the Limits of Philosophy.* Cambridge, MA: Harvard University Press.

Wittgenstein, Ludwig. 1922. *Tractatus Logico-Philosophicus.* Translated by D. F. Pears and B. F. McGuinness. 1961. New York: Humanities Press.

———. 1953. *Philosophical Investigations.* Translated by G. E. M. Anscombe. Edited by G. E. M. Anscombe and R. Rhees. Oxford: Blackwell.

Wolf, Susan. 1982. "Moral Saints." In *Ethics.* Edited by Steven M. Cahn and Peter Markie. Oxford: Oxford University Press.

Wong, David. 1984. *Moral Relativity.* Berkeley: University of California Press.

Index

academic specialization, xi

action, 95, 103, 110n1, 110n2, 110n3, 112n19, 113n19, 143; causation of, 12; and emotions, 99, 106. *See also* motivation

affirmative action, xviii, 161

agreement. *See* consensus, social

Aikin, Scott, 48n45, 83, 84

alienation, 67

Alston, William, 41n1

altruism, 120, 181n20

amoralism, 3, 4, 14n7, 17n21, 29, 59, 67, 84, 91n45, 125, 133n20, 144

analytic/synthetic distinction, 112n15

Anderson, Elizabeth, xvii, xviii, xix, xixn1, 113n25, 133n16

animals, 57n11, 58n11, 88n20, 145, 146, 148n18, 178n2; rationality of, 5

Antony, Louise, xivn8, 133n17

Apel, Karl Otto, 93n65

Appiah, Kwame Anthony, xxn7, 166n17

arbitrariness, 27, 28, 44n20, 117, 141; and contingency, 25, 26, 84

Aristotle, 120

artistic collaboration, 138, 139

Austen, Jane, 109

Austin, J. L., 15n12

autocracy, 149, 150, 154, 164n1

Ayer, A. J., 17n21

bad faith, 54, 88n20, 105, 109, 110

Bagnoli, Carol, 72

baseball, 39, 40, 101, 122

Basques, 160

beauty, 163

beliefs, 5, 6, 9, 31 56, 61, 62, 63, 71, 80, 91n50, 92n50, 92n52, 96, 97, 100, 102, 113n20, 131, 167; division of labor in, 47n43, 82, 83, 85n5, 89n33, 90n33, 93n63; effects of, 39; false, 61; as maps, 63, 64. *See also* holism; system of, 60, 61, 63, 67; and truth, 21; web of, 72

benevolence, principle of, 181n20

Bentham, Jeremy, xivn5, 136

Berlin, Isaiah, 166n12

bias, 107, 108, 113n25, 113n26, 118, 127, 157, 161, 169, 172, 173, 175–77

the Bible, 135, 136, 147n13

bigotry, 160

bivalence, 92n57, 93n63

Brahms, Johannes, 104

Brandom, Robert, xivn4, 48n49, 76, 77, 85n2, 85n7, 86n9, 87n14, 89n32, 90n41

brotherhood/sisterhood, 138

Browning, Robert and Elizabeth Barrett, 23

Buber, Martin, 58n12

191

Buckwalter, W., 113n26

callousness, 137
capacity to suffer, 136, 137, 142, 146, 162
capitalism, 159
categorical imperative, 54, 120, 121, 139
causal *vs.* logical contingency, 43n18
character, 110n1
Chrisman, Matthew, 87n14, 87n16
circularity, 19, 28, 37, 41n1, 44n24, 47n45, 76, 111n7
citizenship, 161
civic education, 153
class, 109
coercion, 126, 127
cognitive hedonism, 92n52
cognitivism, moral, 27, 59, 77, 80, 81, 92n57, 95. *See also* morality, skepticism
collective goods, 53
commodification, 159
communication, 112n18
communist tyrannies, 166n10
community, 4, 70, 76, 80, 83, 108, 109, 139, 178n1; Christian, 126; formation of, 56; Jewish, 126; Muslim, 126
companions in guilt, 92n57, 124, 125
compatibilism, 14n5. *See also* free will
compositionality, 87n14
computers, 5, 88n20
Confucians, 126
consensus, social, 34, 37–40, 48n49, 73, 85n7, 89n33, 90n33, 98–101, 108
consequentialism, 120, 122, 124, 128. *See also* rule consequentialism; utilitarianism
considerateness, 137–39
consistency, 9, 10, 15n17, 51, 82, 93n63, 98–100, 111n12, 112n12, 112n14, 116–19, 128, 137, 144, 157; practical, 100; practical and theoretical inconsistency, 112n19, 113n19
constructivism, 58n12, 72, 73, 89n31

contingency: and arbitrariness, 25, 26, 28, 84; of moral beliefs, 25; and moral principles, 26
Copp, David, 73–75
correspondence theory of truth, 21, 24, 42n8, 48n46, 77, 79, 84, 86n10, 111n8
causal theories of, 23; plausibility of, 63
cosmopolitanism, 149, 160–62, 166n17; and sovereignty, 161
credibility, 138
cruelty, 115, 116, 137
cultural traditions, 160

Danto, Arthur, 148n16
Darwall, Stephen, 54, 57n10, 89n31, 111n7
Davidson, Donald, 46n40, 57n9, 85n8, 112n18
deduction. *See* logic
deductive-nomological model. *See* explanation
deliberation, 108, 152, 177
democracy, 149, 150, 152–54; liberal, 149, 155, 162, 164n1, 165n1
Denmark, 126
Dennett, Daniel, 14n5, 76, 77, 85n7, 86n9, 86n11, 89n32, 90n39, 90n41, 111n6
Descartes, Rene, 47n45, 48n45
desires, 56, 96, 97, 111n3, 111n7, 111n8, 111n10, 131, 147n10, 168–71, 180n11; initial (basic), 169, 174, 179n7; second order, 143
desire theory of motivation, 96–98
determinism, 2
Dewey, John, 58n13, 58n15, 91n48, 111n10, 113n20, 132n3, 180n11
difference principle, 166n11
dignity, 136, 154, 155
direction of fit argument, 43n11, 111n8
disabilities, 154
disability rights, 161
discourse ethics, 77, 78
dismissiveness, 137

dissent, 40. *See also* consensus
distribution, 158, 159
divine command theory, 88n18
dogmatism, xix, 156
double standards, 116, 117, 119, 121, 124, 127–30, 133n12, 138, 139, 144, 157

Eastern thought, 14n1, 145
egalitarianism, 153, 157, 166n12
egoism, 51, 54, 57n3, 57n4, 111n9, 119, 132n4
elections, 150, 154
Emerson, Ralph Waldo, 98
emotions, 130, 132, 133n20, 133n21, 133n22, 137; and action, 99, 106. *See also* passion
emotivism, 17n21
empiricism, 38
Epstein, Brian, 179n3
equal concern for all, 173, 176
equality, 116, 119, 126, 138, 154, 160, 162, 164, 166n12, 174, 175; before the law, 153; formal, 158; material, 157–59, 166n9, 166n12, 166n13; Error theory, 84. *See also* amoralism
essential indexical of "I", 50
ethical theory, xi, 140, 141
evidence, 78, 80, 91n46, 144; historical against democracy, 164n1, 165n1
evolution, 86n9, 91n46, 144
experience, xix, 91n48, 100, 101, 119, 130, 136, 144, 151, 154, 162, 180n11
experimental philosophy, xivn3, 103, 104
expertise, 138
explanation, 10–12, 16n20, 44n20, 80, 84, 88n20; causal, 11; deductive-nomological model of, 10, 16n20; formal, 10; informal, 10; and justification, 16n20
expressivism, 95, 17n21
extensional equivalence, 41n4, 42n4
the external world, 54–56, 77, 83, 101, 129, 144, 145, 162

facts: facticity, 78, 87n15, 125; fact-value distinction, 33, 44n25, 77, 79
fairness, 170, 180n16, 181n21
fallibilism, 34, 35, 70, 84, 115, 141, 155, 156, 164, 166n5
false consciousness, 151, 152
fanaticism, 148n15
favoritism, 161
fellowship of truth, 92n57, 125
feminism, 128, 130, 133n14
Fesmire, Steven, 147n6
Feuerbach, Ludwig, 136
fictionalism. *See* Joyce
folks psychology, 97
forced choice, 111n12
foreigners, 161
formal languages, 100
foundherentism, 112n14
Franklin, Benjamin, 9
freedom, 2, 136, 163, 176, 180n16; and association, 153; and speech, 153
free will, 2, 3, 14n5. *See also* compatibilism
Freud, Sigmund, 109
Fricker, Miranda, 88n20, 147n6
Fukuyama, Francis, xi
fundamental moral principles, 44n22, 115

Galileo, Galilei, 22
Garfield, Jay, 14n1
Garner, Richard, 14n6
Gilligan, Carol, 133n14
the given, 48n49
Gladstone, Ora, xiv
goals, 32, 35, 37, 45n30, 49, 110n3, 140, 142, 147n10, 155, 157, 162, 168, 169, 179n8; achievement as test of truth, 29–32, 36, 39–41, 46n41, 51–53, 61, 62, 70, 74, 75, 80, 82, 83, 91n48, 92n52, 92n56, 99, 100, 131, 132n4, 133n21, 142, 147n5, 149, 159, 165n1, 167; clashing, 50; immaterial/spiritual, 158; proximate, 37; weighing, 46n42, 167, 168, 177, 178

god's image, 135, 136, 138
the Golden Rule x, 50, 139
Goldhammer, Arthur, xiii
the good, xvii, 163
Goodman, Nelson, 44n24
Gould, Stephen, 102
government neutrality, 153, 154
Greifinger, Joel, xiii
Grice, Paul, 15n12, 86n10

Haack, Susan, 112n14
Habermas, Jurgen, 77–79, 90n42,
    93n60, 93n65, 147n9
habits, 104, 113n20
Haidt, Jonathan, 106, 113n24, 113n28
heaven, 140
hedonistic calculus, 180n16
Hegel, G. W. F., 58n12, 58n13, 77
Held, Virginia, 133n14
hell, 140
Heney, Diane, 132n8
Herrick, Paul, 15n13
historical understanding, xvii, 164n1,
    165n1
Hobbes, Thomas, 58n12, 125, 126
holism, 31, 64, 79, 80, 82, 85n2, 88n18,
    141
homophobia, xviii
humans' social nature, 2. *See also* others
Hume, David, 14n5, 44n24, 48n45, 65,
    87n15, 88n18, 96–98, 111n4, 111n9,
    130, 131
humiliation, 142. *See also* moral
    principle, to not humiliate
humility, 142
Hutchenson, Francis, x, xivn5
hypocrisy, 105
hypothetical imperative, 88n19

idealism, 58n13, 75, 76, 163
idealizng: ideal chooser, 168–75,
    177, 180n13, 181n20; idealized
    Reason, 7; ideal moral theory,
    xv, xvi, 179n6; ideal observer
    theory, 173; ideal theory, xvii; and

non-ideal theory, xv; and progress,
    xvii
Ideal Measure of Value Procedure
    (IMVP), 168–73, 175, 176, 178,
    179n6, 180n16
imperfect duties, 147n14
improving life, 171, 172
impulse, 169
IMVP. *See* Ideal Measure of Value
    Procedure
incest, 106, 113n28
incest, 106, 113n28
individuality, 53, 129, 153, 180n15
individuals, 58n15, 125, 126, 128
induction. *See* logic
inference relation, 68, 86n10, 100, 122,
    132n1
inferentialism, 59- 64, 66, 70, 85n2, 87n14,
    87n16, 88n18. *See also* meaning
inquiry, 79
instinct, 52, 101–4
instrumental rationality, 41n1, 45n27,
    98, 172, 176
the intensional stance, 111n6
intersubjectivity, 41, 55, 153
intuitions, xv, 99, 135, 143, 147n14;
    formation of moral, xix; moral,
    xvii, xix, xixn1, 106, 107, 112n13,
    113n325, 141, 143
irrationality, 103, 104, 106, 109, 130,
    137; poor probabilistic reasoning, 104.
    See also rationality, pseudo rationality;
    rationality, quasi rationality

James, William, 45n32, 89n26, 89n31,
    91n43, 111n12
Johnson, Mark, 147n6
Joyce, Richard, 14n6
juries, 152
jury deliberations, 107, 152
justice, 136, 181n21
justification, 3, 5–12, 14, 15n11, 15n12,
    15n13, 16n20, 19–21, 36, 37, 39,
    44n20, 44n22, 46n42, 64, 67, 71,
    73, 78, 81–83, 85n4, 86n10, 88n20,

90n33, 91n47, 92n50, 102, 106, 110, 113n29, 115, 118, 121–23, 130, 139, 162; arguments and, 6, 15n12, 15n13; and explanation, 16n20; of self, ix, xii, 4; sufficient, 70–72, 85n6, 86n12
justified social system of belief (TSSB), 60, 61, 68, 85n4, 90n33, 116, 118, 120, 123, 124, 127, 133n12, 141, 168, 169, 179n4

Kahneman, Daniel, 113n24
Kant, Immanuel, x, xivn5, 48n45, 54, 84, 88n18, 89n1, 116, 118, 120, 121, 127, 147n14, 149
Kantianism. *See* Kant, Immanuel
Kazez, Jean, 180n12
kibbutzim, 166n10
Kirkham, Richard, 19, 20, 42n6, 91n47
knowers, 136, 138, 147n6, 162. *See also* verifiers
Korsgaard, Christine, 54, 57n6, 58n17, 89n30, 89n31, 148n18
Kripke, Saul, 48n46
Kuhn, Thomas, 112n18, 147n12
Kupperman, Joel, 38, 113n22
Kymlicka, Will, 166n17

labor, intensity of, 158
Lackoff, George, 147n6
Lande, Nelson, xiii
language, 100, 102, 112n16, 112n17, 116, 133n12; natural, 100; non-verbal assertion, 139, 148n18; and relativism, 24, 43n15; *See also* compositionality; inferentialism; meaning; propositions; sentences
Lee, Spike, xii
Levine, Steven, xiii, 48n49, 58n14, 91n48
Lewis, David, 65
liberalism, 152–56, 166n5; and government neutrality, 153, 154
life stage, 170–72, 180n13
Lillehammer, Hallvard, 36, 43n11, 92n57, 124

Lloyd, Genevieve, 133n15
Locke, John, 125, 127, 128
logic: deductive, 44n24; inductive, 44n24; of moral reasoning, 13, 100, 101
love, 136, 138, 163, 174, 175, 177, 181n21

Macbeth, 147n3
Machery, E., 113n26
Mackie, John, 14n6, 132n7
markets, 159, 166n14
Marks, Joel, xiii, 14n6, 48n50, 132n9, 133n20, 133n22
Marx, Karl, xv, 58n13, 109, 126, 147n2, 157
materialism, 157, 162, 163
maximax strategy, 177
maximin strategy, 176, 177
Mckim, Robert, 166n17
Mead, George Herbert, 58n16
meaning, 59, 61, 63–66, 68, 70, 86n10, 87n14, 88n18, 112n18; literal, 88n18; of moral terms, 65, 66. and truth, 41n3. *See also* inferentialism
mercy, 136
meritocracy, 118
metaethics, x, xi, 13, 20, 50, 55, 73, 135, 145, 157
metaphors, 146n1
metaphysical assumptions, 84, 162
Mill, John Stuart, xivn5, 113n23, 165n3, 165n4, 166n6, 168
Millikan, Ruth, 43n13, 48n46, 86n10
Mills, Charles, xixn1
Milton, John, 137
minorities, 154, 160
Misak, Cheryl, xivn4, 48n49, 79–81, 83, 84, 91n43, 91n44, 91n45, 91n47, 91n48, 92n51, 92n52, 92n57, 93n60, 93n62, 93n63, 93n64, 93n65, 132n8
mitochondrial Eve, 60
modal terms, 64, 65
Montezuma, 167

moral disagreement, 25, 53. *See also* consensus

moral eliminativism. *See* amoralism; morality, skepticism; moral nihilism, 95

moral intuitions. *See* intuitions

morality, 3, 10, 29, 75, 83, 115, 119, 121, 125, 128, 130, 132, 135, 143, 162; and objectivity, 28; and perception/imagination, 110; and rules, 120, 123; scope of, 145, 146; skepticism of, 3, 13, 17n21, 48n45, 59, 60, 65–67, 84, 95. *See also* relativism

moral judgments, 95–97, 101, 107–10, 121, 122, 127, 137, 138, 162

moral nihilism, 3, 91n45

moral objectivism, xii, xivn2. *See also* objectivism; objectivity

moral principles, 13, 22, 35, 124–27, 131, 132, 133n12, 139–41, 143, 147n14, 157; conflicting, 147n14; to enable others' projects, 143, 144; to not humiliate, 142, 143; to reduce serious suffering, 140–44; truth of, 35

moral saints, 143, 148n15

moral terms, 65, 66, 87n16

More, Thomas, xvi

motivation, 95, 101, 103, 105–7, 110, 110n3, 111n3, 111n7, 111n8, 111n9, 111n10, 119, 120, 147n10, 150, 155, 176, 179n7

Nagel, Thomas, 25, 33, 57n8, 111n8, 132n10, 180n14

the nation-state, 160

naturalism, 74, 75, 86n10, 129

natural languages, 100

natural law, 127, 128

natural sympathy, 97, 111n9

nepotism, 118

Nietzsche, Friedrich, 45n37, 58n12, 109, 163

Noddings, Nel, 133n18

non-ideal theory, xv. *See also* idealizing

Norman, Daniel, 46n39

normative ethics, x, 50. *See also* moral principles; ethical theory

normativity, xv, 72, 74–79, 87n15, 145; procedural, 155

North Korea, 126, 166n8

Nozick, Robert, xivn6, 14n8, 41n1

objective truth, xivn1. *See also* truth

objective weights, 172

objectivism, x, xii, xivn2, x, 59, 79–83, 120

objectivity, 28, 32–38, 40, 43n11, 46n38, 46n41, 46n42, 153, 157, 162, 164, 173, 177, 178, 180n13, 180n16

Occam's razor, 78

open borders, xviii

oppression, 110

original position, 166n9, 176, 177, 181n20, 181n21

Othello, 11, 64

Others, 49–51, 53, 56, 76, 83, 93n65, 110, 118, 119, 129, 133n12, 135–38, 143, 149, 157, 162; recognitions of, 70, 143, 157

ought/is derivation of, 44n23, 65–69, 87n15, 87n18, 88n18, 88n19

pandering, 151

Parfit, Derek, xivn3, xxn6, 14n2, 14n8, 111n8

passion, 96, 106, 111n4, 111n9, 130, 139, 140, 147n10. *See also* emotions

past persons, 178n2

paternalism, 152

Peirce, Charles Sanders, 45n29, 45n32, 45n34, 91n47, 91n48, 132n8

perfect lives, 174

Perina, Mickaella, xii

Perry, John, 47n43

persons, 49, 75, 83, 88n20, 135, 136, 144, 145, 157, 162, 170

perspectivism, 25, 28, 33, 40, 46n37, 55, 56, 82, 152–54, 162

philosophy as dogmatic ideology, xix

Plato, 22
pluralist teleology, 74, 75
politics: political commitment, 155; political epistemology, 149; political norms, 125–28; political sovereignty, 161; political strategies, xvii; political telos, 162; political values, 149; politicians, 150–52, 165n2
Pölzler, Thomas, 148n16, 178n2
Popper, Karl, 147n11
possibility, xvi, xxn7
possible worlds, 65; best, 175
poverty, 165n1
practical rationality, 5, 9, 29, 45n27, 56, 57, 67, 97, 98, 101, 103, 119, 129, 143; and factual reasoning, 13; and judgments, 105, 112n12; marginality of, 103; moral reasoning, 27
pragmatic justification, 30, 31, 35, 36, 38, 40, 70, 75, 88n18, 89n32; soundness of, 13
pragmatic theory of truth, 29, 32, 43n8
pragmatism, x, xv, xxn7, 57n4, 73, 75–77, 79, 80, 84, 85n2, 124, 125, 132n8, 155, 162, 163
preferences, 171. *See* goals; values
prejudice, 108
prima facie duties, 147n14
primary goods, 181n19
principles of justice, 127, 176, 181n20
Prinz, Jesse, 130, 133n20
probabilistic reasoning, 104
procedural normative realism, 89n31
procedural norms, 155
productivity, 158
proper biological function, 86n10
propositions, 5, 6, 15n10, 38, 64, 65, 68, 78, 87n14; propositional content, 112n19
proto-rationality, 169, 170, 172, 176, 180n13, 180n14
proximate goals, 37
prudence, 57n8, 66, 150, 169, 180n14
pseudo-rationality, 7–10, 103–5, 107, 109

public reason, 152, 153
purpose of philosophy, xi, xii
Putnam, Hilary, 43n11

quantum mechanics, 22
Quine, W. V. O., 72, 112n15, 147n12

race, 109
racism, xv, 137, 160
rational causation, 6, 8
rational commitment, 93n65
the rational community. *See* the social system
rationalism, 75, 76, 84, 105
Rationalist Pragmatism, x, xivn4, 72, 74, 75, 77, 79, 80, 82–84, 89n31, 120–25, 127–32, 140, 141, 143, 145, 149, 152, 155–60, 168
rationality, 5, 7, 9, 53, 54, 63, 67, 90n33, 99–102, 108, 128, 129, 135, 140, 162; subject, incoherence of, 51; proto-rationality, 169, 170, 172, 176, 180n13, 180n14; pseudo-rationality, 7–10, 103–5, 107, 109; quasi-rationality, 7, 67, 104, 109. *See also* reason
rationalizations, 7
Rawls, John, xxn2, 89n31, 125, 127, 166n6, 166n11, 166n13, 176, 177, 180n16, 181n19, 181n21
realism, 35, 36, 38, 62, 70, 73, 75–77, 133n20, 162
reality, 39, 40, 63, 162; appearance and, 55, 119; as constraining factual and practical principles, 15n18
reason, 3, 4, 5, 6, 10, 41, 56, 71, 75, 77, 96, 98, 99, 101, 102, 111n4, 113n23, 117, 118, 121, 128, 130, 139, 143, 149; agent relative, 57n2; and morality, ix; and truth, 27, 53. *See also* rationality
recognition of others, 143, 157
regret, 80, 81
relativism: burden of maintaining, 28–29; general, 22, 24, 25, 32, 35,

46n43, 47n43, 93n63; moral, 3, 4,
   14n7, 17n21, 21, 23–25, 28, 29, 31,
   32, 37, 38, 43n10, 44n26, 51, 85n3,
   95, 131, 133n20, 155, 156
relativity theory, 22
relevance, 105, 106, 119, 146
resentment, 140, 144
responsibility, 110n1
Richard, Mark, 43n15
risk-taking, 158
risk-tolerance, 176
Rorty, Richard, 46n38, 48n49
Ross, W. D., 147n14
Rousseau, Jean Jacques, xxn2, 125–28,
   155
rule consequentialism, 122–24
rule of law, 126
Russell, Bertrand, 43n12 48n46

saints, moral, 143, 144
same sex marriage, 161, 166n6
Sartre, Jean Paul, 109
Satan, 137
Satz, Debra, 166n14
Schmitt, Karl, 91n45
science, 71, 93n64, 99, 108, 109,
   113n29, 132, 141, 154, 162, 163;
   credibility of, 71
Schwitgebel, Eric, 113n24
self (selves), xii, 1–3, 5, 14n1, 45n35,
   49, 54, 55, 58n15, 83, 128, 129,
   133n12, 144, 145, 148n16, 162,
   170, 172; created by distancing, 56;
   formation of, 14n4. *See also* others
self consciousness, 136
self delusion, 54, 105. *See also* bad
   faith; pseudo rationality
self determination, right of, 160
self expression, 156
self interest, 110, 128, 129, 150, 158,
   176, 177, 180n16, 181n20
self justification, ix, xii, 4
Sellars, Wilfred, 48n49, 87n16
sentences, 5, 6, 65, 69, 87n14
Sepeille, Andrew, 91n50

sex, 109
sexism, 71, 137, 154
Shakespeare, William, 79, 109
Sidgwick, Henry, 180n17
Silver, Hadass, xiii, xiv, 11n7
Silver, Isaac, xiv
Silver, Mitchell, 14n3, 58n16
Singer, Peter, 143, 148n15, 166n17
slavery, 54, 88n20
Smart, R. N., 147n11
Smith, Adam, 126
social conflict, 164
social contract theory, 120, 124–29, 149
social cooperation, 120, 124–29, 149
social domination, 109
social harmony, 163
social identities, 109, 110, 160
social institutions, 156
socialism, xv, 157–59
socialist values, 149, 157
social system, 4, 5, 60, 67, 68, 71, 77,
   85n3, 99, 120, 130, 145, 148n16,
   155, 161, 167, 172, 173, 178n2,
   179n4; possiblility of multiple,
   178n3
social system of belief, 60, 61, 67, 68,
   72, 82, 84, 86n12, 89n33, 90n33,
   92n50, 116, 119, 122, 124, 133n12,
   167–69, 178n2. *See also* beliefs,
   division of labor in; holism
social tradition of metaethics, 54, 58n12
social utility, 125–27
social values, 157
soft-determinism. *See* compatibilism
solidarity, 46n38, 48n49
solipsism, xii, 52, 53, 55, 111n9, 119,
   129; infantile, 119; practical, 51,
   57n3; *See also* egoism
Somalia, 126
spirit, 157, 163
standards, 129, 135, 155
state of nature, 126
Stevenson, C. L., 17n21
Stich, Stephen, 111n5, 113n26
Strawson, Peter, 58n14

subjective truth, xivn1, 32
subjective value, 169–72, 174–76, 180n18; maximization of, 180n18
subjectivity, 32–34, 45n35, 51, 55. *See also* perspectivism
subject rationality, incoherence of, 51
substantive realism, 89n31
sympathy, 97, 111n9, 130
syntax, 116

Tarski, Alfred, 41n3
theoretical reason, 45n27, 100
thick concepts, 68
thin theory of the good, 166n9, 176
ticking-clock hypotheticals, 92n58
tolerance, 156
tragic choice, 80, 82, 92n57, 93n63, 142
transcendental arguments, 47n35, 83, 84, 93n65
transcendental conditions, xii
transcendental moral standards, 3, 4, 24
transition programs, xvii
trial and error introspection, 106
truth, xivn1, xxn7, 13, 38, 46n40, 54–56, 59, 60, 62–65, 73, 77, 78, 81–84, 86n10, 89n31, 93n60, 99–102, 119, 122, 123, 125, 127, 128, 131, 133n12, 136, 138–40, 144, 145, 149, 152–55, 162–64; bearer of, 60, 79, 80, 82, 96; deflationary concept of, 37, 38; as disquotation, 41n13; fellowship of, 92n57, 125; of moral principles, 35; objective, xivn1; subjective, xivn1, 32; umpires of, 41
truth, theories of, 19; correspondence, 21, 23, 24, 42n8, 48n46, 63, 77, 79, 84, 86n10, 111n8; disquotational, 41n13; essentialist, 20, 85n4, 91n47; extensional, 20, 91n47; pragmatic, 29, 32, 43n8; realist, 42n8; semantic, 20, 41n3
TSSB. *See* justified social system of belief

ultimate position, 176–78, 181n20, 181n21

umpires, baseball, 40
unconscious rationality, 107
underdeterminism, 80, 81
utilitarianism, 116, 118, 148n15, 149, 160, 180n15, 180n16; negative, 147n11
utility, 31, 125, 127, 128, 158; monster, 132n4; predictive, 76, 92n51
utopia, xvi
utopian socialism, xv

Vaihinger, Hans, xxn7
value, xvi, 45n30, 102, 130, 131, 133n21, 135, 136, 139, 168–72, 175, 177, 178, 179n8, 180n16, 181n20; of best life, 170, 172, 174, 175, 178n8; choice of life, 170; continuum, 168; instrumental and intrinsic, 113n23, 176, 180n8; pluralism of, 81, 166n12; subjective, 169–72, 174–76, 180n18. *See also* goals
Vedantist, 22
veil of ignorance, 176, 181n20
verifiers, 54, 83, 137–39, 142, 148n16, 162, 178n2. *See also* knowers
virtue, 135, 136
virtue ethics, 120
Voltaire, 109

Wanderer, Jeremy, xiii, 85n2, 86n10, 87n14
Washoe, 5
Watson, 5
web of belief, 72
weighing goals, 46n42, 167, 168, 177, 178
Williams, Bernard, 57n2, 89n23
Wittgenstein, Ludwig, 48n46, 57n6, 110n1
Wolf, Susan, 148n15
Wong, David, 43n17, 45n28
world government, 161, 162. *See also* cosmopolitanism

Zurn, Chris, xii

About the Author

Mitchell Silver holds a PhD in philosophy from the University of Connecticut and is currently teaching at the I Can Academy of the Suffolk County Jail after retiring from a thirty-five-year career in the Department of Philosophy of the University of Massachusetts Boston. He has also taught at Tufts University, Virginia Tech, Massachusetts General Hospital Institute of Health Professionals, and the Stella Maris University of Monrovia, Liberia. He is the author of *The Veterans of History* (2014), *A Plausible God* (2006), and *Respecting the Wicked Child* (1998).

www.ingramcontent.com/pod-product-compliance
Lightning Source LLC
Chambersburg PA
CBHW022313280326
41932CB00010B/1080